Facebook®, Twitter®, and Instagram® For Seniors

3rd Edition

by Marsha Collier

Facebook®, Twitter®, and Instagram® For Seniors For Dummies® 3rd Edition

Published by: **John Wiley & Sons, Inc.,** 111 River Street, Hoboken, NJ 07030-5774, www.wiley.com

Copyright © 2019 by John Wiley & Sons, Inc., Hoboken, New Jersey

Published simultaneously in Canada

For general information on our other products and services, please contact our Customer Care Department within the U.S. at 877-762-2974, outside the U.S. at 317-572-3993, or fax 317-572-4002. For technical support, please visit https://hub.wiley.com/community/support/dummies.

Wiley publishes in a variety of print and electronic formats and by print-on-demand. Some material included with standard print versions of this book may not be included in e-books or in print-on-demand. If this book refers to media such as a CD or DVD that is not included in the version you purchased, you may download this material at http://booksupport.wiley.com. For more information about Wiley products, visit www.wiley.com.

Library of Congress Control Number: 2018962323

ISBN: 978-1-119-54141-7; ISBN: 978-1-119-54139-4 (ePDF); ISBN: 978-1-119-54143-1 (ePub)

Manufactured in the United States of America

V10006228_112119

Contents at a Glance

Introduction 1

Part 1: Getting Started with Social Networking 9
CHAPTER 1: Getting Equipped for the Internet. 11
CHAPTER 2: Connecting to the Internet 25
CHAPTER 3: So Much About Email (and Safety) 41
CHAPTER 4: Speaking the Social Networking Language 59
CHAPTER 5: Sharing in the 21st Century: Acronyms, Posts,
Photos, and Videos 73

Part 2: Putting Your Face onto Facebook 93
CHAPTER 6: Signing Up and Prepping Your Facebook Profile 95
CHAPTER 7: Preparing to Share Info. 113
CHAPTER 8: Connecting with Friends and Family. .135
CHAPTER 9: Adding Photos and Videos to Facebook. 155
CHAPTER 10: Exploring the Extras: Groups, Events, Watch, and Games 173

Part 3: And Now, It's Twitter Time 189
CHAPTER 11: A Beginner's Guide to Twitter. 191
CHAPTER 12: Conversing on Twitter with Friends, Family, and Even
Strangers 217
CHAPTER 13: Gathering Tools of the Twitter Trade .235

Part 4: Instagramming with the Pros (Your Kids) 263
CHAPTER 14: Where Only Visuals Will Do . . . Instagram. 265
CHAPTER 15: Posting and Perfecting Your Pictures 283
CHAPTER 16: Socializing and Fine Tuning Your Instagram 301

Index 313

Table of Contents

INTRODUCTION. 1

About This Book 2
Conventions Used in This Book 3
Foolish Assumptions 5
Icons Used in This Book 5
Beyond the Book 6
Feedback, Please 7

PART 1: GETTING STARTED WITH SOCIAL NETWORKING 9

CHAPTER 1: **Getting Equipped for the Internet** 11
Select Hardware to Match Your Needs. 12
Know What Options to Look For 16
Shop for Your Device of Choice 19
Browse for a Browser 20

CHAPTER 2: **Connecting to the Internet** 25
Select an Internet Service Provider 26
Choose a Broadband Network Option 29
Connect a Powerline Network 31
Set Up a Wireless Network 33
Protect Your Privacy and Stay Safe Online. 36

CHAPTER 3: **So Much About Email (and Safety)** 41
Check Out Places to Get Your Email Service 43
Choose a Web-Based Email Provider 44
Pick a Pick-Proof Password. 48
Sign Up for a Gmail Account. 50
Add Your Contacts 54
Compose and Send an Email 55

CHAPTER 4: **Speaking the Social Networking Language** 59
Gather on Facebook 60
Communicate through Twitter. 62
Video-Chat with Friends and Family on Skype. 63
Get Connected on LinkedIn 64

See It All on YouTube. 65
Have Your Say on Blogspot. 67
Archive and Share Pictures on Google Photos 68
Stream Music on Pandora 69
Stream TV and Movies on Hulu, Netflix, and Amazon Prime. . . . 71

CHAPTER 5: **Sharing in the 21st Century: Acronyms, Posts, Photos, and Videos** 73
Give Credit When You Share 74
Make Your Links Short. 77
Internet Slang Is a Language of its Own 82
Find and Share Videos on YouTube. 84
Pin a Few of Your Favorite Things 89

PART 2: PUTTING YOUR FACE ONTO FACEBOOK 93

CHAPTER 6: **Signing Up and Prepping Your Facebook Profile.** 95
Sign Up for a Facebook Account 96
Upload Your Profile Photo 98
Find Friends Initially. 101
Add Your Personal Information 103
Confirm You Are You 104
Fill Out Other Profile Information 106
Edit Your Timeline Later 111

CHAPTER 7: **Preparing to Share Info**. 113
Get Your Privacy Settings in Place 114
Meet Your Facebook Home Page. 123
Review Your Timeline Page. 126
Update Your Status 129
Delete a Status Update or Other Post. 131
Add a Photo to Your Timeline 132
Add Life Events to Your Timeline 132
Share a YouTube Video on Facebook 133

CHAPTER 8: **Connecting with Friends and Family**. 135
Make the Navigation Bar Your First Stop 136
Find a Friend with Facebook Search 139
Send a Friend Request. 141
Find Friends in Other Friends' Lists 142

Respond to a Friend Request 143

Make Facebook Lists 145

Hide a Friend's Posts 146

Send Direct Messages to Friends. 148

Retrieve a Private Message. 149

Chat with Friends or Video Call 150

Post Updates on a Friend's Wall. 152

Comment on a Friend's Status 152

Remove Messages from Your Wall 153

CHAPTER 9: **Adding Photos and Videos to Facebook** 155

Upload a Photo to Your Account 156

Create a Photo Album 159

Tag Photos. 163

Untag Yourself in a Photo 166

Delete a Photo 167

Upload a Video to Facebook. 168

Broadcast Live Video on Facebook 169

CHAPTER 10: **Exploring the Extras: Groups, Events, Watch, and Games** 173

Find Your Favorite Things on Facebook 174

Join a Facebook Group 177

Start a Facebook Group 179

Communicate with Group Members. 183

Create an Event Invitation. 185

Review Upcoming Events and Birthdays 186

Watch Facebook TV 187

PART 3: AND NOW, IT'S TWITTER TIME 189

CHAPTER 11: **A Beginner's Guide to Twitter** 191

Register with Twitter 192

Adjust Your Account Settings. 200

Take Charge of Your Privacy. 203

Set Up Notifications for Web and Mobile 206

Review Terms and Privacy Policy. 207

Find People to Follow 208

Tour Your New Twitter Profile 212

CHAPTER 12: **Conversing on Twitter with Friends, Family, and Even Strangers** 217

Follow Basic Guidelines for Conversing 218
Pass Along a Chosen Tweet 223
Like Your Favorite Tweets 224
Search for Tweeted Topics 225
Know What to Tweet About 226

CHAPTER 13: **Gathering Tools of the Twitter Trade** 235

Save Data on Mobile with Twitter Lite..................236
Enhance Your Tweets with Emoji.....................239
Read and Follow Foreign Language Accounts 244
Find Trends and Friends with Twitter Search..............246
Discover What Is Trending 249
FollowFriday, FF, and Other Hashtags....................251
Connect and Chat with People....................255
Solve Customer Service Issues Online 257
Keep Track of Hundreds, Thousands of Friends? 258
View Your Friend Lists 260

PART 4: INSTAGRAMMING WITH THE PROS (YOUR KIDS).........263

CHAPTER 14: **Where Only Visuals Will Do . . . Instagram** 265

Set Up Your Instagram Account....................266
Complete Your Profile in a Browser 269
Check Through the Privacy Settings 272
Should You Use Instagram on a Desktop or Mobile Device?....................276
Find Friends and People to Follow.....................277

CHAPTER 15: **Posting and Perfecting Your Pictures** 283

Make a Difference with Simple Photo Tips..................284
Post Photos Taken on Your Phone 285
Take Photos and Videos in the Instagram App 291
Post Your Stories on Instagram 292
Learn to Take a Selfie 297

CHAPTER 16: **Socializing and Fine Tuning Your Instagram** 301
    Learn the Social Media Shorthand: Hashtags 302
    Interact with Friends and Photos. 306
    Comment on a Photo or Video. 307
    Respond to Follows, Likes, and Comments 308
    Follow Those Who Have Followed You 310
    Send and Read Private Messages 310

INDEX 313

Introduction

Welcome to the third edition of this book. I'm honored that I have been able to help thousands of people get online and use social media safely. Now you hold this power in your hands, too.

I've been working and playing online since the mid-'80s. I started out using CompuServe from my old Kaypro II with a 300-baud modem. I'd log on to my computer in the evenings when I had some quiet ⌐⌐⌐ ⌐⌐⌐⌐ my daughter was asleep.

⌐⌐gh CompuServe had no fancy pages, ⌐⌐osphor-green text on a tiny screen. ⌐⌐any better technology, so we commu- ⌐⌐ss the country and around the world. ⌐⌐d joined groups to discuss our hobbies

⌐⌐ere have been related social communi- ⌐⌐e have been connected computers. Even ⌐⌐ they invented the current online world, ⌐⌐ the 21st-century continuation of a com- ⌐⌐te a while.

⌐⌐ne then (in the early '80s) are still online ⌐⌐e may also (after a long career) want to jump back ⌐⌐⌐ ⌐ feeling of an online community. So, even though this book title says *For Seniors*, you should know I don't like that term. This book is for those with experience.

Although a persistent rumor claims that only the youngsters go online, actually online participation is growing faster in people over 50. There are more online users over 40 than under 25. Perhaps these people were so busy living their lives and bringing up their children that they didn't have extra time for themselves then — but they do now. And just as in the '60s or '70s, they don't want to be left out of anything. They want to be smack dab in the middle of the online revolution.

Unfortunately, a lot of what they encounter when they go online is unfamiliar stuff. So (naturally enough) some of the experienced, graying generation experience a feeling of trepidation when it comes to the Internet — most of all, they're a bit unsure about getting on Twitter, Facebook, and Instagram.

I have to say: *Why?* Participating in social media is freeing — and can bring so much into your life! You can't *not* be there! This book will give you the tools to stay safe and find joy sharing on these sites.

I encourage you: Join your extended family, your children, and your friends online. By participating in social media, you'll find many of your old friends. In a world where people don't chat on the phone much anymore, the online arena is the perfect place to connect.

And you will also make *new* friends. I am blessed enough to have met many of my online friends in person. The online world has given me a whole new group of humans that I can call on for advice — or, better yet, go out to brunch with — in the real world.

Twitter is pretty straightforward — once you get the hang of it, you'll be Tweeting like a pro in no time. Instagram is sort of magical. I often browse the photos at any time of day, just to relax. But a website that's as complex as Facebook has many nooks and crannies that can confuse new users (and even experienced ones). Think of this book as a roadmap that can help you find your way around in the social media world, getting just as much or as little as you want from the trip. Unlike an actual paper road map, you won't have to fold it back to its original shape (whew). Just close the book and come back any time you need a question answered.

About This Book

Remember those open-book tests that teachers sprang on you in school? Well, sometimes you may feel like Facebook pop-quizzes you while you're online. Think of *Facebook, Twitter & Instagram For Seniors For Dummies* as your open-book-test cheat sheet with the answers.

You don't have to memorize anything; just keep this book handy and follow along whenever you need to.

With this in mind, I've divided this book into pertinent sections to help you find your answers fast. I'll show you how to

» Set up your computer for the ultimate online experience.

» There's a short tutorial on emoji, so you'll understand the meaning of 💪, 👋, 😼 and 😄.

» Set up a new account on Gmail to handle all your new communication.

» Join social media by registering to meet old (and new) friends.

» Post to your friend's Facebook walls and send private messages.

» Find people you haven't heard from in years and catch up with their lives.

» See what's going on with your children and grandchildren online — and join the party.

» Share photos and videos online (or just view ones from your friends).

» Become a part of a unique community of people!

Do not reach for your glasses. To protect the privacy of the online community, the screen images (commonly called *screen shots*) that I've used in this book blur private information on purpose. That's to protect the innocent (or not so . . . what the heck, cue the *Dragnet* theme).

Conventions Used in This Book

Anyone born before 1960 grew up in an analog age. Televisions were big, bulky affairs; the first remote controls ca-chunked each time they changed the channel (and they only had four buttons). Families woke up and went to sleep seeing a test pattern. Cameras (the good ones) were solid, heavy devices, and movie cameras whirred along with a comfortable mechanical hum. Typewriters clacked in a danceable rhythm.

Then life turned digital without anyone's permission — even without folks noticing until it happened. The comfortable mechanical sounds of everyday appliances seemed to go away. Whirring, buzzing, and beeping replaced familiar sounds. Everything got more complex: the button count on my TV remote control went from four to a gazillion! It seems as if everything we use has gotten smaller. The digital camera on my phone looks so small and cheesy that I'm shocked it can take a good picture — but it does. (It takes great ones!) Even the type on a page, it seems, has gotten smaller — which is why my publisher has graciously set this book in a type that will permit you to read something, glance at your computer, and look back again without having to pick your glasses off the top of your head.

Here are a few conventions to look out for as you read this book:

» **Online addresses:** The online location (or address) of a website is called a Uniform Resource Locator (URL). These online addresses — as well as email addresses — appear in a `monofont` typeface, as follows:

`www.facebook.com`

» **What to type:** When instructions for a task require that you type something on your keyboard, that something appears in **bold** typeface.

» **On-screen buttons with long labels:** When an on-screen button is labeled with a phrase instead of a single word, I put it in title case, like this: Click the Do This Silly Digital Thing Now button. That ought to head off confusion at the pass.

Foolish Assumptions

I'm thinking that you've picked up this book because you heard that the immediate world has jumped online and maybe you feel a little left out. Perhaps you already like to send text messages and think this Twitter thing might be for you? If either of these assumptions is true, this is the right book for you.

Here are some other foolish assumptions I've made about you (I'm famous for my foolish assumptions . . . you too?):

» You have access to the Internet so you can get online and start to socialize.

» You have an interest in communicating with people, and you want to find out more about what you can do online — without asking your children.

» You want tips to help you get online without looking like a newcomer, or *newbie* (the kids call them *noobs*). I can relate. We have a lot in common.

» You're concerned about maintaining your privacy and staying away from shysters.

Icons Used in This Book

When something in this book is particularly valuable, I go out of my way to make sure that it stands out. In this book, I use the tip icon to mark text that (for one reason or another) *really* needs your attention. An example of this icon:

Tips save you a lot of time and keep you out of trouble.

Beyond the Book

In addition to the content in this book, you'll find some extra content available at the www.dummies.com website:

> » **For the Cheat Sheet for this book, visit** www.dummies.com/ and search for *Facebook, Twitter, and Instagram For Seniors For Dummies 3rd edition cheat sheet.*
>
> » **For updates to this book, click my blog on my website at** www.marshacollier.com.

Like everything else in the world, Twitter, Facebook, and Instagram have an ever-changing nature. And for Facebook — because the website is more complex — this is even truer. (That's annoying, isn't it?) These social networking sites are always trying to improve the user experience, but sometimes such changes can be confusing. My job is to arm you with an understanding of basic functions, so you won't be thrown by any minor course corrections on the site's part. Don't look at this book as a deep dive; it's just enough to help you remove your training wheels when you're done. If you hit rough waters, just look up the troublesome item in the book's index.

Most of all, don't get frustrated! Keep reviewing topics before you feel fully comfortable to take the plunge on the sites. Perhaps even start off with baby steps — there's no need to start off with a bang. No one will notice that you're just a beginner.

A persistent piece of Internet lore quotes Albert Einstein as saying, "I never commit to memory anything that can easily be looked up in a book." But nobody seems to know exactly when he said that. No problem. You and I know that books are handy to have around when you're learning new things. I'm all about that. So is this book. Use your highlighter.

Feedback, Please

I'd love to hear from you: your successes and your comments. I'm on Twitter every day as @MarshaCollier (http://twitter.com/marshacollier). Feel free to join me on Facebook: I have my personal page, a book fan page, and a community page set up by Facebook with my biography. I love making new friends and will be glad to help you whenever I can.

Contact me at mtalk2marsha@coolebaytools.com or on my site, www.marshacollier.com. I can't always answer each and every question you send. But do know that I promise to read each email and answer when I can.

Visit my blog at http://mcollier.blogspot.com, and if you'd like to learn about eBay, check out my website at www.coolebaytools.com. I also wrote *eBay For Seniors For Dummies*, so if you're looking to make a little spare cash, that book will definitely simplify selling (and buying) on eBay for you.

Welcome to the future. It's actually a very fun place.

1

Getting Started with Social Networking

IN THIS PART . . .

Getting yourself ready for the Internet

Connecting to the Internet

All about email and online safety

Speaking the social media language

Sharing in the modern age: acronyms, posts, photos, and videos

Chapter **1**

Getting Equipped for the Internet

D on't worry, I'm not going to tell you that you need really fancy equipment to get started online, but you must *have* a computer, tablet, or at the least a smartphone. These days, there are more choices than you can imagine for joining the online social scene. If you're in the market for some technology to get you there, you've got a few choices, which I tell you about in this chapter.

Shopping for a computer or other Internet-capable device can be a dizzying experience. In fact, it's downright confusing. I suggest you go to a store and kick a few tires (or try out a few keyboards) before you make a decision. Also, recognize that your decisions about digital equipment depend on how and where you plan to connect online. Follow my advice in this chapter to evaluate your computer use and find the right source for your equipment.

Along with your hardware of choice and an Internet connection (see Chapter 2), you need just one more item — a software program or app — to interact with online social media sites. In this book, *social media* is considered Facebook, Twitter, and Instagram. When you get a computer or tablet, you get an Internet browser for free. A *browser* is the software program that lets you talk to the Internet. An *app*, or application, is a standalone program on mobile devices which you download from Apple's App Store or Google's Play Store. They're like having your own private cyberchauffeur. In this chapter, I also tell you a little about the common browsers and apps that are readily available.

Select Hardware to Match Your Needs

1. I confess, I have two desktop all-in-ones with 27-inch screens, three laptops, two tablets, *and* three smartphones — and I use each one at different locations and for different reasons. You certainly don't need to have all varieties to participate in social media; simply decide on which types are right for you. Think through the scenarios in this section and see which one matches your plans. Then go find the hardware that fits.

2. If you are one who likes to sit at a desk or table, or wants a regular place to use your computer, you'll be happy with a desktop variety. Also, if you like to have all the power of today's computing at your disposal, you might want to get a desktop. *Desktop* computers are larger than their portable cousins.

TIP

You can buy a package that combines a monitor, keyboard, and computer module (which houses the processor that is "the brains") or pick up an "all-in-one" that combines the requisite parts into one unit.

TECH-LITE ECONOMICAL SOLUTIONS

You may not have the budget, or even want to get involved in technology past your smartphone, but you may find your phone's screen too small. There are options for you, too:

- **Chromebook:** If you prefer laptops, consider a small Chromebook, which you can purchase for under $200. All you need is a Google account and you can be running the Google Chrome OS immediately. Higher-priced models can include a hard drive for keeping copies of your work. Chromebooks need to be connected to Wi-Fi almost all the time, and the software comes from the cloud.

- **Amazon Fire Tablets:** Although Amazon's tablets run the Amazon OS, you can still install apps from Amazon's Android App Store. So if you have an Android phone, the tablets will be second nature to you. A 10-inch HD version with 32GB of storage is currently about $140.

These economical devices can fulfill many needs. Search Amazon to find the latest iterations of these devices as well as the latest advances and processes.

3. If you're looking for a computer that will allow you to sit seductively at Starbucks — looking cool — you'll have to get a laptop — or perhaps a tablet. How about if you just want to use the device from *anywhere* in your home other than your desk (say, the kitchen counter)? The major difference between a desktop and a *laptop* (as shown in **Figure 1-1**) is that everything you need is combined in one compact, lightweight package. Also, you'll be able to use your laptop to go online anywhere a wireless (Wi-Fi) connection is available. Wi-Fi readiness is built into all laptops.

Also consider the following if you're leaning toward getting a laptop:

- You'll find that keyboards can get progressively smaller, depending on the size of laptop you buy. So if you have big fingers, be sure to test out the offerings in a store before buying one.

- You'll find smaller monitors on today's laptops, so they can be portable. It somewhat defeats the portability purpose when you have to lug around a 17-inch, 6-pound behemoth. Keep in mind that web browsers allow you to easily increase the size of the text you see (more about that in the task "Browse for a Browser" later in this chapter).

FIGURE 1-1

TIP

I've taken my laptop or sometimes my tablet out by the pool when I'm on vacation, and at home, I sometimes *Tweet* (send a message on Twitter) from my garden. Portability is a wonderful thing.

4. If you're looking for extra portability and convenience, think tablet. *Tablets* are handheld devices that are much smaller than laptops (they generally have 8- or 10-inch screens), you can slip one in a purse or shopping bag, and you can buy one for as little at $100. They are a great deal: lots of capability in not much space. My 6.4-inch screen smartphone (a Samsung Galaxy Note 9) 8.4-inch screen Huawei MediaPad M3) is shown in **Figure 1-2** next to a 9.7-inch screen iPad Air 2. The Note 9 weighs about 7 ounces, the MediaPad about 11 ounces, and the iPad a pound.

Due to size limitations, there are a few tasks that a smartphone or tablet can't perform, as illustrated in **Table 1-1**.

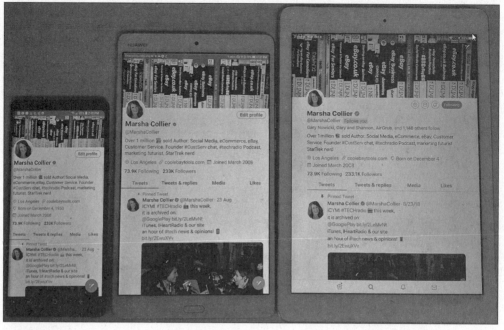

FIGURE 1-2

TABLE 1-1   What a Laptop and a Tablet Can Do

Task	Tablet	Laptop
Email, chat, instant messaging	X	X
Social networking, blogging	X	X
Surfing the web	X	X
Streaming audio or video	X	X
Using word processors, spreadsheets, and small business programs	X	X
Capturing live action with a built-in web cam	X	X
Playing games	Via apps	PC games
Editing videos and photos	Light editing only	X
Seamlessly watching HD movies	Depends on the quality of the Wi-Fi connection	X
Running complex software		X

5. If you want to access social media from your pocket, you can also do so from any of the current smartphones. A *smartphone* is a mobile personal computer that fits in your hand, and you can also use it to make phone calls and texts. Smartphones contain mini versions (*apps* just like those you'd use on a tablet) of almost every piece of software you have on your laptop. When your Wi-Fi connection is out, or if you have the need to connect from a restaurant, your mobile provider can connect you. **Figure 1-3** shows my Android phone ready for action.

FIGURE 1-3

Know What Options to Look For

1. Before you purchase one of the different types of equipment I outline in the previous section, think about some of the options you need to look for on any computing device that you plan to use for interacting with your pals on social media.

   When it comes to a computer, look for one with a large hard drive. The more time you spend using — and collecting pictures, videos, and other important stuff on — your computer, the more Blob-like your hard drive's contents become. (Remember that 1950s horror movie, *The Blob,* where an alien life form just grows and grows?)

A hard drive with at least 160 gigabytes (GB) of storage space should keep your computer happy, but you can get hard drives as big as a terabyte (TB). You're probably going to be storing photos and videos (yes, you will — I promise), so I suggest that you buy one with the most storage available.

2. One USB port is *never* enough. These days, it seems that every peripheral device you need connects to your computer through a Universal Serial Bus (USB) connection. You may end up with an external hard drive for backup, a mouse, a printer, and a digital camera that you need to connect (so you can download pictures).

   Figure 1-4 shows a common peripheral device: a USB flash drive. Make sure that the desktop or laptop computer you get has at *least* two USB ports. You can plug and unplug from these at will or attach a USB hub to one for temporary connections.

FIGURE 1-4

3. Make sure the central processing unit (CPU) is fast. A *CPU* (also known as a *chip*) is your computer's brain. It should be the fastest you can afford. The higher the processor speed is in any device, the faster it processes data. That means less waiting and more time to enjoy what your device can do for you.

4. You must have a keyboard for a computer. No keyboard, no typing. The basic keyboard is fine. You have a basic choice of "clicky" mechanical keyboards (they feel like an old IBM Selectric typewriter) or flatter models that you touch lightly with a tapping motion. Tablets and smartphones put virtual keyboards onscreen, or you can purchase a Bluetooth keyboard for your mobile device. Try them out at a store to see which suits your style.

5. Media-card reader. Your tablet, digital camera, or smartphone may have a memory card in it where it holds all the pictures you take. You may prefer to pop out the card and slip it into your computer than

mess around with connecting cables to archive your photos. If that's your thing, be sure any computer you buy accepts the same type of cards as your mobile devices (and that includes digital cameras).

6. You need a pointing device that moves the pointer around the computer screen; it's usually a *mouse*. Laptops come with touchpads or trackballs designed to do the pointing and give you a quick way to select options by clicking or tapping. I personally find that a mouse is a better choice.

TIP

To save possible pain in your hands, I recommend you use an ergonomic mouse like the Contour Mouse from Contour Design (www.contourdesign.com/product/contour-mouse). I've used one for over a decade (see **Figure 1-5**). The Contour Mouse fits your hand and is available in five different sizes for right and left hands. This mouse reduces or eliminates the grip force required to navigate and click traditional mice, and its sculpted design supports your hand comfortably without the need to clutch the mouse to control it.

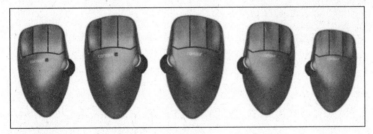

FIGURE 1-5

7. When buying a monitor to go with a desktop computer, size counts! A monitor that has at least a 17-inch screen can make a huge difference in your comfort level after several hours of rabid Tweeting, reading your friends' Facebook posts, or looking at pictures. Anything smaller, and you could have a hard time actually seeing the words and images. The good news: Monitors have become so inexpensive that you can find a 27-inch-or-larger variety for about $200.

Shop for Your Device of Choice

1. These days you can find computers and tablets at many brick-and-mortar retailers, including Target, Walmart, Apple Store, Best Buy, and Costco. Try out each and ask questions. Buying online may be common these days, but "try before you buy" is still wise, and retail stores are more than willing to show you the models they offer.

2. You can also go online and find sellers who may have even better deals on new, used, or refurbished equipment. Some websites that sell these items are Amazon (www.amazon.com), Overstock.com (www.overstock.com), BestBuy.com (www.bestbuy.com), and even at Walmart.com (www.walmart.com).

3. If you don't feel comfortable buying used equipment (but want to save money), you may want to consider a factory-refurbished model. These are new machines that were returned to the manufacturer for one reason or another. The factory fixes them so they're good as new, and then sweetens the deal with a warranty. What you're getting is a new device at a deep discount because the machine can't be resold legally as new. Here are some things to know about refurbished technology:

   - **They're rebuilt and come with warranties.** For the most part, refurbished computers are defined as returns, units with blemishes (scratches, dents, and so on), or evaluation units. The factories rebuild them to their original working condition, using new parts (or sometimes used parts that meet or exceed performance specs for new parts). They come with 60-to-90-day warranties that cover repairs and returns. Warranty information is available on the manufacturers' websites, so be sure to read it before you purchase a refurbished digital device.

   - **You can get name brands.** Major computer manufacturers, such as Dell (www.dellrefurbished.com), HP (www.hp.com/sbso/buspurchase_refurbished.html), Lenovo (www3.lenovo.com/us/en/outletus), and Apple (www.apple.com/shop/browse/home/specialdeals/mac) provide refurbished computers. Check whether your chosen manufacturer's website has an outlet store (**Figure 1-6** shows one example) for closeouts and refurbished goods — I've never been burned!

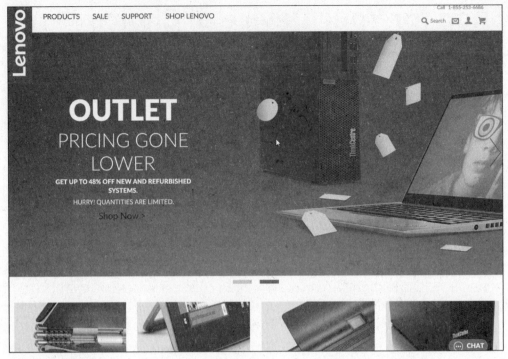

FIGURE 1-6

TIP

Because the inventory of refurbished items changes daily (as do the prices), there's no way of telling exactly how much money you can save by buying refurbished rather than new. I suggest that you find a new unit that you like (and can afford) in a store or a catalog, and then compare it with refurbished systems of the same brand and model.

TIP

If you're thinking about buying from the web or a catalog, don't forget to include the cost of shipping in the total price. Even with shipping costs, however, a refurbished item may save you between 30 and 60 percent, depending on the deal you find.

Browse for a Browser

1. The two most popular *browsers* (the software programs that help you read what's on the Internet) are Google Chrome and Firefox; both are available for Mac and PC. (They are to browsers what Coca-Cola

and Pepsi are to the cola wars.) Both programs are powerful and user-friendly. Type the address (also known as the *URL,* for *Uniform Resource Locator*) of the website you want to visit, and boom, you're there. For example, to get to Twitter's home page, type `www.twitter.com` in the browser's address box and press Enter. (It's sort of a low-tech version of "Beam me up, Scotty!" — and almost as fast.)

The most popular browsers for desktop and mobile are Chrome, Firefox, Edge, and Safari. **Figures 1-7** and **1-8** show you the Chrome browser and how it displays pages on both a computer and a tablet. (Sit, browser! Now shake! *Good* browser!) The one you choose is a matter of preference — I use them both!

FIGURE 1-7

FIGURE 1-8

2. You can get a variety of browsers for your mobile device or computer for free. To find out more information (or to make sure you're using the most up-to-date version of the software), go to

- `www.google.com/chrome` for Chrome
- `www.mozilla.com/firefox` for Firefox
- `www.apple.com/safari/` for Safari
- `www.microsoft.com/en-us/windows/microsoft-edge` for Microsoft Edge

3. If you want to add speed to your browsing and cut down your desk time, get comfy with using keyboard and mouse shortcuts. I'm all about using keystrokes instead of always pointing and clicking! I also love the controls available on my mouse. **Table 1-2**, **Table 1-3**, and **Table 1-4** give you a list of the shortcuts I like to use. You'll see that all browsers share similar shortcuts.

TABLE 1-2   Microsoft Edge Shortcuts

Press This	Edge Will
F1	Open a help window.
Ctrl and F	Open a Search box so you can perform a search for a specific word on the current page.
F4	Open your URL list so you can click back to a site that you just visited.
F5	Refresh the current page.
F11	Display full screen, reducing the number of icons and amount of other stuff displayed.
Esc	Stop loading the current page.
Home	Go back to the top of the web page.
End	Jump to the bottom of the current page.
Backspace	Go back to the last web page you viewed.
Ctrl and + (plus sign); Ctrl and – (minus sign)	Enlarge or reduce the text on the screen.
Ctrl and D	Add the current page to your Favorites list.

TABLE 1-3   Firefox Shortcuts

Press This	Firefox Will
Backspace	Go to the previous page you've viewed.
Ctrl and O	Open a window to open files from your computer.
Ctrl and U	View Page source (to study HTML).
F11	Display full screen, reducing the number of icons and amount of other stuff displayed.
Esc	Stop loading the current page.
Ctrl and P	Print the page.
Ctrl and S	Save the current page to a file on your computer.
Ctrl and + (plus sign) or Ctrl and – (minus sign)	Enlarge or reduce the text on the screen.
Ctrl and F	Find a word on the current web page.

TABLE 1-4 **Chrome Hot Keys**

Press This	Chrome Will
Alt and Home	Open a web page that shows either a preset home page or thumbnails of the sites visited most often from that computer.
Ctrl and O	Open a window to open files from your computer.
F5	Refresh current page.
Ctrl and U	View Page source (to study HTML).
F11	Display full screen, reducing the number of icons and amount of other stuff displayed.
Esc	Stop loading the current page.
Ctrl and 1 through Ctrl and 8	Switch to the tab at the specified position number.
Ctrl and 9	Switch to the last tab that is open in your browser.
Ctrl and Shift and T	Reopen the last closed tab.
Ctrl and P	Print the page.
Ctrl and D	Bookmark the current page.
Ctrl and S	Save the current page to a file on your computer.
Backspace	Go back to the last viewed web page.
Ctrl and Shift and N	New Incognito window: websites you browse in this tab will not be recorded in your Internet history.
Ctrl and T	Open a new tab in the browser so you can visit another web page while leaving the current one open.
Ctrl and + or Ctrl and – (minus sign)	Zoom to enlarge or reduce the text onscreen.
Ctrl and 0	Return to browser's default text size.
Ctrl and F	Find a word on the current web page.

IN THIS CHAPTER

» **Select an Internet Service Provider**

» **Choose a Broadband Network Option**

» **Connect a Powerline Network**

» **Set Up a Wireless Network**

» **Protect Your Privacy and Stay Safe Online**

Chapter **2**

Connecting to the Internet

You're settled on your devices, and you're ready to get started with social connections on the web. Before you start visiting sites such as Facebook, Twitter, and Instagram, you need *access* to the Internet. Your smartphone will automatically connect to your telecom provider, but what about at home? The way to access the Internet through other devices is through an *Internet service provider,* or ISP. If you don't already have access to one, don't worry; joining is easy, as I describe in this chapter.

ISPs offer two basic types of connections: DSL (slower, but less expensive) and broadband (faster and pricier). In this chapter, I fill you in on some details to help you decide what's right for you. Also, I tell you about the wired or wireless networking methods that complete the setup you need for easy access from home.

Over the years, I have written what seems like volumes of tips to keep people safe online. I know this book won't have to give you all the whys and wherefores — you've been around the block (as have I) — so I give you just a few easy-to-follow best practices for staying safe during your online social interactions.

Select an Internet Service Provider

1. If you live in a rural part of the country, there may be no broadband Internet in your area. You may need to connect through a slow, telephone dial-up ISP, such as EarthLink (www.earthlink.net/internet). Dial-up requires no additional equipment or connections in most older computers; just load the software from the provider and follow the registration steps that appear on your computer screen.

TIP

When you go to a computer store or buy a computer, you're hit with all kinds of free trial offers that beg you to "Sign up now, first month free!" You can find free introductory deals everywhere! Read the section further on in this chapter about privacy before you sign up for anything.

2. If you have a need for speed (and trust me, you will), you may want to look into getting a broadband connection. The quality of the different types of broadband (DSL, fiber, and cable) can vary greatly from area to area, even from street to street. Before you decide what kind of broadband connection you want, use your local library or friend's computer and go to www.dslreports.com, shown in **Figure 2-1**.

DSLReports
Welcome · log in · join | Q Search dslreports.com

| Home | Reviews | Speed Test new | Tools | News | Forums | Info | About | Join |

Happy Customers	Mixed	Unhappy
PA Verizon FiOS new	CA Cox HSI	WA Frontier Communications new
TX Suddenlink	MO Mediacom new	MI AT&T DSL new
IL Comcast XFINITY	MS MaxxSouth Broadband new	MI Comcast XFINITY
TX Comcast XFINITY new	GA Comcast XFINITY new	TX Frontier Communications new
IN Charter new	US Optimum Online new	VA Verizon FiOS new
TX Time Warner Cable	WA Comcast XFINITY	IL RCN new
CA AT&T FTTP new	NC Time Warner Cable new	MN CenturyLink new
NC Carolina Mountain Cablev..	NY Time Warner Cable new	NY Charter new

FIGURE 2-1

Scroll down the page and look for the Review Finder. Type your zip code in the text box, press Go, and click the headlines to read the reviews from other users in your area. You can post questions, and get the information you need to decide what kind of high-speed connection will work best for you.

3. Broadband (high-speed) connections can save you bunches of time when you're flying through Instagram photos. Here's the skinny on the different types:

- **DSL:** Short for *Digital Subscriber Line*. A DSL line is the least expensive high-speed connection you can get. It will average around 10 to 40 Mbps download and 3 to 10 up. A DSL line is available almost anywhere in the country because it accesses the Internet over existing copper phone lines.

- **Cable:** An Internet cable connection is a very reliable (and fast) method for Internet access if you have digital cable TV available in your neighborhood. It can also be the most expensive. The Internet connection runs through the same cable as your television, connecting to a modem, and it's regulated by your cable TV provider. Speeds can easily exceed 100 Mbps. With the advent of digital cable, this Internet connection is an excellent alternative. (See my www.dslreports.com/speedtest results from my network in **Figure 2-2**.)

- **Fiber:** The newest entrant into the broadband market uses fiber optic cable and is complicated and expensive to install. That's why it's not yet available in most markets. It is the gold standard of the future, but current hardware can't take advantage of its higher speeds of 500 Mbps to 1 Gbps.

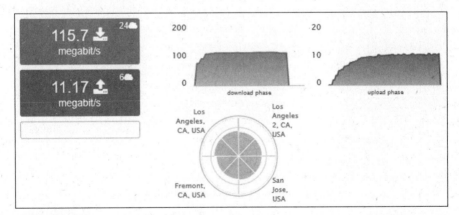

FIGURE 2-2

4. You have one more type of Internet connection to consider: public Wi-Fi. *Wi-Fi* stands for Wireless Fidelity, which describes a particular (and common) wireless technology for local networking without wires (that is, via a radio frequency). There are many public places where you can find free (or very low cost) wireless Internet access. If you decide on a mobile device (see Chapter 1) and don't plan to spend a great deal of time online, you may not need an ISP of your own. All you need is a portable device — with a wireless connection.

To find free Wi-Fi when you want to go portable, find your nearest coffee house (Starbucks, Coffee Bean and Tea Leaf, Panera Bread) or local library and take advantage of their free Wi-Fi connection. Get connected and visit www.wififreespot.com. At this site, as shown in **Figure 2-3**, you can look up restaurant, hotel, and retail chains that offer Wi-Fi in all their locations, along with a state-by-state listing of small businesses and other locations that offer free Wi-Fi. Read further in this chapter for security tips to remember when you're connecting to a public Wi-Fi hotspot.

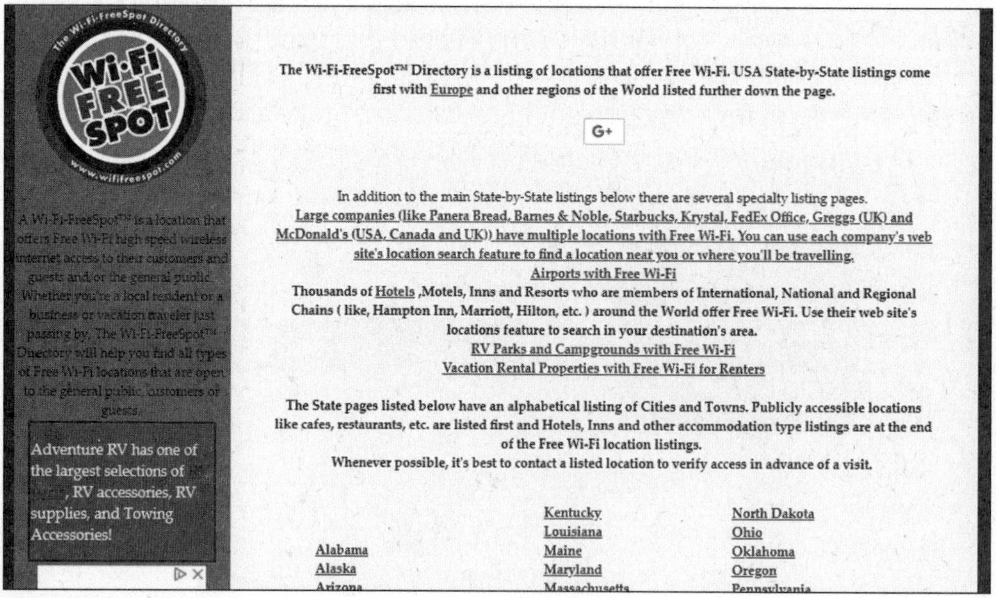

FIGURE 2-3

TIP

Apps that locate free Wi-Fi zones are available for tablets and smartphones. Use one if you must, but first read the section in this chapter on wireless safety.

Choose a Broadband Network Option

1. When you set up your Internet connection, you're actually setting up the beginnings of a home network. By networking your home, you can save time — not to mention gain convenience — because you add the flexibility of connecting to the Internet from different rooms or locations. You can also Tweet from out by your pool (or in your backyard) during summer!

TIP

A *network* is a way to connect computers so they can communicate with each other as if they were one giant computer with different terminals. The best part of this idea is that a network lets many devices share a high-speed (broadband) Internet connection — you can share printers, televisions, and gaming devices as well. When you set up a computer network, your home can become your personal Wi-Fi hotspot!

2. You have a choice of three types of home networks: Ethernet, powerline, and wireless. See **Table 2-1** for a quick rundown of some pros and cons of each.

TABLE 2-1   **Network Pros and Cons**

Network type	Pros	Cons
Ethernet	Very fast, cheap, and easy to set up	Everything must be wired together; cables run everywhere
Powerline	Fast, reliable, because your home is prewired with electrical outlets	Electrical interference may degrade signal
Wireless network	Fast, no ugly cables to deal with	More expensive, possible interference from other devices

While you make a decision about the type of network you want to use, consider the following points:

- The wireless network is the standard. If you have a device and a high-speed connection, you deserve to have Wi-Fi in your home. You'll have many options and can stream video from your tablet to your television or use one of the Amazon Fire TV Sticks. Wi-Fi can do that and more!

- With broadband over powerline networking, you get high-speed Internet directly through your home electrical system. Just plug in your powerline boxes (more on that later) and you're up and running!

3. Regardless of the type of network you choose, all networks need the following two devices:

- **Router:** A router allows you to share a single Internet connection among multiple devices. A router does exactly what its name says: It routes signals and data to and from the different devices on your network. If you have a computer, the router can act as a firewall or even as a network device, allowing you to have a wireless printer (I have one — it's great) and a connection for a gaming device.

TIP

You can connect as many computers, tablets, smartphones, printers, or game systems as you like, and reach the Internet from anywhere in your home or garden. You can also watch TV through Wi-Fi if you have a new, Internet-enabled television.

- **Modem:** You need a broadband modem for a high-speed Internet connection, and you get one from your cable or phone company. To install, plug the modem into an outlet with cable (just like your TV) or into a phone jack with the phone line for DSL. The modem connects to your router with a short length of Ethernet cable.

TIP

If you have broadband, you don't need to have a computer turned on to access the connection from anywhere in the house. As long as they are plugged in, the router and modem will work in tandem to distribute the signal.

Connect a Powerline Network

An ingenious invention, a *powerline network* uses your existing home power lines to carry your network and your Internet connection. Powerline networks have been around for a while.

When deciding what kind of network to set up, consider these benefits of a nifty little powerline system:

» **It's inexpensive.** A pair of requisite powerline magic boxes costs as little as $35. You need one for each computer.

» **It's fast,** as fast or faster than other network connections. You could stream DVD movies from one room to another.

» **It doesn't consume extra electricity** because the networking connection is made through your existing electrical wiring.

» **Installation is easy.** Just plug a cable into your router, and connect the cable to the powerline adapter. Plug the powerline adapter into the wall outlet.

1. To set up a powerline network, you need the following items along with a router and modem (which you need for any network):

   - **Electrical outlets:** I'll bet you have more than one in each room.

   - **An Ethernet connection on each computer (or device):** All computers come with an Ethernet outlet.

   - **Powerline Ethernet adapter for each computer:** You plug an Ethernet cable from your computer into the powerline Ethernet adapter, a small box about the size of a smartphone that plugs into any two- or three-prong electrical outlet. See **Figure 2-4**.

2. Hooking up a powerline network is so easy that it's a bit disappointing — you'll wonder why it isn't more complicated. If you have a high-speed Internet connection, you received a modem when you signed up. Because it's not common to connect the modem directly to your computer (a router does the network routing for you), you may already have a router.

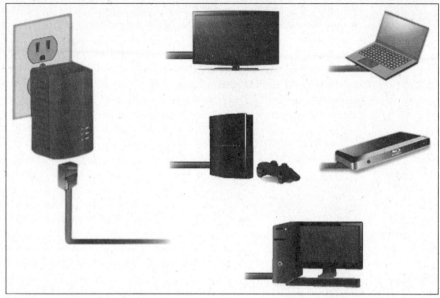

Photo courtesy of Linksys

FIGURE 2-4

The integration works like this:

a. *The high-speed connection comes in through your DSL or cable line.*

b. *The cable (or DSL) line plugs into your modem.*

c. *An Ethernet cable goes from your modem into a router.*

d. *One "out" Ethernet cable connection from the router goes to a local computer.*

e. *Another "out" Ethernet cable goes to the powerline adapter.*

f. *The powerline box plugs into a convenient wall outlet.*

g. *Another powerline adapter plugs into a remote outlet and picks up the signal sent from your router. Connect it to another device with an Ethernet cable.*

3. When you want to connect the computers in other rooms to the network, just plug in a powerline box. **Figure 2-5** shows you a typical setup for (say) a home office. Other rooms need only a powerline adapter that you connect to a computer, game device, and so on, running an Ethernet cable from the adapter to the device's network connection.

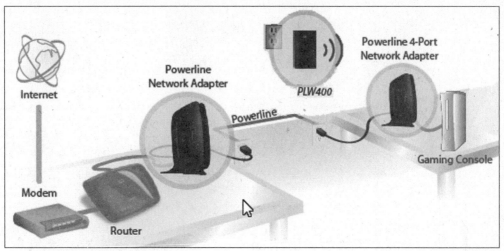

Figure courtesy of Linksys

FIGURE 2-5

Set Up a Wireless Network

1. Wireless networking (also known as Wi-Fi) is the most convenient technology for all kinds of networks. It's an impressive system, with no cables or connectors to bog you down. You're probably more familiar with wireless technology than you may think at first. If you've ever used a wireless telephone at home, you've used a technology similar to a wireless network. Most home wireless phones transmit on the radio frequency band of 2.4 GHz (gigahertz) and offer an option to choose from several channels automatically to give you the best connection.

TIP

Here's an FYI on all those signals running around and about your house. AM radio broadcasts from 53 kHz (kilohertz) to 1.7 MHz (megahertz); FM radio, television, cell phones, GPS, and the International Space Station broadcast in megahertz. One gigahertz (GHz) is a thousand kilohertz, so it won't be interfering with other radio frequency signals.

2. The two most prevalent forms of wireless networks also work on the 2.4 GHz band; the channel will be preset when you set up the system (but you can change it later if necessary). There are four types of wireless formats, and the newer types are *backward-compatible* (that means the newer types work well with the older types). Be sure to check your various computers, devices, routers, and so on that you want to connect in your network; in particular, find out which wireless format(s) they use. The most common formats that you will find are

- **802.11g:** This incarnation of Wi-Fi uses the 2.4 GHz band; its nickname is "the g band." It speeds data to a possible 54 Mbps, and is backward-compatible with 802.11b service. Many older Wi-Fi networks and gaming devices work on the g band.

- **802.11n:** This mode — the newest — builds on the previous standards by adding multiple-input multiple-output (MIMO) technology. MIMO uses multiple antennas (usually built into the router) to carry more information than previously possible with a single antenna. It uses the 5 GHz band (an improvement on the old 2.4 GHz band). It also increases speed through connection to 100 Mbps.

- **802.11ac:** Also nicknamed *Gigabit* or *5G* Wi-Fi, this is the newest flavor of Wi-Fi which supports better range and is the fastest to date. It incorporates the MIMO standard on the 5 GHz band (no competition from household appliances), increases the streams, and is more reliable.

TIP

For maximum speed, your entire network needs to be running on the latest form of 802.11 on a 5 GHz network. In my house, my 802.11ac network doesn't work at full speed because I adapted my devices to 802.11ac. For my older laptops, I purchased an inexpensive USB dongle that upgrades it to the fastest connection possible. **Figure 2-6** shows you how simple it is. Once it's plugged into a USB port, your computer will immediately recognize the new standard. I'll continue with a mixed 802.11g/n/ac network until I upgrade my televisions and other devices with 802.11ac. Until I do that, my home network won't run at the top advertised speeds.

Figure courtesy of Linksys

FIGURE 2-6

3. Before you start worrying about sending your data over the airwaves, you'll be glad to know that wireless networks are protected by their own brand of security.

- **WEP (Wired Equivalent Privacy):** This original technology led the way in-home Wi-Fi security. WEP encrypts your wireless transmissions and prevents others from getting into your network. Sadly, hackers broke into WEP; it got so that a high-school kid could crack this system, so now home Wi-Fi users have WPA (and even WPA-2) instead. For more about those, read on.

- **WPA (Wi-Fi Protected Access):** This utilizes a *pre-shared key* (PSK) mode, where every user on the network is given the same passphrase. In the PSK mode, security depends on the strength and secrecy of the passphrase. So to link your laptop or desktop to a wireless network with WPA encryption, you need to find out the predetermined passphrase. Just enter it during setup on every computer that uses the network, and you should be good to go.

TIP

Most Wi-Fi hotspots you come across may not have any encryption, and some may be free for all to use. Just be aware that some miscreants drive through neighborhoods with a Wi-Fi scanner looking for open wireless networks. These *war-driving* scammers then attempt to connect to an unprotected network to hack into personal information. Be sure to set your security settings to protect your network.

4. With a wireless network, you have to hook your computer (a laptop works best) to a wireless router to perform some beginning setup tasks such as choosing your channel and setting up your WPA passphrase. When you complete the setup and turn on your wireless router, you have created a Wi-Fi hotspot in your home or office. Typically, your new hotspot will provide coverage for at *least* 100 feet in all directions, although walls and floors cut down on the range. Even so, you should get good coverage throughout a typical home. For a large home, you can buy signal boosters to increase the range of your hotspot.

5. The following steps, although simplified, outline the process for how you configure your wireless network.

   a. *Connect an Ethernet cable from your laptop to your router.*

   b. *The setup program may run automatically (or the documentation that came with your router will tell you how to invoke it). Set your security protocol and passphrase.*

   c. *Follow router instructions as to whether you need to reboot the router.*

   d. *Run a cable from your DSL or cable jack to your modem.*

   e. *Connect an Ethernet cable from your modem to your router.*

   f. *Type the passphrase into all devices on the network, one at a time.*

Protect Your Privacy and Stay Safe Online

I'm always upset when I see legitimate publications (online or in print) featuring articles spreading fear about using the Internet. These articles particularly prey on those who are not tech savvy. Here I will give you legitimate solutions and resources so that you can stay safe online. You've been on this planet many years and have learned lots of lessons. There's no need to talk down to you. So the two most important pieces of advice I can give you?

» Never share information on the Internet that you wouldn't tell to anyone but your closest circle of friends and family.

» Do not add free apps to your devices that you are not sure you really need. For example, I only load my airline's app when I'm traveling and then delete it from my phone when my trip is over.

With this advice firmly in your mind, the following are truths to remember about being safe online.

- » **Nothing on the Internet is free:** I'm sure you've figured this out — there is no free lunch. There are no free websites and especially not apps that you load on your phone or to your browser.

- » **Just because you pay for a service, doesn't mean there's *less* chance you'll be taken advantage of.** After the Facebook data scandal hit the news, you might feel that viewing ads is your "payment" for accessing free sites and apps. That's only partially true. The truth is, the customer's data is the product. You may not think you've given data away, but in fact, many apps and websites can track your habits to learn more about you.

- » **Every smartphone gives up data about your location — even if you have your GPS and Wi-Fi turned off.** Apps and operating systems take advantage of this data all the time. Some miscreants will also sell this data.

- » **You can't assume that every provider on the Internet will follow privacy laws to the letter.** You know in your heart, that's just not going to happen. There's always a bad apple. Every time you start up a new device, use new software, go to a new website (or load up a new app), you are presented with some reference to accept the platform's Terms of Service (TOS in tech parlance). You may even just see a sentence or two, and be prompted to click through and read the entire policy. What's more, the likelihood that your data may be shared with a government agency (now or in the future) is a real possibility.

I don't want to scare you, but someone with just a few bits of information about you can get a lot more data than you can imagine. The Internet has plenty of sites (for example, Google maps) that will even show people a photo of your house. Always be cautious and remember the following:

1. When using Wi-Fi in a public place, use a VPN (Virtual Private Network). Don't freak out — I did when I first heard of it. A VPN is a service that sends your Wi-Fi data to an encrypted server that the provider operates. The data is then sent to the public Internet. Your data can now only be traced back to the VPN server, not to you.

WHEN DID YOU LAST READ A COMPLETE TOS?

TOS's are usually many pages long and filled with legalese. In 2016 a fictitious website was set up and 543 undergraduate university students were invited to a pre-launch evaluation of a social network. The students were presented with a Privacy Policy which (buried in the legalese) said that their data would be given to the NSA and employers. Also the TOS said they would have to give up their first-born child as payment (if they didn't have a child yet, the clause would remain active until 2050). 98 percent of the participants skipped through the legal jargon and signed up for the website.

No one actually reads a TOS. Most existing policies would take up to an hour to read! It is worth your while to go over a Terms of Service and Privacy Policy when you are presented with one.

As you may have figured out by now, not all VPNs are created equal (even the ones you pay for). Security pros recommend checking a VPN out at the website `https://thatoneprivacysite.net/simple-vpn-comparison-chart` to see any pitfalls of a commercial VPN. At the top of the page, indicate to show ALL entries and you'll be presented with a very thorough list of VPNs. The highest rated have green blocks across the board.

Even though I use a VPN, I limit my Wi-Fi hotspot dealing to reading news, social updates, and general (not too personal) information. Wi-Fi hotspots are open networks; there is no security to keep your data safe. Therefore, when you connect in public, nothing is really private. So Starbucks (and other public zones such as hotels or airports) are not the appropriate place to perform financial transactions or to send anything over the network that might reveal your personal information.

2. **Don't click links or open attachments you receive in email messages.** Even if you get an email message from someone you know, don't click any links and email the person back questioning any attachments. There's no way to know for sure that the person's account hasn't been hacked; if it has, chances are you're being directed to a site that can do you serious damage. Here are specific examples of email messages with links that you might receive:

   - **Phishing emails:** These emails purport to be from your bank, your investment broker, or even your insurance company. They ask you to click a link, and when you do, you arrive on a page where you have to log in. *Do not log in* (if you've gone this far). Bad actors can replicate a web page to look very official, and what they really want is your log-in information — in particular your passwords, account information, or social security number.

   - **Emails that you think are from friends:** You may get a link in an email message that you think is from a friend. Don't click it unless you are sure! Sometimes these links take you to a website where you can get a Trojan (a sneaky program that gives a hacker remote access to your computer), a virus (when unknowingly downloaded, replicates itself to wreak havoc on your programs or data), a worm (a variant of a virus that replicates itself transparently until it takes over all your computer's memory and possibly your hard drive), or heaven knows what. Stay safe.

   - **Emails from your bank or someone that you do business with:** Instead of clicking a link in the email, go to the bank or business website by typing the web address into your browser address bar as you usually do. If the bank or business has some sort of special message for you, it will show up when you sign in to your account. Most times, you will not receive an email link unless you sign up with the business for automatic payments or notices.

3. **Stay safe with friends.** You'll find that you will have more "friends" getting in touch with you on social media because it's a bit more impersonal. The fun of social media is being able to hear from many people from different places. Also, your online bio is only a sentence or two long and it doesn't (or at least shouldn't) give away any secrets about you.

TIP

Facebook's info page *does* show a lot of information. You might not want everyone on your friend list to be able to see everything — perhaps only your closest friends. Use Facebook's security controls (see Chapter 7) to set controls for who can see what when they visit your Facebook pages.

4. Don't give away (or even type in an email) too much information on any Internet site. Don't give away any bit of information that makes you feel uncomfortable. Be careful who you trust online with your home address and other contact information. *And never give away your social security number!*

Email Service

» **Choose a Web-Based Email Provider**

» **Pick a Pick-Proof Password**

» **Sign Up for a Gmail Account**

» **Add Your Contacts**

» **Compose and Send an Email**

Chapter 3

So Much About Email (and Safety)

I know, I know, you've got sending and receiving email down. But did you know there's a bit more to it? You can use email to send messages, but you can also subscribe to news lists and feeds on the Internet. In fact, social media uses your email account to send you notifications of activity on your (and your friends') pages, private messages, and more if you request them. You'll be surprised when your email becomes your pipeline to the news that your friends post on the sites. Let's get into the full picture now!

I'm sure you know that your email address consists of two parts. The part before the @ sign is the local part (usually your name, personal ID, or nickname) so the server knows who to send the email to. After the @ sign is the *domain address* — which tells the domain name system which mail transfer agent accepts mail for that domain.

Every website has a URL (its address online), and every email address has a domain component. When requests for web pages or emails are launched into the ether of the web, the routing system needs to know where they should be sent. So if you're using the email address that your Internet service provider (ISP) assigned you, the email is sent to your user ID (your name) @ your ISP domain — literally your address on the web.

Then the mail transfer agent (MTA, a type of software) uses your online name and address to transfer electronic mail messages from one computer to another.

Also know that your email address (the local part) can use any name you want, as long as someone else at the domain isn't using it. It's usually best to have at least one address with your real name for public and official use. You might want to add a second (or third, fourth, or fifth) address with different *noms de plume* for family members, friends, and newsletters you subscribe to. For example, I have the following names on different services:

mcollier1	eBay4Dummies
Marsha.Collier	eBayGal
Talk2Marsha	OnlineCustserv

There may be six different names, and all are accessible online, but they all can download into Outlook, an email program that's part of Microsoft Office on your PC, or be read online in a browser or app.

In this chapter, I tell you about where you can get free email service and take you through the basics of signing up and using Gmail, the free email service from Google. Having a Gmail account is not only cool, but it's very convenient. You might prefer to give out this anonymous email address to online sites for privacy reasons. It's just an extra convenience. Check out this chapter for more of the benefits.

Check Out Places to Get Your Email Service

1. You can start your search for an email account with your Internet service provider (ISP). When you signed up for your Internet service, you were probably allotted five or more email accounts for different members of your family. Your ISP also assigned (or allowed you to select) a user name when you signed up. My ISP gave me my user name, but I wasn't aware that it would be the name in my email address, too. (Seriously, *mcollier1* doesn't have much of a ring to it.)

   Your ISP will have a web interface where you can check your email online, but it's far more efficient to forward that email to a web based solution for *all* your email addresses.

2. Understand that the email account from your ISP has pluses and minuses, as follows:

   - **Minus:** You may change Internet service providers in the future. Hence, if you're using the ISP email address as your own, you'll have to change it. This will force you to contact everyone who has the old email address and ask them to change it in their records. I've been with my ISP for over fifteen years; the thought of having to send a change of address to *every single one* of my contacts is beyond loathsome.

   - **Plus:** Your ISP is going to be a lot more helpful when you have a problem or a question than the web-based free services I mention in the next step. Service providers are invested in keeping you as a paying customer. They have a customer-support staff that you can contact with problems.

3. Consider using one of the popular web-based email services. More and more people have found Internet-based email accounts the convenient way to go for general email. They can access these accounts online from any computer (or mobile device through an app). They offer excellent spam and virus protection, too.

   Notice that (in the preceding step) I didn't say all web-based email accounts were *free*. Although the providers don't ask for money, they do expose you to ads while you go through your email.

4. The benefits of having a web-based email address is that you can change your home ISP any time you want, and you won't have to notify hundreds (perhaps thousands) of connections to give them your new email address. In the next section, I give you an overview of the leaders in the online email arena who are jockeying for your business.

Choose a Web-Based Email Provider

1. Yahoo! Mail from industry veteran Yahoo! (founded in 1994, which is ancient by Internet standards) is now owned by Verizon. The home page for your email is a mélange of news tips, weather reports, trendy topics from the Internet, an editable calendar, ads (of course), and (finally) your email boxes, as shown in **Figure 3-1**. It's very popular and the free service has these features:

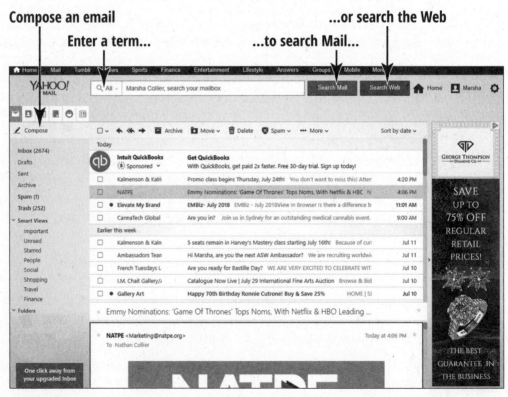

FIGURE 3-1

- **1 terabyte of email storage:** This means you may be able to keep your emails and attachments on Yahoo forever if you want. A terabyte (TB) of storage is equal to approximately 1,000 gigabytes (GB) or a million megabytes (MB) — that's a whole lot of storage space.

- **Huge file attachments:** If you want to attach videos or other large files to your emails, it's easy on Yahoo! Many servers limit the total size of the files you can send through email. Yahoo! limits attachments size to a 25MB (megabyte) maximum.

- **Robust Help area:** Notice the cog icon in the upper right corner of the screen? Click it to see a drop-down menu. Click Help to be transported to a simple-to-understand tutorial and help area.

  To access Yahoo! Mail, go to `http://mail.yahoo.com`.

TIP

2. Microsoft Outlook is another popular online email service. If you've used Outlook on your Windows computer as part of Office, you'll find the free online version very intuitive. Various Microsoft email addresses such as @hotmail.com, @live.com, and @outlook.com live online under the Microsoft Live umbrella. You can sign up at `https://outlook.live.com` for email and any other Live services you might want to use (as shown in **Figure 3-2**).

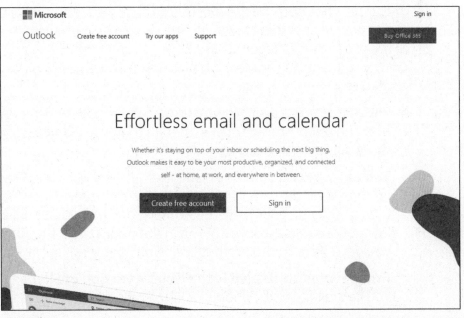

FIGURE 3-2

TIP

First off, you need to know that the service is only run by Microsoft, who don't fuss over what kind of computer you use. You can use either a Mac or a Windows PC and still avail yourself of these services. You may know of people who have msn.com email domains, which are also served up by the Hotmail servers.

Here are the special features of the no-cost Hotmail service:

- **Microsoft offers 15GB of email storage space to start:** Office 365 Home and Office 365 Personal subscribers get 50GB of space.

- **Skype Messenger service and Video Chat:** Once you've signed up, you then have access to IM through Skype. Learn more about using Skype in Chapter 4.

- **Integration with Outlook and Office 365** for email and calendar, using the Outlook Hotmail Connector tool.

- **15GB of email storage space:** You can get an additional 5GB of storage when you sign up for Microsoft's OneDrive. You get an extra 3GB when you use the mobile app to upload your pictures.

- **Import from other online email services:** With an easy tool, you can import other online email services into your Outlook page.

3. Google Mail (Gmail) — the newcomer begun in 2004 as an invitation-only test — has become the most popular of the free email platforms (and my personal favorite). The Google home page has a box at the top right (see **Figure 3-3**) where you can easily access any of Google's other free services. What makes Gmail popular is the array of features:

- **15GB of storage and growing:** Google's founders say no one will ever run out of storage space (though they'll be glad to sell you more space if you need it).

- **Tabbed Inbox:** No need to wade through emails to find the important (or personal) messages you want to see. Gmail uses tabs to divvy up your mail into Primary, and editable Social and Promotions tabs. So if you're not in the mood to go shopping, you don't have to see promotional email until you feel like it.

- **Gmail Hangouts, which is the Google version of Skype:** You can initiate texts, phone, or video calls to other Gmail users from your page.

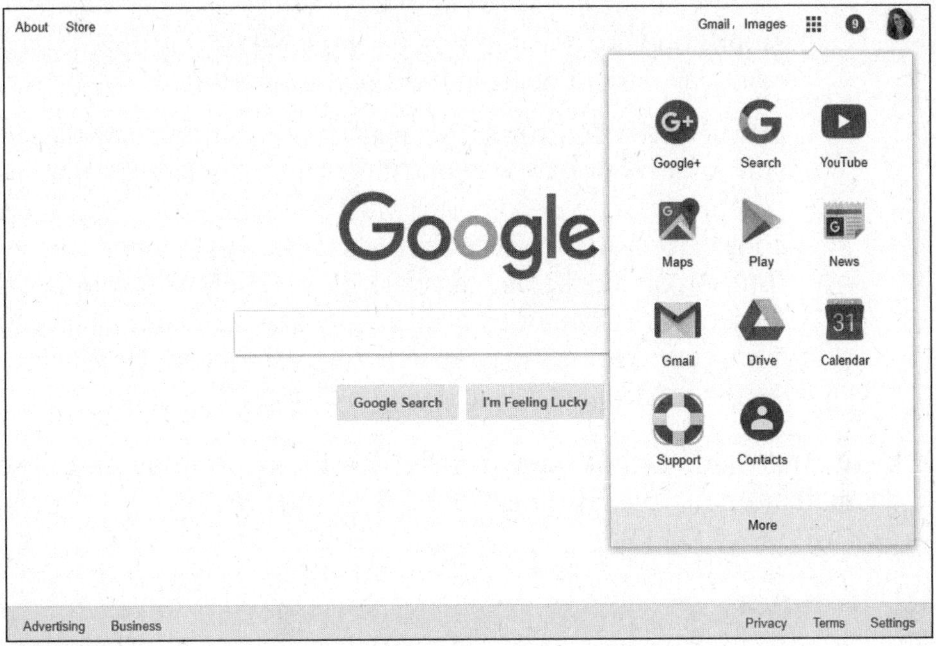

FIGURE 3-3

- **Google Voice:** Get a free phone number! You may connect any of your phone numbers to this service to act as an answering machine for your calls. You will receive transcriptions of voice mail through your Gmail account. (Learn more at www.google.com/voice.)

- **SMS (Short Message Service), or text messages:** You can send these to any other Gmail user through Google Hangouts on the Gmail desktop interface. All you need to do is click the Hangouts icon to find their name in the lower left corner and click to send an SMS or video call.

- **A great spam filter.** *Spam* is the name for advertising email that is sent to you unsolicited by unscrupulous vendors to try to sell you goods or even to defraud you. Gmail smartly places spam in your Spam folder for you to review and will be deleted automatically within 30 days.

- **Google Calendar:** An online calendar is automatically yours when you have a Gmail account. You can opt to share your calendar with someone, or keep it private. And you can access your calendar from the drop-down menu as shown in **Figure 3-3** that also appears on your mail page. Calendar syncs with your tablet and smartphone so you can view — and interactively update — your calendar without being in front of a computer.

- **Connectivity features:** These include instant synchronizing (sync) with smartphones and connecting with the email program on your computer. Gmail sends your email to your desktop and keeps a copy on the Gmail server until you choose to delete it. The sync function on mobile devices work interactively with your desktop. (When you delete an email from any device, the email disappears from your screen and goes into the trash of your Gmail account; you can always retrieve it if you've deleted it in error.)

All that said, Gmail is currently the most popular and flexible free email service. In a later section, I show how to set up a Gmail account.

Pick a Pick-Proof Password

When you set up an email account — or any account — on the Internet, you will have to set a *password,* which is the keyword you type in to confirm your sign-in along with your user ID. Passwords are used not only in email, but also on almost every website of which you become a member.

If you have a strong password, hackers will pass by your account and attempt to hack an easier target — so here's where I get into giving your password some muscle.

Picking a good password is not as thought-free — but *is* twice as important — as it may seem. Whoever has your password can (in effect) *be you* anywhere on the web — posting comments, sending spam email messages, and leaving dangerous messages (which can range from pranks to scams or worse) for others to see. Such an impostor can ruin your online reputation — and possibly cause you serious financial grief.

My best tip for a password is to use the initials from a memorized passphrase. For example, "I went to the University of Miami," which becomes the password *IwttUoM.*

PROTECT ALL YOUR ACCOUNTS WITH TWO-FACTOR AUTHENTICATION

Because data breaches have become a common occurrence, many websites allow (and encourage) two-factor authentication. Once you activate this, your accounts will be doubly safe.

It works by your adding your mobile phone number to your online account. If you request to reset your password (because you forgot it) or try to sign in from a new device, a code will be sent to your smartphone via text message. Type that code onto the platform and you've been authenticated.

Here's how to use it:

- Google: Set it up at www.google.com/landing/2step and it will protect you on *all* your Google services.
- Facebook: When you run into a problem, you can request a code be texted to you *or* go to the mobile app on your phone. On the Facebook mobile app, click the hamburger menu in the upper right. Under Settings & Privacy, click Code Generator. A code will appear that will change every 30 seconds.
- Instagram: Go to settings and enable Require Security Code. Once you do this, you'll have to type in a code each time you sign on (remember that mobile apps stay signed in unless they are updated). After you enable it, the app will give you 5 codes and prompt you to take a screenshot for future use.
- Twitter: On the desktop (or mobile app) click your profile photo to see the Settings & Privacy option. Choose Account ⇨ Security ⇨ Login Verification. Once you enable this, Twitter will text a code to your phone to verify that it's you.

Setting up 2FA is not only safe, it's the smart thing to do.

With any online password, you should follow these commonsense rules to protect your privacy:

> » Don't pick anything too obvious, such as your birthday, your first name, your address, or (never, never!) your social security number. (**Hint:** If it's too easy to remember, it's probably too easy to crack.)

» Make things tough on the bad guys — combine numbers and letters and create nonsensical words. Use upper *and* lower cases.

» Don't give out your password to *anyone* — it's like giving away the keys to the front door of your house.

» If you even suspect someone has your password, immediately change it.

» Change your password every few months just to be on the safe side — maybe rotate a group of passwords over the various accounts you use.

Sign Up for a Gmail Account

1. I like Gmail above the other online email service providers because it has great features and is easy to use. So start here to set up a Gmail account. Open your web browser and type this URL in the address line:

   `http://mail.google.com`

   You'll see a page that looks like **Figure 3-4**. Click Create an Account to begin. Read the information on the next page and then click the New Features link near the center of the screen. Should there be any updates you need to know about, the latest news will be on this page.

2. In the upper right part of your screen, see the box that reads Create an Account? Yep, that's the one; click the Create an Account button and get ready for the magic to happen. By getting your own Gmail account, you get access to Google's world of cloud web tools, such as Google Calendar (an interactive online calendar you can share with your family), free Blogger blogs, YouTube, and Google Docs (a suite of free online programs very similar to Microsoft Office).

FIGURE 3-4

3. The resulting Create your Google Account page (see **Figure 3-5**) is where you type your information:

- **Your name:** First and Last.

- **Desired Login Name:** Fill in what you want to become your local address and name at the Gmail domain. In **Figure 3-5**, I selected *marshaismyfavoriteauthor* as my sample name. My email address will be `marshaismyfavoriteauthor@gmail.com`.

   After you type your desired name, Gmail automatically lets you know if the name is available. If it isn't, Google will make suggestions that you probably won't like. Put on your thinking cap and come up with a good login name. This name will be with you for a long time; there's no changing it later.

TIP

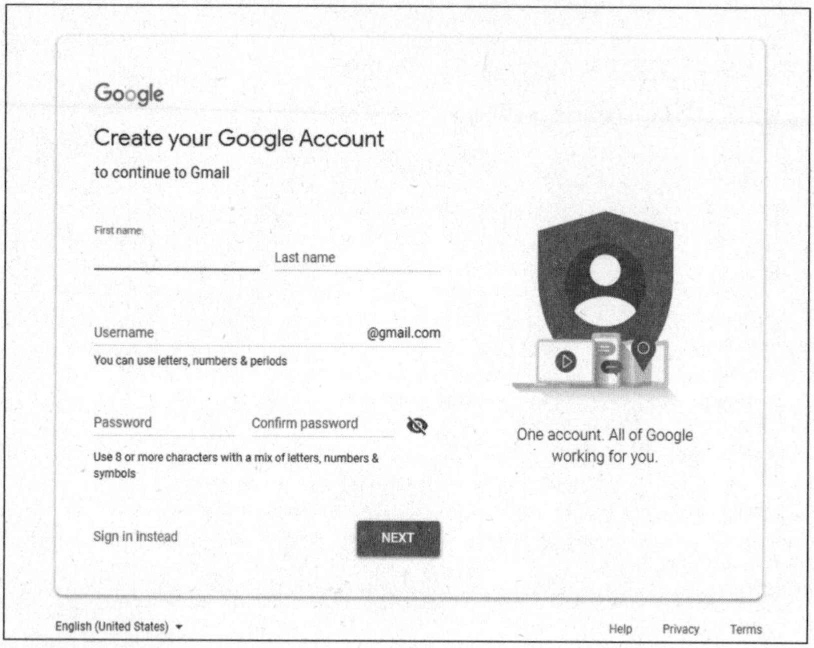

FIGURE 3-5

- **Choose a Password:** Refer to the preceding section and type your password in the box; make sure it's at least eight characters. You'll notice (as you're typing) that Google tells you whether your selected password is Weak or Strong. Go Strong! Also, type your password again — carefully! — to confirm it where prompted.

- **Birthday:** Google wants your birth date. Use the drop-down menu to select your birth month and fill in the date and year.

  It might be okay to fib about your age, but be sure you remember the date you give Google. Should you ever forget your password, or if your account gets messed up in some way, you're going to have to supply this information. If you can't remember it, you're out of luck.

- **Gender:** Male or female? Google also provides an Other option for all the others in the world.

- **Mobile Phone:** Adding your mobile phone number here puts it on record with Google and offers the opportunity for them to send security notices or password-reset instructions to your phone if they're ever needed.

- **Your current email address:** Type your ISP email address so that Google can send you an email message to authenticate you.

- **Word verification:** You'll see a bunch of semi-legible letters in a box. (They're called *Captcha* codes, and you can find out about them more in Chapter 6.) Try to read them — and if you can make them out, type them in as prompted. If you're wrong, the page refreshes and you get a new set of letters. If it causes you problems, you can skip this form of verification. Google will then text a code to your mobile phone to enter on the site.

- **Location:** In this box, the United States is filled in by default. If that's where you are, fine. If not, type your country.

TIP

Never use your mother's maiden name as a security question on the web. That information should be between you and your bank.

- **Terms of Service:** Here Google outlines its Terms of Service (TOS). Any website you sign up with has such terms. Read the TOS and print them if you'd like, but if you don't agree to them, you can't have a Gmail account.

- **Personalization Option:** You may see a box asking if Google can use your account to personalize content and ads on other sites. Check this option if you want Google to scan your email box to identify things that might interest you and deliver ads that match those interests. Deselect if you'd prefer that they keep out of your business.

4. Click the Next Step button.

TIP

The next page requires you to select some security questions and allows you to add a photo to your account. Follow the instructions to upload a pic if you want that extra level of personalization. If you're fine being an anonymous blue silhouette, click Next Step again. You're given the option to Continue on to Gmail and your new email account.

Add Your Contacts

1. When you first arrive at your Gmail page, take a deep breath and look around before you start to click anything. **Figure 3-6** shows you some of the important points to take in. Get familiar with the page; there's a lot to look at. When you first sign up, you'll notice that the fine folks at Google have sent you some introductory emails. So why not start there?

Read your e-mail messages

Compose an email   **Search**   **Incoming mail sorted by tabs**

FIGURE 3-6

2. One of the emails you have received after initially signing up has instructions on how to import your contacts. Move your cursor over the email list. Your cursor turns into a small hand with a pointing finger. Click your mouse once and the email opens!

3. You can import your contacts and existing mail from Yahoo!, Hotmail, AOL, and your ISP accounts. If you indicate that it's okay to do so, Gmail will continue to import your mail from the other servers for the next 30 days. For now, I suggest that you just close the email by clicking the Back to Inbox link on the top left of the email. You may just want to input your contacts manually.

4. When you're back at the Inbox, look at the icon box drop-down menu on the upper right side shown in **Figure 3-3**. Click the Contacts icon from that menu, then click New Contacts on the new screen and prepare to add a contact.

5. Fill in your contact's information on the new screen. You can add the name, email address, phone, address, birthday, website (if the person has one), and any notes you want to make. When that's done, click Add to complete other fields that don't show up on the main screen. Gmail automatically saves the info as you complete the fields and adds the contact to your list.

6. Select the contact's name from your contact list at any time to make changes or to add information to the contact. Return to your Inbox by clicking the Contacts drop-down menu in the upper left and selecting Inbox.

Compose and Send an Email

1. If you're following along, then you're probably about to send your first Gmail email. Click the link that says Compose (at the upper left of the screen), as shown in **Figure 3-7**.

2. The email form opens. In the To box, type the name of one of your contacts or type someone's email address.

3. Type the subject of the email in the Subject line.

4. Type your email message into the text box below the Subject line. If you want to add interest to your text, you can change the typeface, its size, make it Bold, Italic, Underlined, or change colors by using the format bar. Want to get fancy? Try these tricks on for size:

   a. *Highlight the text by clicking your mouse button (and holding it down) at the beginning of the text you want to edit.*

   b. *Keep the mouse button down as you drag the mouse pointer across the text.* Lift your finger off the mouse button when you come to the end of the text you want to fancy up.

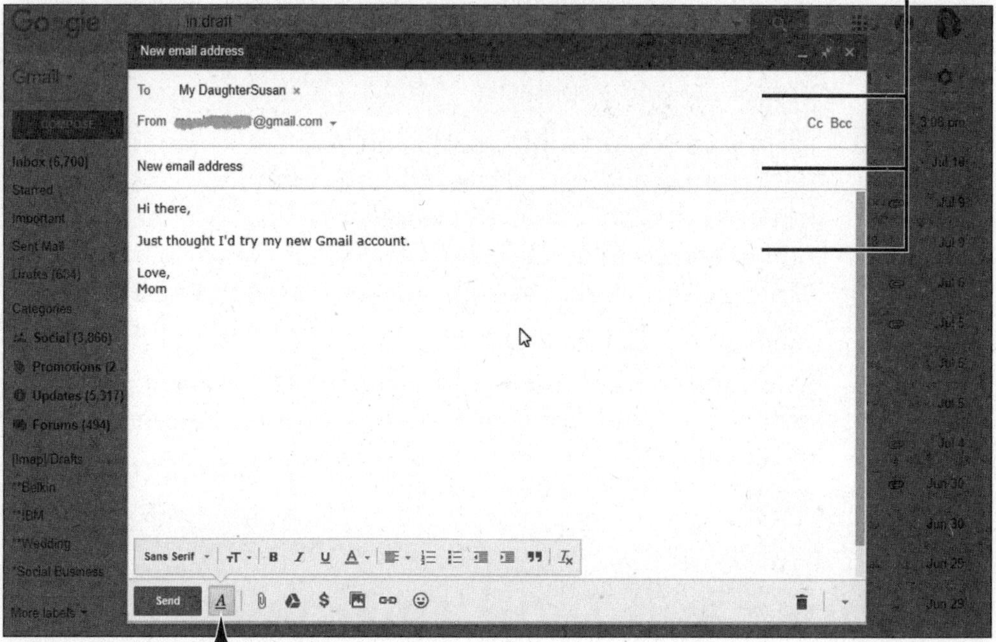

Fill in a recipient, subject, and message

Bring out the format bar

FIGURE 3-7

    c. *As shown in **Figure 3-8**, click the capital A (indicating text attributes) at the bottom of the email box. Select the formatting option you want to apply from the format bar that appears.* In this example, I plan to change the type to **bold.**

    d. *You can also select the font (or color if you're using the color selector) by clicking it, and magically your text changes.*

5. When you finish writing and formatting your email, click the Send button in the lower left corner of the email form.

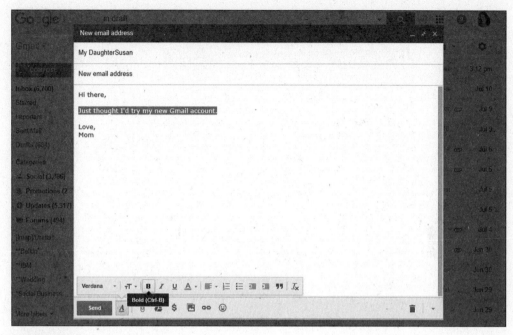

FIGURE 3-8

» Gather on Facebook

» Communicate through Twitter

» Video-Chat on Skype

» Get Connected on LinkedIn

» See It All on YouTube

» Have Your Say on BlogSpot

» Archive Photos with Google

» Stream Music on Pandora

» Stream TV and Movies

Chapter **4**

Speaking the Social Networking Language

You probably suspect that the online social network includes a whole lot more than Twitter, Facebook, and Instagram. And you're right! I suspect that once you get involved on the web, you're going to want to spread your wings and take off to some other fun venues.

There are quite a few more sites where you might want to participate with your friends. In this chapter, I give you a very quick overview of the most fun sites I've found in the *interwebs*, or *cyberspace* — both terms are slang for the Internet. Just to keep you up on what the cool kids say and where they hang.

So, in no special order . . .

Gather on Facebook

Because a large section of this book is about Facebook, I won't go into much detail, but know that as of March 2018 the site has more than 2.23 billion (with a *B*) active users per month. That's a lot of people. You never know who's going to show up on the pages.

Facebook is a place where you can find your family (I connected with relatives across the country and in Europe), new people with common hobbies and ideas, and old school chums as well. Best of all? You can view old friends' photos and see how they aged over the years. Since anyone over the age of 13 with a valid email address can join, most kids are members. Which benefits us parents: We can benevolently follow our kids' and grandkids' pages to see some of what they're doing and watch out for them a bit. (I love looking at my daughter's page.)

Facebook is a community where, if you want, you can share online contact on a daily basis. You can check in at any time and see what's happening in your friends' and family's world. The benefit of Facebook over Twitter is that you can see all your friends' posts on their page or your news feed.

Figure 4-1 shows my Profile page. I've been a Facebook member for quite a while; as you can see, Facebook reminded me I've been on Facebook for 11 years.

Figure 4-2 shows you my "Fan" Page that the *For Dummies* people set up for me. You can find these types of Pages for many of your favorite public figures, products, and businesses. Liking a Fan Page makes you part of an online community, and you can communicate directly with the brand. Feel free to find my page www.facebook.com/ MarshaCollierFanPage on Facebook and post; I always love meeting my readers and hearing your social media stories.

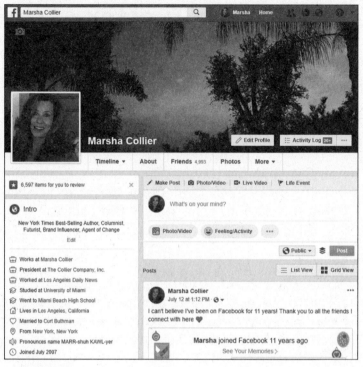

FIGURE 4-1

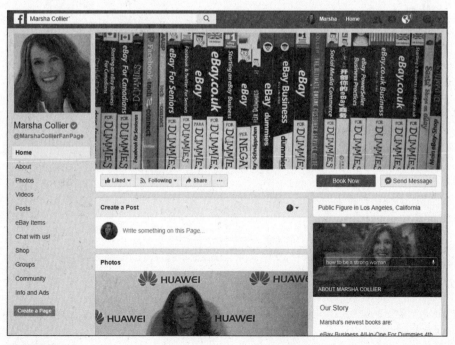

FIGURE 4-2

Communicate through Twitter

Have you sent a text message on your smartphone? Of course you have! People send more text messages than they make phone calls these days. As far back as September 2008, Nielsen reported that a typical U.S. mobile subscriber placed or received 204 phone calls each month. In 2017, it was reported the average user sends 72 text messages a day.

Twitter is a variety of an SMS (for Short Message Service) on the Internet. I tell you more about that in Part 3 of this book, but I know you'll have lots of fun checking in every day to see what the rest of the world has to say.

Figure 4-3 shows my Twitter Profile page, along with some of my *Tweets* — the Twitter term for posts or short messages and replies. Though these can't go over 280 characters, you may be surprised at how much information fits into that format. It makes you a more concise writer.

FIGURE 4-3

After you set up a Twitter account, you can start to "follow" other Twitter members (a process I explain in Chapter 13) and have other members follow you, as well. One of the fastest growing demographics on Twitter is the 55 year and over age bracket.

Once you begin to tweet, you can have real-time conversations with people online — and build up an online community this way.

Video-Chat with Friends and Family on Skype

Remember back in the old days when we thought how cool it would be to make video calls? Fifty years ago we saw George and Jane Jetson chatting with friends on their videophones. Even our parents saw Charlie Chaplin using videotelephony in the 1936 movie *Modern Times*.

Today, computers, tablets, and smartphones all have cameras and microphones and are capable of making that video calls. Since 2003, Microsoft's Skype has been the most popular and easy to use VOIP (voice over the Internet) client program.

On your computer, go to Skype.com to get started; on your mobile device, just download the Skype app. Once you've connected with your friends, you can make voice or video calls from one Skype account to another for free. **Figure 4-4** shows me initiating a Skype call on my Wi-Fi-only tablet.

These calls are best made over a Wi-Fi connection. Visit the website to get more information. But now? There's hardly any excuse for not chatting with a faraway family member.

Skype is also useful for making international phone calls. If you make regular calls to landlines in the United Kingdom, for example, you can subscribe to a monthly service that gives you unlimited minutes for only $2.99 per month, or purchase Skype Credit for as little as $10 and then landline calls are 2.3 cents a minute.

FIGURE 4-4

Get Connected on LinkedIn

If you have (or had) a business career, I know you're going to enjoy LinkedIn. It's a business-oriented social network with over 500 million users. If you have a job, you should be on the site. If you're currently "at liberty," semiretired, or interested in consulting, you should also be on the site. Just think — you can probably connect with most of the colleagues and heavy hitters you've worked with over the years. Your friends may be connected to some smart new folks who just might be looking for your kind of experienced help.

After you register with LinkedIn, you can type in your résumé, fill in information about yourself and your talents, and look for former acquaintances whom you've lost track of. You can search (try to remember everyone you've ever worked with) and connect with people you know and trust in business. These become your *connections.* You can invite anyone (whether a site user or not) to become a connection.

TIP

Connections are not automatic. When you locate someone you know on LinkedIn, you have to ask the person to connect with you. And don't attempt to connect with someone you don't know. Instead, find someone you already know, connect with him or her, and let that person connect you with new parties. That's the purpose of making connections.

My daughter's LinkedIn profile is shown in **Figure 4-5**. I enjoy being connected to the people I've worked with and get notices when they change jobs, update their profiles, or join one of the many groups on the site.

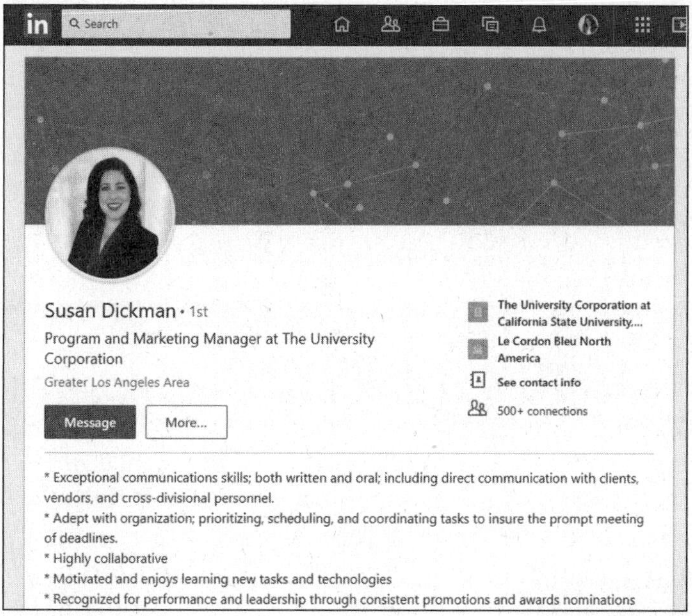

FIGURE 4-5

See It All on YouTube

You're going to love YouTube — a video-sharing website where users can upload and share videos. You can browse almost any subject and find a video you'll enjoy. Want to watch a Harrier take off from an aircraft carrier? Check. Want to see Sonny & Cher's last performance of *I Got You Babe* on the David Letterman show in 1987? You'll find it at `https://youtu.be/c4EaFzRVj1M`. (You're welcome.)

Want to see your grandchild take those first steps? That's up to your son or daughter. Most content on YouTube is uploaded by individuals, but the major media corporations including CBS, BBC, and other organizations offer some of their videos, movies, and music on the site. YouTube is the second most visited website on the Internet, right behind Google.

TIP

I really hope you set up an account on YouTube. You don't have to register to watch videos, but if you'd like to comment and rate videos, you need to have an account. *Entertainment Weekly* magazine put YouTube on its "Best of the Decade" list, saying, "Providing a safe home for piano-playing cats, celeb goof-ups, and overzealous lip-synchers since 2005." It's really a lot of fun!

When you register for any Google service, you're automatically part of the site, and you get your own channel. **Figure 4-6** shows my channel and some of my favorite videos. I just know you'll spend hours on the site watching vintage commercials, TV shows, and more.

FIGURE 4-6

Have Your Say on Blogspot

Have you ever considered writing a blog? The term *blog* is a shortened version of *web-log*, originally a place where people would write and post short stories on the web. Your blog could be that (short stories) — or a personal journal, random musings, or writings devoted to a specific subject (perhaps a hobby of yours)? It's free to set up and run a blog on Google's Blogspot, `Blogger.com`.

As you join more social networking sites, you can link to any blogs as you post them. And you may be surprised at the number of readers you draw. You could develop your own community where regular readers comment on your blog posts (if you want).

I have a blog on Blogspot (see **Figure 4-7**). Check it out at `http://mcollier.blogspot.com` — maybe you'll get an idea of what you'd like to write on yours.

FIGURE 4-7

Archive and Share Pictures on Google Photos

I used to worry that all my precious photos taken on digital would disappear in a hard drive crash one day, but no more. When you sign up for your Google account, you're given 15GB of storage for Gmail, Google Drive, and Google Photos.

There's a pleasant loophole here. If you upload photos to Google Photos, you'll get free unlimited storage for all photos up to 16 mega-pixels and videos up to 1080p resolution. If a photo is larger than 16 megapixels, it will be compressed to save space. This shouldn't be a worry because quality prints can be made up to 24 inches from the 16-megapixel size. If you actually do run out of space, you can buy 100GB of storage for under $20 a year.

To get started with Photos, download the web app (Backup and Sync) to your computer from https://photos.google.com/apps. After you've installed the app, tell the app which folders to back up, and select the Photo & Video upload size. Once you've set it up, your photos will back up to the Google cloud immediately.

TIP

I only sync photos from my Pictures folders (I keep temporary photos in a folder on my desktop that doesn't sync with Google Photos). I also select High Quality for uploads. The original qual-ity will fill up your storage rather quickly, so why bother?

Getting the app for photos taken with your mobile devices is equally simple. You'll find the app in Google Play (for Android) and the App Store (for iOS). The setup is easy, and you can configure the uploads to occur only when you're charging your device and only over a Wi-Fi connection.

Aside from keeping a lifetime of photos (even traditional photos you've scanned), Google offers amazing features.

Google learns from your photos (I told you nothing is free on the Internet) and you benefit from that feature. You may search your

Photos page for places, graduations, babies, pets, and even specific names if the person is also on Google.

Figure 4-8 shows a search of my Google Photos for cats. Google will pick up every photo in my archive of a cat. Real or porcelain.

TIP

You can also share photos (or a folder of photos) with someone else who is on Google. They will have access to that folder and none of your other pictures.

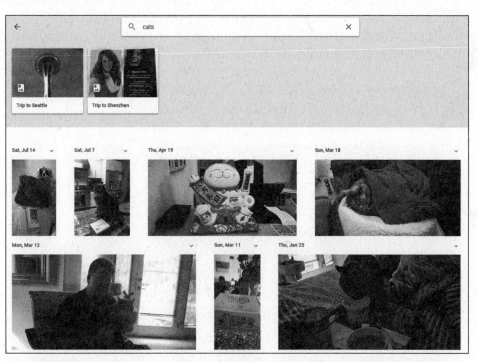

FIGURE 4-8

Stream Music on Pandora

Visiting Pandora.com is like having a radio in your computer. When you arrive at the home page, just type in a favorite song or artist, and Pandora builds an online radio station for you; it broadcasts songs that you will like. (I promise.)

This magic result is based on the Music Genome Project, the most comprehensive analysis of music ever undertaken. Pandora's team of musician-analysts listens to music, one song at a time, to study and collect hundreds of details on every song. According to the Pandora site, it takes the analysts "20-30 minutes per song to capture all the little details that give each recording its magical sound — melody, harmony, instrumentation, rhythm, vocals, lyrics, and more — close to 400 attributes!"

Amazing, no? Once you register, you can create up to 100 stations to fit your many moods. If the music Pandora selects isn't just what you want, let the team know with a click of your mouse and they'll refine the choices selected for your station.

Figure 4-9 shows one of the custom radio channels shared with me by my daughter, Rat Pack radio, on Pandora.

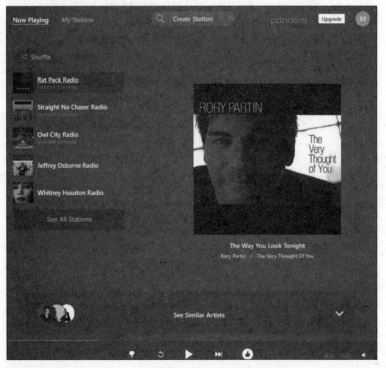

FIGURE 4-9

Stream TV and Movies on Hulu, Netflix, and Amazon Prime

There are three key players in the Wi-Fi video-streaming segment of the online world: Hulu (www.hulu.com), Netflix (www.netflix.com), and Amazon Prime on Amazon.com. At all three sites, you can find TV shows and movies online.

» **Hulu** no longer offers a free service which allows you to watch TV shows on a computer. To watch any of Hulu's offerings (commercial-supported streaming video of TV shows and movies from NBC, Fox, ABC, and many other networks and studios) on a mobile device or smart TV, you'll have to pay for a membership. A paid membership to Hulu ($7.99 a month) gets you full access to their entire library of current season episodes, full series runs of older shows, and hundreds of classic films.

» **Netflix**, the folks who used to mail out DVDs, now has a paid streaming service. They not only have a massive library of TV shows and movies, but they are known for creating award-winning original content that you can only see through Netflix. Our family subscribes to Netflix, for two screens at HD. That costs $10.99 a month.

» **Amazon Prime Video** is a free service that's a benefit of an Amazon Prime membership. You pay $119 a year (or $12.99 monthly) and get all sorts of goodies . . . too numerous to list here. Here's my favorites:

- Free two-day shipping on all Amazon orders

- Access to stream their massive selection of movies and original content on Prime Video to your devices or TV

- A huge selection of music streamed free on Prime Music

To see a complete list of Amazon Prime benefits, go here: www.amazon.com/gp/help/customer/display.html?nodeId=200444160.

» **Make Your Links Short**

» **Discover How Internet Slang Is a Language of its Own**

» **Find and Share Videos on YouTube**

» **Pin Your Favorites**

Chapter **5**

Sharing in the 21st Century: Acronyms, Posts, Photos, and Videos

One of the most fun ways to share online, in Twitter, Facebook, and Instagram, is using your favorite music and images. In this book I've talked about sharing your own photos on Facebook and Instagram, but how about treating your online friends to some of the unique items you run across elsewhere on the web? You could share a news story, a song, or a funny video — pretty much any cool thing you find!

I've spent many evenings online with friends, pointing from a picture to a video to a story. It's the 21st-century version of a coffee klatch; it's also like sharing a bottle of wine with friends (only you get to drink the entire bottle if you want).

In this chapter, I give you some advice for mannerly and efficient sharing, go over some great places to find material to share, and tell you how to easily transport the treasures you find to your Facebook or Twitter pages or blog.

Give Credit When You Share

1. I want to talk a little about the conventions — or, better yet, the etiquette — for sharing what you find online. Odds are, if you hijack someone's article or photo from somewhere on the Internet, that person may never know it — but *you* will. Good manners (believe it or not) are still in fashion on social media, but they follow new rules. Please credit any website and the person behind the post when you share the content. You can generally do so by including a link back to the original posting of the content, and in the case of Twitter, why not thank the person who originally posted it.

TIP

I posted a video of Chris Edmunds to a couple of places: my Twitter feed, Facebook page, and my own blog. **Figure 5-1** shows how I handled giving credit while composing the Tweet.

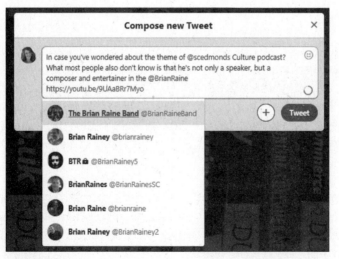

FIGURE 5-1

2. When you want to link to a YouTube video (see the later task "Find and Share Videos on YouTube" for more information), you can type the @ (at-sign) before you type the name you want to credit. When you do that on Facebook, the names of friends show up in a drop-down menu just like on Twitter. **Figure 5-2** shows how that works. When you see the person's name you want to include, click it, and the full name appears in your post. Doing this also causes the post to appear on your friend's Timeline page. It's what the kids call *giving a little Facebook love*.

Start typing a name here...

...and choose from your friends list

FIGURE 5-2

3. Suppose you want to share a video elsewhere online, as I did a few days later when I posted Chris's video on a blog (yes, I *really* liked it). Besides mentioning the original poster by name in your blog text, you can include the name in the keywords area of your blog.

4. When you're looking around on the web, you'll no doubt see a Creative Commons license badge on independent websites. *Creative Commons* is a nonprofit organization that works to increase the amount of content "*in the commons* — the body of work that is available to the public for free and legal sharing, use, repurposing, and remixing." When you see a Creative Commons license icon, click it, and you'll be brought to a page where the actual license appears. This license tells you if there are any restrictions about the content that you may want to share.

The Creative Commons license is represented by three basic icons; the license details are based on the order in which the icons appear. **Table 5-1** outlines a simple shortcut to the Creative Commons license rules.

TABLE 5-1   **Creative Commons License Icons**

License Icon	Stands For . . .	Which Means . . .
	Attribution	You may distribute, remix, tweak, and build upon the work, even commercially, as long as you credit the original creation.
	Attribution — Share Alike	All the above, with this caveat: You credit and license new creations under the identical terms.
	Attribution — No Derivatives	You may redistribute, commercially and non-commercially, as long as the work is passed along unchanged and in whole, with credit to the author.
	Attribution — Non-Commercial	You may remix, tweak, and build upon the work non-commercially only.
	Attribution — Non-Commercial — Share Alike	You may remix, tweak, and build upon the work non-commercially, as long as you credit and license new creations under the identical terms. You can download and redistribute the work as is, but you can also translate, make remixes, and produce new creations based on the work.
	Attribution — Non-Commercial — No Derivatives	This license is often called the *free advertising license* because it allows download of works and sharing as long as the distributor credits and links back to the original. The work can't be changed in any way or used commercially.

Make Your Links Short

When you've found something you want to share, you'll need to share it via the Internet address of the post (the URL) by copying and pasting. There's the rub — have you ever noticed how long some URLs can be? Even in email messages and web postings elsewhere, typing in a gigantic URL can be a real chore. The solution is to shorten them.

When we're talking Twitter, you have only 280 characters for every Tweet. So Twitter uses its own shortening service. When you paste a URL into a Tweet, Twitter alters it and shows only the first 22 characters (which can look a bit sloppy as well).

But there is a solution: Several online services will abbreviate any web address to a nice, manageable size. These services began as helpful tools for everyday folks, but now they are more used by marketing agencies because of the valuable metrics they supply.

You may have seen some shortened URLs when you were perusing Twitter. See any web links that look nonsensical, with no legible words? Clicking that silly looking link will get you where you want to go, via the magic technology of the web.

TIP

Two popular URL shorteners — `TinyURL.com` and `bitly.com` — are in use currently. I use bitly because it's integrated into every application I use on my computer and mobile phone. Also, bitly gives you an information page where you can see metrics: how many people click your link after you publish it. (If you use an app to post items in advance, most will automatically shorten your links with bitly upon your request.)

For example, the web address for my podcast is

```
http://wsradio.com/category/technology/computer-and-
    technology-radio/
```

If I use the URL-shortening application from the bitly website, I can assign the following permanent bitlink that I often use, and which I can also reuse over and over. It looks like this:

```
http://bit.ly/tech-radio
```

If I'm Tweeting about my radio show, at least the link from bitly gives me room to mention the guests.

1. Want to give bitly a try? Find a nice, long URL that you'd like to shorten, type **http://bitly.com** into your web browser and press Enter. You'll arrive at the bitly site, as shown in **Figure 5-3**.

TIP

I recommend registering with bitly; the site has never sent me any spam. This way, if you want to use your shortened URL online, you'll be able to send the post directly from the article's page.

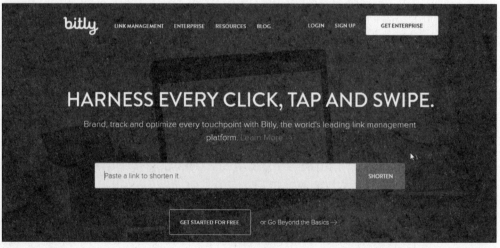

FIGURE 5-3

2. Start the bitly registration process by clicking Sign Up at the top of the screen. On the resulting page, type in a username, email address, and password as prompted. You can also automatically create an account using your existing Google, Twitter, or Facebook accounts.

3. When you're done filling in the usual items, click Create Account, and you're in — that's all there is to it! You're automatically transported back to the bitly home page, but now it will look a little different.

4. There are two ways to use bitly. The choice is yours:

- Copy the URL you want to shorten from its web page: Click to highlight it, and then press the Ctrl and C keys together. Switch over to the bitly site and place your cursor in the text box that says *Paste a link to shorten it*. Paste your long URL in the box by pressing the Ctrl and V keys together.

- Go to your bitly account by clicking the hamburger menu (three or four lines) next to your name and click Resources. From the resulting page, you can get a browser extension for your web browser, or a mobile app for your phone or tablet. This tool allows you to insert a mini bitly gadget (so you don't have to go back to the bitly web page) to make a short link directly from any page on the web.

  Clicking to add the Chrome extension will take you to the Google Play Store where you can add the extension to your browser (shown in **Figure 5-4**).

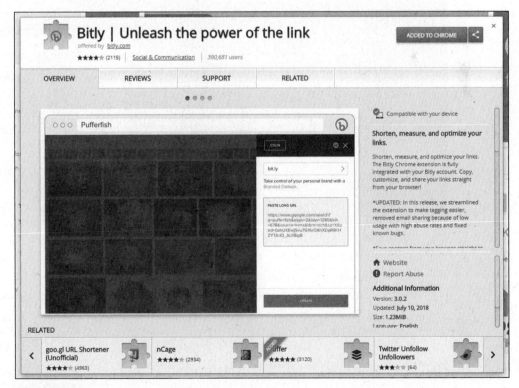

FIGURE 5-4

Once it installs in your browser, you'll see a small *b* in a circle icon in the top right, next to the URL box. Place your mouse pointer over the *b* to create a Bitmarklet, click, and hold down the click. If this is the first time you've used bitly, you'll have to sign in and give the Chrome extension permission to use your bitly account. Voilà! It's now part of your browser, ready for use. Just click the *b* to bitmark (shorten the URL) to share the page you're on.

5. Your long URL turns into a magically shortened one, as shown in **Figure 5-5**. If you plan to use the shortened URL in an email, merely click the Copy button, and the new URL is automatically placed into your Clipboard so that you can paste it into an email or an SMS message.

Click here to create a Bitmarklet

Click to copy or share the Bitmarklet

FIGURE 5-5

6. If you'd like to share the friendlier URL, either on Facebook or Twitter, click the Share button. Click the website you want to share on and then type the rest of your post in the text box (as in **Figure 5-6**). Behold: bitly automatically generates a post with the link embedded. Use bitly each time you come across an interesting news story, article, or video on the web. It'll save you a lot of typing, and it'll make sharing much easier.

7. Click the Share button, and your comment and link will autopost instantaneously to your Twitter-stream or Facebook timeline.

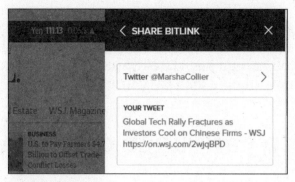

FIGURE 5-6

8. When you go back to your bitly page a little later, you can see how many people clicked your link to check it out. (I checked one of my links and saw the info depicted in **Figure 5-7**.) If you click the View Stats link next to anything you've posted from bitly, you get an hour-by-hour report on the action. You can slow-scroll down the Stats page to find where else your link was shared, and from which countries. Kinda interesting.

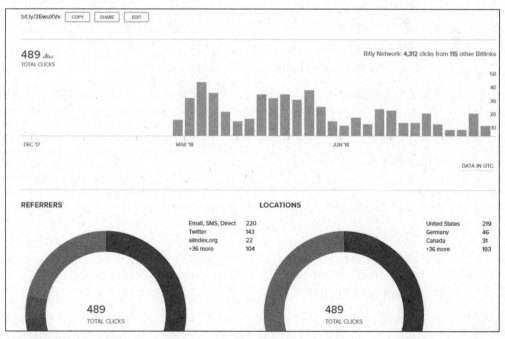

FIGURE 5-7

TIP

Also, using bitly is a great way to shorten your own personal web link in your 160-character Twitter bio. After you've put a bitly link in your profile, you can go back to bitly and view the statistics that show how many people visited your page.

Internet Slang Is a Language of its Own

The Internet, especially social media, has some mysterious words of its own that are not always understood by those over 30. Understanding (and using) these acronyms may help you chip away at a possible bias. Plus, it's an eye-opener when you understand the secret (ever-changing) language kids use today.

These are for intermittent usage; don't use them too often or you'll be deemed uncool. I could probably list a hundred, but for brevity's sake, I'll just list my favorites.

» **AMA:** Ask Me Anything. This started on a website called Reddit, where an authority on a subject takes open questions.

» **BAE:** Before Anything Else. This acronym is generally used when referring to one's sweetie or dear one.

» **DM:** Direct Message (also PM = Private Message). The default way to give permission for someone to message you in private.

» **ELI5:** Explain Like I'm 5. When you want a simple, short explanation of something.

» **Epic:** An adjective to describe anything huge or amazing.

» **Facepalm**: Reaction when someone says or does something incredibly stupid.

» **ICYMI:** In Case You Missed It. When you mention something that you think most people already know or you have said it before. Manners count.

» **IMHO:** In my humble opinion. Use when you're trying to put across a point, but you don't want to be pushy about it.

- » **IRL:** In Real Life. Real life versus Internet life.

- » **JSYK:** Just So You Know. This is the new way of writing FYI.

- » **Lulz:** For the laughs. A derivative of the longstanding LOL (Laughing Out Loud), meaning you did something just for fun.

- » **Lurker:** Someone who follows a chat or a forum but never comments. (This is a perfectly acceptable practice.)

- » **Meme:** Superimposing a snarky comment (or captioning an image) on a photo. I would show you a screen shot, but they are generally NSFW. You can make your own memes on a website: memegenerator.net.

- » **NSFW:** Not Safe For Work. Anything marked NSFW should not be viewed on a big screen in a public environment.

- » **Photobomb:** When someone (human or animal) unexpectedly appears in a photo. Like when your cousin Larry jumped in between you and your Bae while taking a selfie. My husband is expert at this, as seen in **Figure 5-8**.

FIGURE 5-8

- » **PWNED:** When you've been PWNED, you've been defeated or humiliated and your opponent has victory over you. Also used as a noun: PWNAGE.

- » **SMH:** Shaking My Head. Conveys disappointment in something someone does or says.

- » **TBT:** Throwback Thursday. When you want to share something from the past, do it on a Thursday and tag it #TBT.

- » **TL;DR:** Too Long; Didn't Read. If you share an article that seems really valuable, but it went into minute detail, you might not have time to read the entire thing. Mark your comment TL;DR.

- » **TROLL:** Trolls are people who post to annoy or anger you. They can be terribly annoying. The best advice I have is, "Don't feed the trolls." Just block them and move forward.

- » **Well played:** A response when someone does something particularly well.

- » **YOLO:** You Only Live Once. Your excuse to do something incredibly wacky.

There are many Internet slang dictionaries on the web, but I take no responsibility for what you see if you go there (just for lulz).

Find and Share Videos on YouTube

Many more hours are burned these days watching videos on YouTube (www.youtube.com) than listening to songs on a radio. According to YouTube, more than 1.8 billion unique users visit the site each month. YouTube bills itself as "Broadcast Yourself," so you'd think that you might find only homemade videos. That's not the case. Big-time studios post portions of television shows and trailers from films. There are more than 1 billion hours of video watched daily on the site (a month might represent about an hour for every person on the planet). If you haven't visited the site, you should.

Music videos (because there's really no more MTV) are the most popular on the site. As of this writing, the video that's had the all-time most views — 5.4 billion and counting — is "Despacito" by Luis Fonsi featuring Daddy Yankee.

One of my favorite channels, which has a loyal following, is "Lucas the Spider," shown in **Figure 5-9** (an adorable animated, very short — under a minute — series). The creator of this popular video series has had over 23 million views on just one of his animations.

FIGURE 5-9

But, to prove that popularity doesn't belong just to the rock stars with fanatical followings, the fifth most popular (with over 864 million views) is *Charlie Bit My Finger Again*. It's a short home movie about an infant biting his older brother's finger, as shown in **Figure 5-10**. Go figure. I guess there's a big audience for kid videos; after all, the *Little Rascals* episodes are getting harder to find these days (unless you look for a boxed set of DVDs on eBay).

Charlie bit my finger - again !
863,390,281 views 👍 1.8M 👎 244K ➡ SHARE ⊟ ...

FIGURE 5-10

1. To find a video to share, start by typing a keyword in the search box on the home page at www.youtube.com. You can search for topics, actors, singers, politicians . . . just about anything. For example, I typed **Susan Boyle** (of *Britain's Got Talent* fame) in the search box and got more than 396,000 results. And one of my favorite films is *One Six Right,* an independent film on the history of aviation. To find it, I type **One Six Right** into the text box and click Search. Try typing a search term for one of your favorites.

2. On the next page (the search results), you see a list of videos that match your search term. In my example, the videos have *One Six Right* in the title; I clicked the top one and came to the page shown in **Figure 5-11**.

3. To share a video that you find on YouTube, click the Share button that appears below the video viewing window. (Notice that email, Twitter, and Facebook icons appear through the Share button.) A box opens

onscreen, showing you the URL of the video and a collection of buttons that link to various online communities — including Facebook and Twitter.

"One Six Right" Opening Sequence (remastered for Blu-ray)
18,985 views

FIGURE 5-11

4. To share the video on Facebook, click the Facebook button (as shown in **Figure 5-12**); a window appears and offers you two ways to share:

a. *To post the video to your Facebook Profile page, type your message in the text box and click the Share button.* After you click the Facebook icon, a box pops up allowing you to post comments and the video to your timeline.

b. *If you'd prefer, you can send the video link to specific Facebook friends or lists.* Click the privacy icon next to Share and select Custom. You then see a Custom Privacy window, as shown in **Figure 5-13**. Select from the drop-down list and begin to type your Facebook friend's name; a list will appear. Select your friend's name from this list, and the message is ready to send. Click Save Changes and then Share to send it along to your friend's Facebook message center.

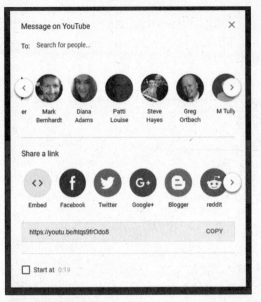

FIGURE 5-12

FIGURE 5-13

5. To share the video on Twitter, click the Twitter button and a second window opens with a message box containing the video's title and URL (see **Figure 5-14**). (If you're not signed in on Twitter, you need to do so in your browser or app, and then go back to YouTube and try again.) Edit the message if you'd rather say something other than the video's title, but don't delete the link. Click Tweet. Your message appears, along with a shortened version the video URL, in your Twitter stream.

FIGURE 5-14

Pin a Few of Your Favorite Things

1. Perhaps you've heard about Pinterest, the virtual scrapbooking site where you can start your own Pin Boards using images from around the web and then share them with friends? My Pinterest Board is at `www.pinterest.com/marshacollier` and is shown in **Figure 5-15**. Please join me on the site; perhaps my Pins will give you inspiration.

FIGURE 5-15

TIP Pinterest allows you to theme your Pin Boards by title, so you can collect various images and categorize them for easy sharing.

2. The first thing you must do to get to the site is to type `www.pinterest.com` into your browser, and go! Look for the Sign Up link and click it. Pinterest asks whether you'd like to join by connecting through your Facebook or Twitter accounts. Realize that this type of sign-up method gives Pinterest some "permissions" on your social network accounts.

You can read the details, but the less permission you give, the less all those big-data algorithms out there will be perusing your friends' information.

3. Sign up with your email address and the process will request a little personal information (such as your gender), so Pinterest gets an idea of who you are. Next, you'll have to upload a photo; the site won't be taking a profile picture from one of your other social media accounts.

4. Pinterest suggests some boards for you to follow; they want you to follow at least five. I recommend following topics that pique your interest. These choices are not set in granite, and you can unfollow anything on Pinterest at any time.

   Once you've made your selections, you will receive an email to verify your email address. Follow the instructions in the email and you will arrive back on Pinterest.

5. Now that you're officially a member, you need to create a *Board*. Or several. Your Pin Boards are where you share images from your computer or from the web. Click the Create Board plus sign (+).

When you have the Create a Board form onscreen, here are the steps to follow:

1. Give your Board a title. Name it something catchy that describes the sort of images you plan to share on the Board.

2. Decide if you want the board to be to be Secret.

TIP

   Secret Boards are handy when you do holiday shopping on the web. No one can see the Secret Boards you create; they're kept hidden from prying eyes.

3. Once you've filled out the form, click Create Board. You'll be faced with a blank Board named with your title, and suggested items to pin (suggestions based on the words in your title) as shown in **Figure 5-16**.

4. Click Add a Pin and you will be able to upload an image from your computer, or from the web by typing in the URL (web address) of the page where the image appears.

FIGURE 5-16

TIP

To make things easy for yourself when you come across an image you want to share, get an add-on (if you're using Firefox) at

```
https://addons.mozilla.org/en-US/firefox/addon/
   pinterest-pin-button/
```

or an extension (if you're using Chrome) at the Chrome Web Store (`https://chrome.google.com/webstore`) and search for Pinterest Save Button.

These sites install a Save button in your browser, so images on web pages will appear with a P button for easy pinning to your Boards.

5. To use the add-on widget extension from a web page, just click the image you want to post and a Pin It icon appears. Click Pin It, and a Pick a Board post form appears. Fill out the form, decide whether you'd like to share to Facebook or Twitter, and click Pin It.

Voilà! You've just pinned your first Pin!

TIP

When you've set up your account, you can find friends to follow typing their name in the search box on the top, as shown in **Figure 5-17**. You can also share Pins from their pages on yours by mousing over the Pin and clicking Share.

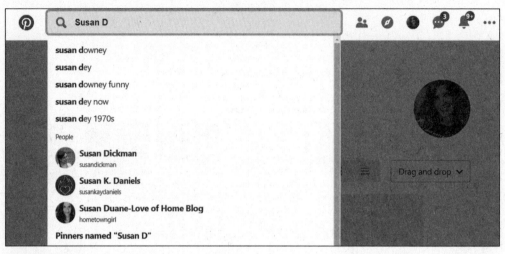

FIGURE 5-17

2

Putting Your Face onto Facebook

IN THIS PART . . .

Signing up and getting your Facebook profile ready

Prepping to share your information

Connecting successfully with friends and family

All about adding photos and videos to Facebook

Exploring groups, events, and games

» **Upload Your Profile Photo**

» **Find Friends Initially**

» **Add Your Personal Information**

» **Confirm You Are You**

» **Fill Out Other Profile Information**

» **Edit Your Timeline Later**

Chapter **6**

Signing Up and Prepping Your Facebook Profile

You've heard about it; it's in the news all the time. Your kids and maybe (if you have them) grandkids all have Facebook profiles, and now it's your turn. I think that Facebook is the best first place to start connecting online because of the friendly atmosphere, so follow my tips for an enjoyable and safe experience. I bet you'll be surprised when you see how many of your friends, past coworkers, and perhaps even past romantic interests await your contact.

To get yourself into the action, you need to sign up and put together your Facebook *profile,* which is where everyone looks to learn more about you. You don't have to fill in your profile information all at once, so don't worry that it's going to be somewhat of a time-consuming task. After you sign up, your Profile page awaits your visits for leisurely updates.

Getting started on Facebook may seem daunting. But when you're ready to take the plunge, I can help you discover what needs to be done. This chapter lays out all the basic Facebook setup instructions in sets of easy steps that enable you to master the basics before jumping in with both feet.

TIP

Know that Facebook may reorder the steps I share with you. They are often tinkering with the site. Just follow the information in this chapter and you'll be just fine.

By the time you're done reading these pages, you'll have all the knowledge and tools necessary to navigate the site like a pro. All you need to add are friends and family! I tell you more about making a Facebook connection with friends and family in Chapter 8.

Let's get moving.

Sign Up for a Facebook Account

1. Open your Internet browser and type in the URL (Universal Resource Locator, the web address) for Facebook, `www.facebook.com`. When you arrive on the Facebook home page, you find the Sign Up area, as shown in **Figure 6-1**, which asks you to fill in several important facts:

- **Your first and last name:** D'oh, that's the very easiest part.

- **Your email address:** You may have more than one email address, but decide which one will become the hub for your Facebook doings, and enter that address where prompted.

- **Your password:** A very important feature, your password is private, and *encrypted* (a technical way of hiding what you type from anyone other than the inner workings of the site itself — think Jack Bauer from the TV show *24*). Never give your password to anyone. You might want to make note of it for your own reference; write it down and put it in a safe place (**not** taped to your computer monitor). You'll have to know your password to sign in to your Facebook account.

- **Your gender:** This is probably the easy part. Nothing much to worry about here. If you want to get fancy, I'll show you how later in this chapter.

- **Your birth date, including the year:** Click the down arrow next to the drop-down menus and select your month, date, and year of birth. Facebook requests your actual date of birth to encourage authenticity and provide only age-appropriate access to content. (You can choose to hide this from your timeline profile if you want.)

TIP

If you're a bit shy of exposing your *real* age, don't feel alone. My age is a secret that I guard tighter than the feds guard the gold at Fort Knox. There is a way around the Facebook requirement. If you use the drop-down menu to select your birth month and date, you can just indicate a year waaaaay back in history. In **Figure 6-1**, I selected a pretty random year — 1980. (Heh, that'll keep 'em guessing.)

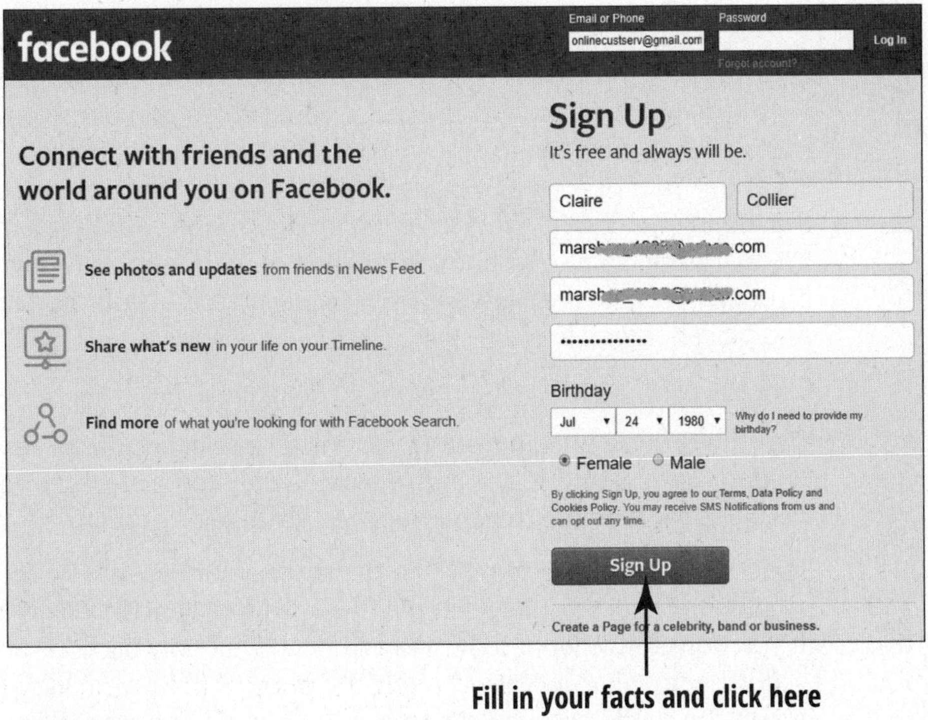

Fill in your facts and click here

FIGURE 6-1

2. After you enter the information in Step 1, click the Sign Up button.

3. Facebook then lands you on a page designed to lead you through a step-by-step process of adding friends, finding even more friends, and filling in profile information (including your picture).

TIP

I cover Facebook's prescribed friend–finding process in the upcoming sections, but I want you to know that you also have the option to skip any or all of the steps and come back to them later.

Upload Your Profile Photo

1. Do you have a flattering picture of yourself on your computer that you'd like to share? If so, follow the simple steps that start here. (If you don't have a photo available and your computer — laptop or phone — has a camera, skip down to Step 7 for those instructions.) Chapter 14 also has tips on how to take a flattering selfie.

TIP

Early in the sign-up process, Facebook says it's time to either *Add Picture* or *Take a Photo* to personalize your profile and home pages. Many people are camera-shy and don't put up a photo for their Facebook friends to see. If that's your inclination, I want to tell you that I think that not posting your picture will make your Profile page pretty boring. So why not be a little daring and put up your picture? If you're not quite ready, you can put up a picture of your dog or cat as a placeholder.

2. Click the Add Picture link, as shown in **Figure 6-2**.

3. Click the Browse button to start your picture selection. The File Upload window opens and a directory of your computer's contents will appear. Go to the folder where you store your photos.

4. Select an image that you'd like to display on your Facebook profile by clicking it. Be sure your selected photo is wider than 180 pixels in size. (If you don't know what that means, or can't tell how big your photo is, don't worry; Facebook will reject the photo if it's too small or too large.) The name of the photo you chose should appear at the bottom of the window in the File Name text box.

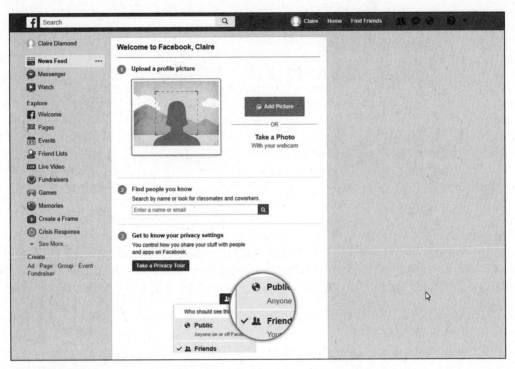

FIGURE 6-2

TIP

If you question whether a photo is too large, its file size (in *kilobytes*, or KB) should be next to the filename in your folder. If it's too big, you can preview the photo in a photo-editing program (for example, Windows Live Photo Gallery) and crop it to a smaller size.

Note: In this chapter, I am showing you figures of the screens I see on a PC that runs Windows 10 or on an Android phone. Depending on what operating system you use on your computer, your screens may look a little different. But don't fear — the steps are the same.

5. Click Open, and the picture you chose begins to make its merry way through the web to Facebook automatically. (Nice, huh?) As shown in **Figure 6-3**, my cat's photo has uploaded to Facebook. I'll put up my own when I've completed my page setup.

FIGURE 6-3

6. If you don't like the photo you selected, you can always change it later in the Edit My Profile area. (You can find the link to this area under your picture on your Profile page.) To go with a different photograph, simply move your mouse over the top of the words *Delete Your Picture.*

7. Alternatively, if you don't already have any photos you like, you can take a picture from your computer web camera (if you have one). Click Take a Photo with Your Webcam (refer to **Figure 6-2**).

8. A window appears asking your permission for Facebook to access your camera and microphone. Click the option button next to Allow.

9. If your webcam is pointing in the right direction, you will now see your image (as you sit in front of your computer) in the Take a Profile Picture window. Well, you kind of see it.

10. You may now pose for your picture. When you're satisfied with how your picture appears, click the word *Take* (next to the camera icon) to "take" the picture.

11. You've taken your picture! If you're happy with it (or as happy as you can be at the moment), click the Set as Profile Picture button and your photo will upload to your Facebook profile. (Remember, you can always swap out this picture later.)

At this point, if you pause and return later, the tasks that follow may come in a different order. No mind, just check back here for any advice and tips. This isn't a race; it's supposed to be fun, so take your time.

Find Friends Initially

1. Facebook takes you to a Find Friends page; **Figure 6-4** (left) shows you how it looks on a tablet. Facebook tells you "Facebook is better with Friends." It is, but if you read the fine print on this page, it lets you know it will be accessing your contacts — on your device or computer.

TIP

I recommend that you **never** give Facebook access to your personal contacts. This will not cause you to miss out on any social media magic, and it will maintain you and your friend's privacy.

2. If you click Get Started, Facebook prompts you to type in your email address and your email account password. If you do this, it links your email account and contacts to Facebook, and allows you to send Facebook friend invitations en masse. I suggest you skip this step (by clicking Skip in the upper right corner of the screen).

3. You will note that once you click Skip, Facebook is relentless; see **Figure 6-4** (right). Clicking Skip again will only bring you back to the same page. The only way to get out of this loop is to click the arrow that now appears in the upper left corner of the window, which returns you to your unfinished Profile page.

4. I give you this advice for a few important reasons:

   - **Complete your profile.** The invitations go out the moment you click to invite. It will look so much better *after* you've added your photo and other profile information.

   - **Find them later.** After you've set up everything, it's very easy to find people on Facebook, and I'm a fan of baby steps.

   - **Privacy.** I'm a big believer in privacy. I don't want to expose my contacts to the Facebook linking.

TIP

I recommend that you click Skip for now, because I recommend setting up your Facebook page completely first, and then finding people you know and adding them as friends on Facebook at your leisure. That way, when they receive your friend invitation, they can see your already completed, nicely laid-out new Profile page. Having your profile completed shows that you know what you're doing and are ready to roll! Perception is (almost) everything online.

5. Okay, you may think you have skipped finding friends, but Facebook won't give up. A pop-up window appears saying: "People who complete this step usually find up to 20 friends, and Facebook is a lot more fun with friends. Are you sure you want to skip this step?" Yes please. Click Skip and move along with the sign-up process.

6. Two things will happen during the sign-up process.

- Facebook sends you an email to confirm your email address. You must confirm this to go ahead with building your profile.

- If you pause and decide not to finish your page right away, Facebook sends you a daily email urging you to return. They will stop after you've completed more of your profile.

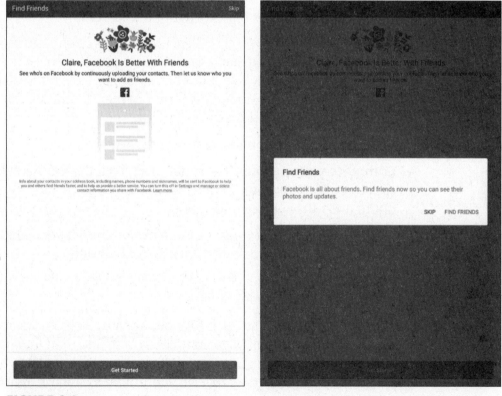

FIGURE 6-4

Add Your Personal Information

1. This is where Facebook content gets *really* personal. Facebook asks you to enter your basic profile information, beginning with

   - The **high school** you attended and your year of graduation. When you begin to type your school name, Facebook suggests schools that match in a drop-down menu.

   - Your **college or university** (if any).

   - The **employer** you work (or worked) for.

   - Your **current city**.

   - Your **hometown**.

2. Facebook's Privacy settings begin to click in at this point, and I go into them in depth in Chapter 7. For now, selecting Friends (because you don't have any at this point) is a safe bet. Facebook uses different icons to represent who will be able to see facts that you add to your profile. Table 6-1 shows the basics:

   TIP Note that in general, the cog icon is a recurring theme almost everywhere on the web. When you see a cog, it means that you can change settings.

   TIP Any of Facebook's Privacy settings can be changed at any time, so decisions made now aren't set in concrete. But do know that if you try to friend someone you knew twenty years ago, the person might not know who you are if he or she can't see some specific data that will identify you, so it's worthwhile keeping some of the basics public.

3. After you enter the requested personal information, a window may pop up with suggested friends. You may want to add some or all of these suggested friends based on your school and employment life. You can choose to befriend any or all by clicking their names. Doing so will *immediately* send a friend request to them. (Be sure you want to connect *before* you click — there's no turning back.)

   TIP If you want, you can skip this step and go on to the next tasks. You can always search for friends later. Just click Skip and move along.

4. There's a page that requests that you choose interests by instantaneously "liking" celebrity and news-source pages. Posts from these pages may automatically show up in your news feed. I don't know about you, but I would rather visit these pages at a later time and see the type of content that they post before cluttering up my news feed. For now, Facebook is for connecting with friends. You may click the word *Skip* to move on.

TABLE 6-1   Facebook Privacy Settings

Icon	Description
🌐 **Public**	When you click the globe icon next to the word *Public* (or *Everyone* in some places), anyone who looks up your page can see this information.
👥 **Friends**	The silhouette of two people, next to the word *Friends*, indicates that only those with whom you connect and "friend" on Facebook can see this information.
🔒 **Only me**	The padlock and *Only Me* mean . . . you guessed it. This information is available only to you and no one else can see it.
⚙ **Custom**	A cog next to the word *Custom* means that you can decide specifically who can see this information. Custom privacy settings become more valuable once you've recruited an extended group of friends. Chapter 7 shows you how.

Confirm You Are You

1. After the steps in the Facebook profile-building process are completed (or skipped, based on your choices), you may come to a page welcoming you to Facebook; in a ribbon at the top of the screen, you see a notification suggesting you go to your email to complete the sign-up process.

2. Go to your email now and find the email from Facebook. This is their way of being sure that you've supplied the correct email address and you are indeed a living person.

3. Open the email, and it should look similar to the one in **Figure 6-5**. Note that the email has a clickable link to confirm your account to Facebook. Click Confirm Your Account in the email and you are taken back to Facebook, with a pop-up indicating that you have confirmed your account.

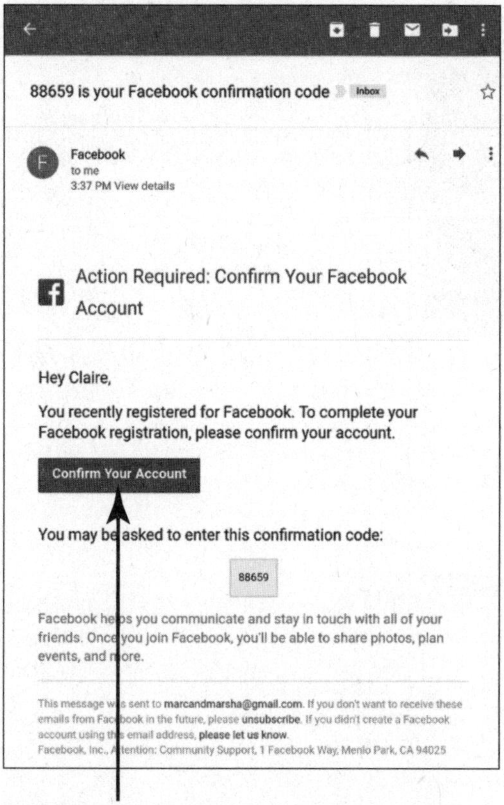

Click here to confirm you aren't a robot

FIGURE 6-5

4. The Facebook landing page welcomes you to Facebook. Steps on this page help you further fill out your Facebook profile. Because you have already completed (or skipped) some steps, either scroll down this page or (preferably) click the link at the upper left of your screen (under your full name) that says Edit Profile. This enables you to add things like personal interests, contact information, and affiliations to your profile.

Fill Out Other Profile Information

Clicking the email link brings you to your profile, shown in **Figure 6-6**. Each box links to the tasks that you need to complete to finish posting your profile. There may be a link to Edit Profile.

FIGURE 6-6

At this point, you have a chance to put together the descriptive part of your personal profile (and correct any not-quite-humorous entries you made previously in jest). You decide what and how much to share: Make your profile as revealing as you like, or (for a little privacy) as vague. You can get all the privacy you want as you fill out the profile details. Each piece of data can be assigned its own privacy level. By clicking the icon that appears to the right of a text field, you see a drop-down menu where you can customize the level of privacy for each bit of information.

1. You've already entered your gender and birth date, so that will be filled in to the About area (if you added your school and employment info, that area will be prepopulated as well). You now have the opportunity to add more information, such as your relationship status, and political and religious views.

TIP

Remember that everything on the About page is optional and that Privacy settings can be set throughout. You are **not** required to fill in dates.

2. Whatever you choose to share, filling in the blanks is simple. Here are the items to consider:

   - **Birthday:** Having the month and day listed is very important. Facebook notifies your Facebook friends about your birthday. They will come to your page and overwhelm you with birthday wishes. So you need to have something here.

     You do have options should you not want to show your birth year (whether real or bogus). You can select who can see your whole birth date, or your birth date without the year. Note that there's a new option: a silhouette of three people. This icon represents Friends of Friends — and now things get complicated. Not only would this information be available to your chosen friends, it would be viewable by all of their friends. In my case, that could add over 54,000 people who could see this data.

   - **Relationships:** You can leave the relationship space blank, or you have an opportunity to be far more specific (or not) than you might ever have imagined. Besides the boring old *Single, Married,* and *Divorced,* the choices on the drop-down menu also include *In a relationship, Engaged, In an open relationship, Widowed, In a domestic partnership,* and even *It's complicated* (which things often are, but note that this term is rather ambiguous and some people may misconstrue it). There are eleven different ways to describe your relationship status as shown in **Figure 6-7.**

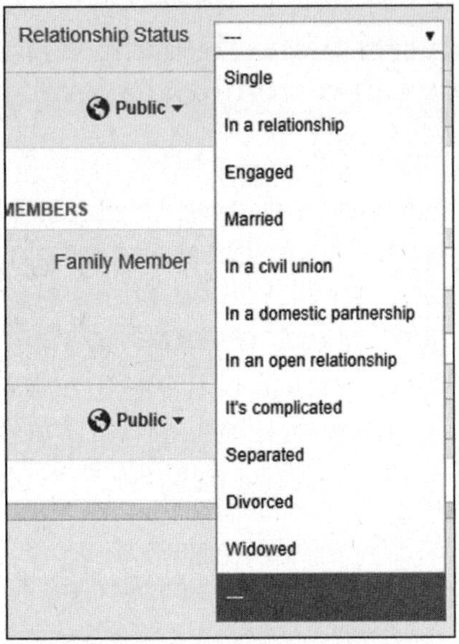

FIGURE 6-7

If you indicate that you're in a relationship of some sort, you can then decide whether to list your anniversary date — either for others or simply to remind yourself. If your significant other (not one of Facebook's options) is already on Facebook, just type in the person's name and his or her photo will appear.

- **Family Members:** With any luck, other members of your family are on Facebook. If your relations do have accounts, then type each one's name in the text box, and select the person's relationship to you from the Choose Relationship drop-down menu, which gives you a dizzying array of options. When you confirm that a Facebook member is one of your relations, a message will be sent to him or her, asking for confirmation of your familial relationship. After your relation confirms to Facebook that you really are related, you get a link to that person's Profile page on yours. Pretty cool.

- **Interested In:** This option is about preferred dating prospects. You can list whether you're interested in Men or Women, or leave these boxes unchecked.

- **Languages:** If you speak more than one language, why not let your friends know? Just fill in the name.

- **Political and Religious Views:** In the Political Views text block, you can type the name of a political party, or a comment that seems funny if you're minded that way. In Religion, type the name of your faith if you want.

3. After you input all the Basic Info you want to enter, click the Save button.

TIP

The idea isn't to reveal so much about yourself that you eliminate any mystery. It's simply to give others on Facebook a semi-definitive and representative picture of yourself, enough so your personality comes to the surface. You can also delay filling in this information until later if you prefer. You may decide to get the lay of the Facebook land a bit more before adding more personal information. Or you might decide never to reveal this stuff at all. It's really entirely up to you.

4. If you haven't already supplied the information, click the Work and Education section link. This section affords you the chance to elaborate on your high-school and college info, as well as what you do (or did) for a living.

TIP

The benefit of including this information is that many people search for Facebook friends by schools or workplaces, and an old school chum may find you by performing such a search.

5. To tell your story, edit the About You and the Favorite Quotations boxes. Write up a short bio; people want to know a little about you. Also, keep in mind that people's favorite quotations say a lot about them. Type in a few quotes that you love, with the appropriate attributions.

6. In the Contact Information section, click the pen to edit, and the form appears onscreen. Your personal email address is hidden from your timeline for privacy (because you confirmed this information earlier).

At this point, you can type in any contact information you want your Facebook friends to see, including your

- **Social links:** Also, you can list your other social accounts through the drop-down menu (see **Figure 6-8**).
- **Mobile phones**

- **Address and zip code:** You may also indicate a "neighbor[hood]" [to] preserve your privacy. Say if you lived in Beverly Hills, it might be safer to list your neighborhood as Los Angeles.

TIP

This is where sharing gets sticky for me. I may make friends on Facebook that I don't want to have my home address and phone number. For the sake of my security, I leave that blank; I really don't want it to appear anywhere. If I want someone to have that information, he or she can always send me an email to request it.

- **Website URL:** If you have a blog or a business page, type the URL in here.

7. Scrolling down the page allows you to add films, TV shows, music, and books you have liked or want to watch. Remember, you can always add this ancillary information later.

WEBSITES AND SOCIAL LINKS

Social Links [   ] [Instagram ▾] ✕

+ Add another social link

✓ **Instagram**
Twitter
Snapchat
YouTube
Twitch
WhatsApp
LINE
WeChat
Kik
Pinterest
Tumblr

🌐 Public ▾ | **Save Changes** | Cance[l]

BASIC INFORMATION

Birth Date   July 24

Birth Year   1980

Gender   Female

+ Add who you're interested in

+ Add a language

+ Add your religious views

+ Add your political views

FIGURE 6-8

Edit Your Timeline Later

1. When you have your information in place, you may decide to make additions and changes. You can always return to edit your profile information by clicking the About link below your profile photo on your Timeline page.

TIP

Remember that any information you enter about yourself — along with your name and friends list — can be as private or public as you want.

2. Information that you may consider sensitive is available only to those whom you have befriended, based on your settings. And that's where the privacy and security settings come in. At any time, you can adjust your global or individual privacy settings for contact and profile information by clicking the down arrow at the top right of any Facebook page, and then choosing Privacy Settings from the resulting menu. See Chapter 7 for a complete look at choosing your privacy settings.

In the next chapter, I guide you through adding your cover photo (what's that?) and how to keep private things private.

Place

» **Meet Your Facebook Home Page**

» **Review Your Timeline Page**

» **Update Your Status**

» **Delete a Status Update or Other Post**

» **Add a Photo to Your Timeline**

» **Add Life Events to Your Timeline**

» **Share a YouTube Video on Facebook**

Chapter **7**
Preparing to Share Info

On Facebook, there are three basic levels of privacy: *Friends*, *Friends of Friends*, and *Public* (anyone who happens upon your page). You hold the key to how much, or how little, information about yourself you allow others to access on the site. The personal information you choose to share is apart from the publicly available information — such as your name, profile picture, current city, gender, networks, friend list, and pages — that helps friends find and connect with you.

On Facebook, your privacy and security settings work as locks that control access to what's revealed about you, and to whom. In this chapter, I show you how to access and edit your privacy and security settings at any time. The idea behind these settings is to give you control of your Facebook experience.

Use these settings so you don't have to worry about your personal information falling into the wrong hands — or having prying eyes access something about you that (for whatever reason) you don't want just anybody to know. You are in charge — and can filter who views your information to increase your feelings of security and privacy online. The trick is finding *all* the controls. Then, with your information secure, you can move on to the fun stuff!

TIP You can set the privacy of your status updates, photos, and information as you post them, by using the privacy selector on the fly, I recommend you never share anything that you wouldn't want published in your local newspaper. Even if you delete a post, some people may still have seen it. Use your good judgment to protect yourself online. Facebook sets the default for posts to be viewable by Friends only.

This chapter also shows you how to make the most of your Facebook pages by posting updates and photos, and by getting into the conversation. I'll get the tough stuff out of the way first.

Get Your Privacy Settings in Place

1. To start the process of checking your privacy and security settings, look at the top right of the screen on any Facebook page and on the navigation bar (Chapter 8 tells you more about using this area), locate the word *Home*. Depending on your activity on Facebook, the area will be populated much as mine is in **Figure 7-1**, or you may just see some grayed-out (or blued-out) text. Bear with me here.

TIP Should Facebook change their navigation, don't fret. The advice that follows will still be valid. If you can't find the "official" settings page (which links to settings mentioned in this chapter), type www.facebook.com/settings in your browser and you'll be all set!

TIP I recommend that you perform the tasks in this section in a web browser, preferably on a computer. The options in the mobile app are far less intuitive (to be kind). Things are laid out more clearly on the web platform. I know this all will be somewhat daunting.

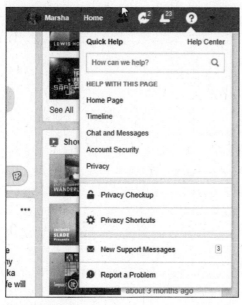

FIGURE 7-1

Facebook is a valuable resource, and I believe that going through all these settings will help you keep your information and data private.

So, if you move your mouse to the far right, the cursor (arrow) will turn into a pointing finger. If you squint really hard you may (or may not) see a downward-pointing triangle on the far right, and a question mark to the left of it. When you click the question mark, a drop-down menu appears, providing access to your Account Security (questions on privacy), Privacy Checkup, and Privacy Shortcuts. The Privacy Shortcuts link (in **Figure 7-1**) is a list of Facebook's suggestions that point to an area where you can adjust your settings.

2. Next to the question mark on the navigation menu, click the grayed-out triangle and you'll see a menu with the word *Settings,* which work in concert with the Privacy Shortcuts on the other menu. This brings you to the main Settings page (shown in **Figure 7-2**), which gives you many more options.

The Privacy Settings enable you to control who can see your profile information, contact you, or look you up on Facebook. This page is set for Facebook's default options; you have to **take action** and change them if you want to tighten up your privacy. There is nothing to be afraid of.

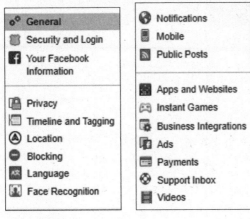

FIGURE 7-2

3. Click the word *Edit* to make any changes throughout the Settings area. For example, under Privacy, *Who can see your future posts?* sets the default for everything you post on Facebook. If you want a specific post to reach a wider (or smaller) audience, you can use the individual controls on each post. When you click Edit in this section, a screen appears (as in **Figure 7-3**). In addition to Public, Friends (those with whom you've connected on Facebook), and Only Me (pretty self-explanatory) in the audience selector drop-down, you now see some additional options.

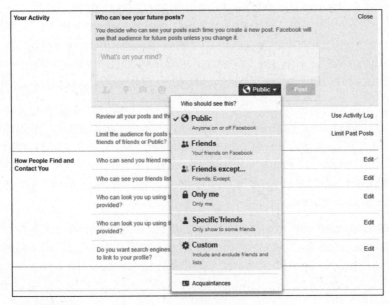

FIGURE 7-3

- **Friends except:** When you're currently in a feud with your next-door neighbor or a friend at work, you can select their names here and exclude them from seeing your post.

When you told your friends you were babysitting but you're out to dinner with other friends, don't post the picture of the group of you in a restaurant. Excluding people from seeing your post in their stream doesn't mean it won't exist. Anyone who sees the post can take a screenshot and innocently post it with a comment for all to see. Heed my words, things can backfire. Don't overshare and you won't need to monkey around with tons of settings.

- **Specific friends:** Clicking this option (whether here or when you are posting updates, photos, videos, or Going Live) produces a searchable list of your friends. Click the dot next to each person's name that you want to see the post and they will be able to view it. Again, if you really don't want others to see it, think twice before posting.

- **Custom:** This is an advanced privacy setting; **Figure 7-4** shows an example of Custom Privacy options. You may select individual groups, lists, or, if your default is to be Friends, you can also include anyone who is mentioned (or whose photo is tagged) in the post — and their friends.

- **Acquaintances:** Acquaintances is one of the lists you can put together on Facebook (which I cover in Chapter 8). *Acquaintances* are folks you don't feel the need to be in close touch with; if you put them on this list, their posts will rarely show up in your news feed. If you select this option, your listed acquaintances will no longer see your posts. Also, they also won't be notified that you've designated them as "acquaintances."

Tightening up your Facebook feed by too much can suck the enjoyment out of Facebook. Consider customizing specific posts as you post them; it will make your time spent on Facebook a lot more enjoyable. This is all supposed to be fun.

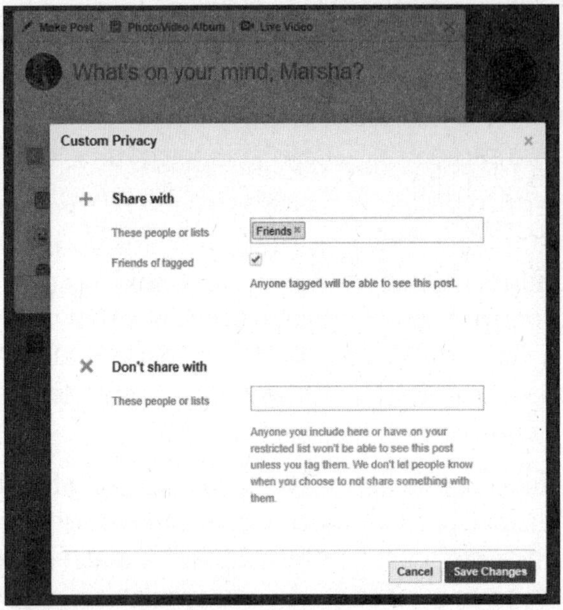

FIGURE 7-4

You can also edit who looks you up on Facebook (and how). This privacy setting controls who can see your name or profile information as search results on Facebook. This setting also indicates whether you allow search engines such as Google to access your publicly available information. Further on, I show you how to see a Public Preview of your timeline.

4. Click the left-side onscreen navigation, shown in **Figure 7-2**, to visit the different areas of the settings. Here's a little more about some of the sections you find here:

- **Security and Login:** Facebook sets your Security options appropriately; go and take a look at them and edit, if necessary. This is where you can lock down your account with Two-Factor Authentication, which I describe in Chapter 3. Under Setting Up Extra Security, a couple of little-known — but very valuable — features appear.

    One is *Get alerts on unrecognized logins*. Should someone log in to your account from a device or browser that isn't identified with your account, Facebook will send you a notification.

The other is *Trusted Contacts*. If you ever forget your password, or can't access your email account due to some sort of computer disaster, special one-time security codes can be sent to your trusted contacts. You can call those contacts to get this code so you can access Facebook again. You must select a minimum of three close (and trusted) friends.

- **Timeline and Tagging:** Part of the fun of Facebook is that other members can post comments, pictures, and video. If another member tags you in a posted item, it will also appear on your wall. Here's the area where you decide who can post (and comment) on your wall and who can view photos of you.

  In the *Review* area, you can indicate that nothing should be posted to your page until you've seen it and approved it in your Timeline Review. This way, when your niece snaps an absolutely dreadful photo of you, it won't be smack dab on your timeline for all to see (stay tuned; later on I show you how to work with your Timeline Reviews to prevent posts from appearing on your page (as well as removing the tag if you must).

  Also in Review, click the View As link next to *Review what other people see on your timeline,* and your public profile will appear as mine does in **Figure 7-5**. Use this link to view what your results might look like when someone finds you in the results from a search engine.

- **Ads:** An important place to visit. There are several sections on this page. Be sure to visit them all.

- **Your Interests:** If you've been on Facebook for a while, you might enjoy clicking here. This is what Facebook thinks you are interested in based on its observations of the stories you read, posts you comment on, and things you've liked on the site. You might find these uncannily accurate and a bit creepy. You are able to delete topics that you're not interested in, and that should adjust Facebook's algorithm. There are several categories here, so click each topic above the picture tiles as shown in **Figure 7-6** and click the X in the upper right corner of any tile you want to remove.

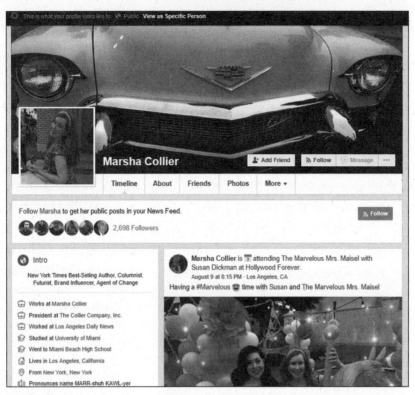

FIGURE 7-5

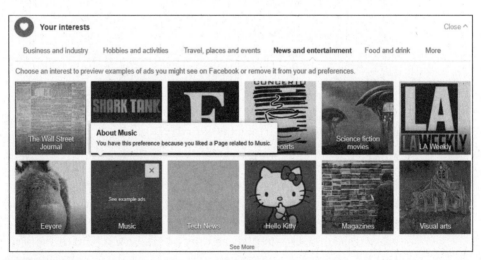

FIGURE 7-6

- **Advertisers you've interacted with:** When you click on ads on Facebook, advertisers (further down on the page) add you to their target list. Feel free to remove any company you're not interested in here in the same way you removed the Interest tiles in **Figure 7-6**. Again, click across and click on the other categories. If you follow my instructions further on, you will have nothing in the other categories, because I'm going to be showing you how to opt-out of this data collection.

- **Your Information:** Here is where you can opt-out for some personalized advertising. This means if you indicate you don't want your marital status used as an advertising identifier, Facebook may show you ads that are meant for single or married people.

- **Ad Settings:** Here you will find three very important settings. These are the settings that protect your name from being used in advertising from advertisers off of the Facebook platform. By denying these permissions, you deny Facebook the right to use information they get from your actions on the site and elsewhere. I have set these all on my account to "Not Allowed" and "No One." Click each heading to read the explanation of how the data is used or shared if you want, or just save time and deny permission.

- **Face Recognition:** Here's where you need to make your own decision. I am not a fan of facial recognition, but I am keenly aware that it occurs everywhere we go. I know I've been scanned at airports and in banks. There is current debate as to whether this practice is an invasion of privacy or a benefit to society.

  I can tell you how it might be a benefit on Facebook. On the Internet there are bad actors who take other people's photos (from Facebook posts, blogs, Google, or websites) and use them as their own. They may use them in profiles to put up a false persona or for other nefarious ends.

  If you allow Facebook's Face Recognition on your photos, you will be notified in your Timeline Review when you appear in photos or videos but haven't been tagged. This gives you the opportunity to report any misuse of photos. No one is permitted to impersonate you on the platform. Also, when someone posts a photo of you, the Face Recognition option will suggest your name for tagging.

Many iPhone users I know are comfortable with unlocking their phones with their face, but some aren't. Whether the benefits of this technology outweigh the perceived risk is up to you.

TIP

To turn Face Recognition on or off on a smartphone, open the Facebook App. Tap the hamburger menu (three parallel horizontal lines) on the screen and tap Settings and Privacy ⇨ Settings ⇨ Face Recognition.

- **Apps and Websites:** In this section, you put controls on what Facebook apps, advertisers, and the websites on which you've used Facebook login can share about you when you're using these applications and websites. You can also block certain applications from accessing your information and contacting you; such applications include games, causes, and surveys. If you simply don't want to be bothered, be careful which games and application invites you get from friends.

TIP

When you visit a website, you might think it easier to sign in with your Facebook account versus typing in your email address and a password. You're right . . . but when you use Facebook login on another site, you may be opening access to your data and lists of Facebook friends to that website. Consider this next time you're looking for a shortcut.

- **Notifications:** If you'd like Facebook to notify you when people mention you or when close friends post, you can edit these settings here. Be sure to click Edit so you can actually see which notifications Facebook wants to send you. Some are worthwhile and others, not so much. If you leave this control unchecked, your mobile device will buzz all day.

An important Notification setting lies in the On Facebook section. Once you go down the list of the many options, be sure to click Edit on the *Tags* line. This will enable you to be notified every time someone tags you in a picture or a post. I recommend changing this to *Anyone* because you never know when someone may mention your name or mistag you in a picture. This way you can swiftly handle these tags in your Timeline Review discussed further on.

- **Blocking:** Click the Edit Your Lists link under Blocking. If there are some folks you'd really rather not interact with on Facebook, this setting allows you to block them from access. Simply type in each name and/or email address that you want to block, and then click the Block button. Once you've blocked someone, that person can no longer see any of your Facebook activity. You can also block apps that you may have used in the past that still have access to your Facebook data.

  Using the Restricted List (in the same section) may be a more palatable way to handle your privacy. Rather than blocking a person, you might Restrict them. By restricting someone's view, they will not see any Facebook post that you share only with friends.

Meet Your Facebook Home Page

1. You have two main pages on Facebook: Home (also called your *News Feed*) and your Timeline. You can select the one you want to view by clicking either Home or your name (for your timeline) in the navigation bar atop any Facebook page. Clicking Home brings you to your news feed. Your home page has links for just about anything you want to do or see on Facebook. In the center of the page is a column for News Feeds, featuring your friends' updates.

2. The left side of this page has clickable navigation links that take you to important areas of Facebook that relate to your account. These areas include the Pages you create, Groups you join, and Lists you curate, as well as your Apps and Interests. Be sure to click the See More . . . link if it appears.

3. By default, the news feed in the center of the page shows the updates your friends have posted that are getting the most attention with replies. There is some mystery algorithm that decides which posts you see. So you may click the down arrow next to *News Feed* at the top left of your navigation links — Most Recent posts — if you'd like to see each post from each of your friends, in the order of posting. **Figure 7-7** shows how it's done.

TIP

Aside from my family, whose posts I request to *See First* (more on that later), I visit my friends' pages by typing their names into the search bar regularly. This way I can see what they've been up to, even if Facebook hasn't deemed their posts necessary for me to see.

FIGURE 7-7

4. On the right side of this page, scroll down to watch a live ticker of your friends' Stories on Facebook. There are also links to see sports scores and to *Watch Latest Episodes* and *Facebook Watch*. These videos are custom created content for Facebook members' entertainment. Click on See All for the latest offerings. Just below this stream, you see some important sections to pay attention to (see **Figure 7-8**):

   • **Birthdays:** Represented by a tiny gift box icon, the Birthdays link shows which of your friends has a birthday today. By clicking the link, you can see the names and be able to post a Happy Birthday wish that shows up directly on their pages. (Also note that you can access your friends' birthdays by clicking the Events link on the left side of the Feed page.)

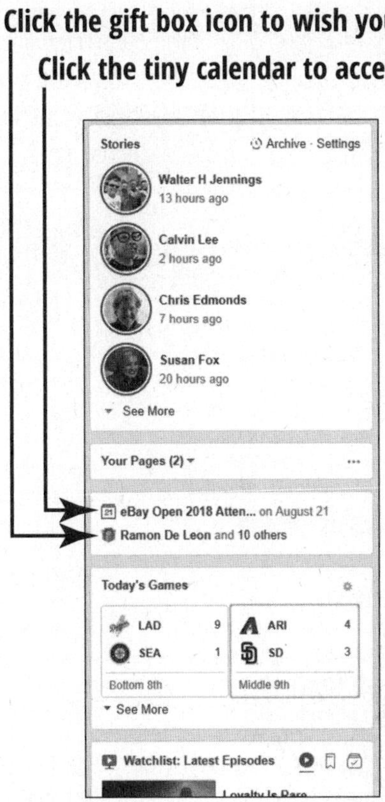

Click the gift box icon to wish your friend a happy birthday

Click the tiny calendar to access upcoming events

FIGURE 7-8

- **Events:** Click the tiny calendar and you see links to upcoming events (in chronological order) that you've been invited to, that your friends may be interested in, or that are going on in your community. Just click the appropriate link on the left side of the page, shown in **Figure 7-9**.

  You can check out the event by clicking on the page link. If you want, you can respond Interested, Going, Maybe, or Can't Go.

- **Chat:** At the very bottom on the right side of the screen is a box marked Chat. Clicking here opens a box that enables you to text with your online Facebook friends or to place a video call. The side chat bar on the desktop can be a bit distracting, so if I want to make video calls, I use the Facebook Messenger app. (Chapter 8 explains how this works.)

FIGURE 7-9

Review Your Timeline Page

1. Click your name at the top navigation bar on any Facebook page, and you arrive on your *Timeline* (the page showing your public profile). Your Facebook timeline is designed to chronicle your travels and activities. It can show how you categorize your life and times and digitally document your entire life, should you wish. The page, as you see it, is your personal view. Click the View As bar at the bottom of your cover photo to see the way it looks to your friends when they visit your page. Notice that there are links just below your name. These are just the start; by clicking the word *More,* you make many other options appear that tie into your timeline.

   Figure 7-10 shows you my page, populated with all the links (my view). This looks closer to what your page will look like after you've been on Facebook for a while.

2. In **Figure 7-10**, you see a large photo at the top. This is your cover image (think of it as a kind of album cover). Your cover photo is the first thing that people see when they come to your Facebook page. Your Profile photo appears in the lower left side, inset into the cover. You can use a personal photo that expresses your mood at the time. Click the small camera that appears grayed out until you mouse over it in the upper left-hand corner of your page.

Click the small camera to upload a cover photo.

↓

Marsha Collier

👁 View As   ✎ Edit Profile   ≣ Activity Log 20+   ···

Timeline ▾   About   Friends 4,995   Photos   🔒 Archive   More ▾

Videos
Check-Ins
Sports
Music
Movies
TV Shows
Books
Apps and Games
Likes
Events
Questions
Reviews
Instagram
Manage Sections

⭐ 6,627 items for you to review   ✕

✎ Make Post   📷 Photo/Video   ◉ Live Video   🏴 Lif

❸ Intro

What's on your mind?

New York Times Best-Selling Author, Columnist,
Futurist, Brand Influencer, Agent of Change

Edit

🖼 Photo/Video   😀 Feeling/Activity   ···

🏠 Works at Marsha Collier

🏠 President at The Collier Company, Inc.

🏠 Worked at Los Angeles Daily News

🎓 Studied at University of Miami

🎓 Went to Miami Beach High School

🏠 Lives in Los Angeles, California

From New York, New York

Posts

Marsha Collier shared a post.
18 hrs · ❸ ▾

Can't wait to see my Dodgers "Big Blue Wrecking Crew,
Garvey, and more along with Rod Carew, Rich Kee and

FIGURE 7-10

TIP

After you have stored photos on Facebook (see Chapter 9), you can change your cover to any of these other photos as well as upload a new one at any time.

3. You will be prompted to upload a photo, and a window on your computer pops up. Go to the folder that holds your pictures, select one, click Upload, and the photo appears on your page.

TIP

The photo appears as 851 pixels wide by 315 deep — but I wouldn't be too concerned about the exact size; just stick to horizontal format pictures. Facebook enlarges your photo to fit the space if it's too small. But the photo has to be at least 720 pixels wide, or Facebook asks you to select a different one. If your image is larger than 315 pixels in height, you have the option to reposition your image.

4. Once you upload an image, you'll see the words *Reposition*. To center your photo vertically, *mouse over* (hover your mouse pointer in) that area; the cursor turns into a hand icon that you can use to drag the image up or down until you feel it's centered just the way you want it.

5. Click the Save Changes button, and your image appears at the top of your Facebook timeline.

6. Small box links appear in the lower right side of your cover photo. These help you manage your page.

   - **View As:** This switches your view from managing your page to Public viewing mode.

   - **Edit Profile:** Here you can make additions and/or deletions to your profile information.

   - **Activity Log:** Clicking here brings you to a page that has a link to your activity on Facebook and a link to your official Timeline Review. This is where you can see when you've been tagged in photos. You can decide whether tagged photos will appear on your page. Even if you don't want these posts to appear on your page, you can Like or comment on the posts right here.

   - **Three horizontal dots:** This box takes you to your Timeline Settings page.

7. The tabs that appear below your cover photo are

   - **Timeline:** Clicking here allows you to choose to view your page's timeline photos in a grid or a list format.

   - **About:** Clicking here brings you to the page that offers a bio and contact information. You can edit this at any time here, too.

   - **Photos:** Here's where you see photos of you that you've posted, and images of you that other people have posted. Photos magically appear here when a friend tags you in a picture. (Check out Chapter 9 for the how-to information on adding photos and tagging friends.) Click here to go to a page with all your photos and albums.

   - **Friends:** As you accumulate friends on Facebook, small versions of their profile pictures appear here. When you click the box, a page with clickable links and pictures of all your friends will appear.

   - **More:** Clicking More produces a drop-down menu listing every section of your profile and connected apps. For example, Check-Ins represents places where you've checked in on Facebook and posted photos or events.

If you click Manage Sections at the bottom of the section list, you can indicate whether to show more or fewer sections — and change the order in which they appear.

Update Your Status

1. Here's where the fun really begins. In the long, thin rectangle that appears at the top of either of your Facebook pages, type in your *status* — some words about what's going on with you at the moment. Inside the status update box, you see the question *What's on your mind?* To answer the question — called *posting* — click inside the box and type any message you want.

TIP

Most people use the update feature to let other people know what they're doing at that given moment — often you see quick notes such as "Baking a cake for my in-laws" or "Going to work out on the treadmill."

TIP

If you're on your smartphone, you also have the option to Check In to a special place you're visiting (see a web example in **Figure 7-11**).

2. You can attach videos, photos, live video, or links to interesting pages on the web. If you're posting your update from your Profile page, you can select color backgrounds, stickers, add animated GIFs, support non-profits, and more by moving the right slider shown in **Figure 7-11** up and down. Click the icon representing the item, should you want to attach something to your comment. To attach a website link to a status update:

   a. *Type your status update into the text box.*

   b. *Navigate in another browser tab to the website you want to share and select its URL by highlighting it in your browser's address bar.* Then copy it by pressing Ctrl+C on your keyboard.

   c. *Paste the URL below your comments by clicking and then pressing Ctrl+V on your keyboard.* A mini-version of your linked page will appear below the comment (see **Figure 7-12**).

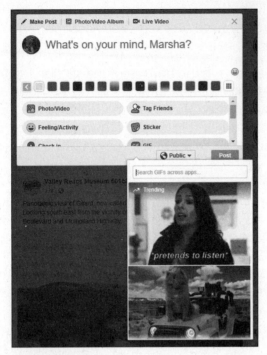

FIGURE 7-11

FIGURE 7-12

    d. After the thumbnail of your link appears in the update box, you can delete the URL. The thumbnail contains the clickable link to the article or page.

3. When you're done typing the message (and attaching a photo, video, or link), check the Privacy selector at the bottom (click the small globe icon) to be sure you've chosen who gets to see the update. Now click the Post button at the bottom right of the status update section.

TIP

The words you typed in your status update (if you did not attach a link or photo) appear with your name at the top of your Facebook timeline.

Delete a Status Update or Other Post

1. Removing the current status update from your Profile page is one of the simpler tasks to perform on Facebook. Move your cursor to the upper right-hand corner of the offending status update.

2. Click the three horizontal dots, and the option to Delete appears, as shown in **Figure 7-13**. (If someone has shared something to your page that you'd rather not see, you have the option to Hide from Timeline, Edit Post, Change Date, and more.

FIGURE 7-13

3. Click Delete and a confirmation window pops up. Confirm that you want to delete the post, and it's gone.

Add a Photo to Your Timeline

1. To post a photo to your timeline, locate the word *Photo* and the row of icons at the top of the status update text box where you see the question *What's on your mind?*

2. Click the Photo/Video icon on your desktop. Doing this opens a menu to upload a photo from your computer. On a mobile device, you will be asked whether you want to take a picture or use an existing one. The procedure is the same as loading a photo for your Profile page.

3. Click Attach Photo, and you see a box that prompts you to browse for a photo or video on your computer. Click the Choose File button to look for a picture on your computer. After you find a photo, click that photo to select it. Then you can put it up on your Facebook wall by clicking the Post button at the bottom of the status update box.

Add Life Events to Your Timeline

1. Life events happen to us all. And in your timeline status box, you have the opportunity to share your special events with the world (or just with your friends). To add a significant event, click the Life Event link above the status update box.

2. Select one of the five main categories that identifies your event. Facebook produces an arrow menu on the right (as shown in **Figure 7-14**), offering a list of options in the main categories.

3. Select the category you want to add, and then fill out the form that pops up; include the city and state in which the event occurred.

4. Add a photo. (You can upload a fresh one or select from photos already uploaded.)

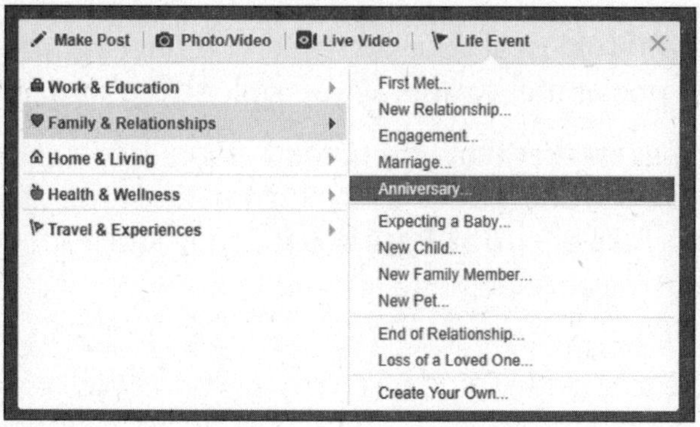

FIGURE 7-14

5. Specify the Privacy setting by clicking the small down arrow to the left of the Save button.

6. When you're all done, click Save and the event will be part of your timeline and on your map.

Share a YouTube Video on Facebook

1. So you just watched a video on YouTube and you can't wait to show it to all your friends. Well, it turns out that Facebook is the perfect place to show a video to the maximum number of friends in the minimum amount of time. Start out by going to YouTube (www.youtube.com) and clicking the video you want to share. Beneath the screen that's showing the actual video, you should see a Share button. Click it, and you get several buttons you can click to share the video on various social networking sites, including Twitter, MySpace, StumbleUpon, and (you guessed it) Facebook.

2. Click the Facebook button, and you're prompted to add a message in a rectangular text box (similar to the status update space). Type in your message and click the Share button at bottom right. Voilà! You've posted a video to your Facebook wall.

You can also copy the URL of your video, and then paste it into a status update, as you would when posting any link. See this chapter's earlier task "Update Your Status" for the steps.

If you want to upload a video of your own that you have on your computer, you can post it the same way you upload a photo.

3. Facebook would much prefer that you upload original videos to the site. They don't give YouTube videos a nice big image as the other posts on Facebook. Take a look at **Figure 7-15**. They look rather small on the bottom once they are posted.

> **Marsha Collier**
> Just now · 🌐 ▾
>
> Have you discovered Lucas the Spider on YouTube?
>
> ⓘ
>
> YOUTUBE.COM
> **Lucas the Spider**
> Meet Lucas the Spider!
>
> 👍 Like   💬 Comment   ↪ Share   ⧉ Buffer   ⬤ ▾

FIGURE 7-15

First Stop

» Find a Friend with Facebook Search

» Send a Friend Request

» Find Friends in Other Friends' Lists

» Respond to a Friend Request

» Make Facebook Lists

» Hide a Friend's Posts

» Send Private Messages to Friends

» Retrieve a Private Messages

» Chat with Friends or Video Call

» Post Updates on a Friend's Wall

» Comment on a Friend's Status

» Remove Messages from Your Wall

Chapter **8**

Connecting with Friends and Family

Now that your Facebook Timeline page is all set up and people can see who you are, it would make sense to have some friends online to connect with. Facebook can be a lonely place if you don't make friends, so in this chapter, I help you find lots of friends: old and new.

So put on your thinking cap. Think of the various offline connections you have — aside from the people in your daily life (and your family) — think back to friends from previous jobs, church, schools, and maybe even summer camp. (I'm friends on Facebook with the girl who used to pick on me mercilessly when I was a kid; she's actually not half bad now!)

Ready? This is going to be fun.

Make the Navigation Bar Your First Stop

1. Whenever you visit Facebook, you see a blue bar at the top of the page. This navigation bar, as shown in **Figure 8-1**, appears on all Facebook pages. The navigation bar does just what its name implies: It allows you to navigate to different pages on Facebook quickly. From here, you can get a brief view of what's going on with your account and friends. At the top right are icons that may have small red squares with white numbers in them, also shown in the figure.

See requests, messages, and notifications here.

Edit Account drop-down

FIGURE 8-1

2. Check out the activities available from the navigation bar. From **Figure 8-1**, I can see that I have 2 new friend requests, 3 new messages, and 88 notifications. Clicking these icons gives you different results (keep in mind that anything you can do by clicking these icons you can also do from any page):

- **Friend Requests:** An icon silhouette of two people represents Friend Requests. When you click here, you'll see a drop-down menu showing the people who have requested your friendship online. You may click their names to go directly to their timelines.

- **Messages:** A red square with a number over the cartoon voice-bubble indicates that you've received private messages. The number represents how many messages from Facebook members are in your message area. Click here and you'll get a drop-down menu. If you've viewed a message on another device (such as your tablet) the link will have a white background. If you haven't read a message, the link will have a light blue background.

TIP

When you read a private message on Facebook, the other party can tell just by looking at the message — provided the sender is viewing it on a mobile device that can track the opening of messages. (Most Apple devices do.)

TIP

In the mobile app, tapping the Messages icon (on the top of the app) requires you to download the Messenger app, Facebook's version of texting or iMessage. The app only works with friends through Facebook, and you need to download this app from the Play Store or App Store. If you do not want to download the app, you'll have to go to Facebook in a web browser in your mobile device to read or answer any incoming messages.

- **Notifications:** You'll see an icon of a bell if someone has posted a note on your wall, invited you to an event, commented on a post of yours, or commented on a picture you're in; it's a notification of activity that references your account. Pictured in **Figure 8-2**.

3. Are you looking on Facebook for a friend, your local coffee shop (if it has a fan page, it may post coupons), or your favorite movie or author? Try out the Facebook search feature. Just start typing the name or topic in the *Search for people, places and things* text box, and a drop-down list appears. As you type the words, Facebook uses the drop-down list to suggest a name (or topic) that matches what you're typing. If you see what you're looking for, click that name or phrase. If the name doesn't show up, click See All Results at the bottom of the drop-down list and search from there.

FIGURE 8-2

If you don't see a *See all results* link at the bottom of the menu, odds are there's no match on Facebook. You can still try to search by clicking the little magnifying glass in the Search box.

4. Clicking the word *Home* takes you to your home page, the hub for your news feed and (most important) the organization area on the left side of the screen. This area gives you access to other Facebook activities, including photos to view and friends to contact. (Later sections in this chapter cover these activities.)

5. Clicking your name links you to your Timeline page. From there, you can see what your friends have posted on your wall, as well as edit any information on the page.

6. Clicking the question mark takes you to Quick Help where you can report problems, go over your privacy shortcuts, and set your preferences to control how you operate on Facebook — including how private you want to be. (I cover the details in Chapter 7.)

7. The next grayed-out item (blued-out on Facebook) is a down-pointing arrow that takes you to pages and groups (if you make any — see Chapter 10 for instructions), your Activity log that lets you know everything you've been doing on the site.

Find a Friend with Facebook Search

1. Think of a small group of your friends and write down a list. Then sign in to your Facebook account; you'll land on your home page. From here, you have two ways of finding people; start by using the Search box. Type one of your friend's names in the Search box, as I've done in **Figure 8-3**. Just as when you're searching for anything on Facebook, a drop-down list appears — this one with semi-matching names.

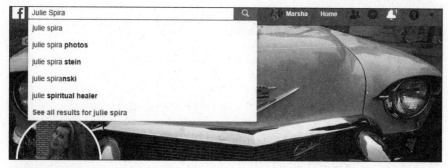

FIGURE 8-3

If you're not sure how to spell your friend's name, just type in as many characters of it as you think may be right. Facebook will pick up the slack.

2. If your friend is not on the Suggested list, click the See All Results link. You'll then see a page (or many pages) with results that match what you've typed. You should be able to find your friend if he or she is a member of Facebook.

TIP

The regular Facebook Search box does not always show every John Doe that is on Facebook; even when you click See All Results. (See how to use the advanced version of searching for friends further on.)

3. Here's the second way to find friends: Look at the blue bar at the top of the page for the Friend Requests (two people) icon. Click the icon and a drop-down menu appears, showing any friend requests you may have (to the right of the words *Friend Requests* you will see a link to Find Friends). Click there and you come to a page with a tool on the right that allows you to *Add Personal Contacts* as Friends (shown in **Figure 8-4**).

If you select any of the services listed, you'll be asked to type in your ID and password. Facebook will import your contacts automatically.

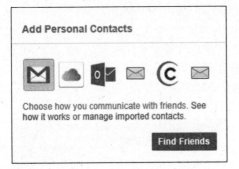

FIGURE 8-4

This Facebook feature that imports contacts is called Friend Finder. It's perfectly safe, and Facebook does not store your password. Even so, I don't like it; here are some reasons why:

- As I said in Chapter 6, I'm a stickler for privacy and do not want to share my online contact lists with anyone.

- Friend Finder makes automatic connections based on the email addresses in your address book. Facebook says: "Facebook won't share the email addresses you import with anyone, but we will store them on your behalf and may use them later to help others search for people or to generate friend suggestions for you and others." If you don't want Facebook to store this information, visit this page to Remove All Imported Contacts: www.facebook.com/contact_importer/remove_uploads.php.

4. If these features are fine with you, feel free to add your online contact list. I can tell you that Facebook won't blatantly lie, but be sure you read every notification message before agreeing to any Facebook activity.

5. If you search for a friend and can't find them from the Search box, click on People and you'll see a column on the left that is an even better way to search for a long-lost friend. **Figure 8-5** shows you an advanced search where you can select as many details as you know about someone to narrow down a search. This helps especially if your friend has a common name.

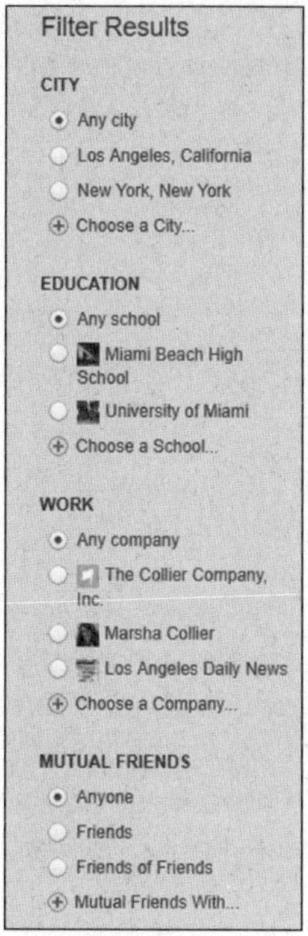

Filter Results

CITY
- Any city
- Los Angeles, California
- New York, New York
- Choose a City...

EDUCATION
- Any school
- Miami Beach High School
- University of Miami
- Choose a School...

WORK
- Any company
- The Collier Company, Inc.
- Marsha Collier
- Los Angeles Daily News
- Choose a Company...

MUTUAL FRIENDS
- Anyone
- Friends
- Friends of Friends
- Mutual Friends With...

FIGURE 8-5

Send a Friend Request

1. When you find someone on Facebook you'd like to add as a friend, doing so is a pretty simple task. After clicking the link to your prospective friend's Timeline page (to double-check that he or she is the person you're looking for), you may see an Add Friend box next to the name as in **Figure 8-6**.

2. After you click the Add Friend button, the words *Friend Request Sent* appear. Also, to the left of the Add Friend button is a list of friends you have in common. Success at growing your circle of friends can come pretty quickly.

3. After you send your request, a friend request is posted to the recipient's Facebook notifications.

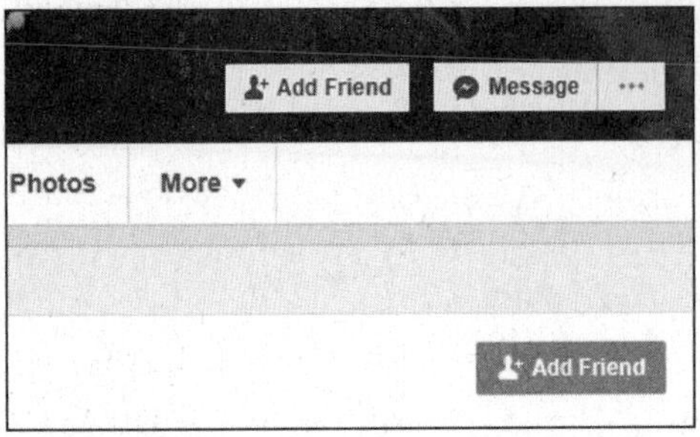

FIGURE 8-6

Find Friends in Other Friends' Lists

1. Odds are that the friends you have on Facebook are connected to other people you may know already. Would you like to make those people your friends on Facebook, too? It's easy. Facebook Timeline pages have Friends links you can find below the cover photo (unless the member has chosen to block the box from view). If you have Facebook friends in common, you'll see the number of mutual friends on the box, as shown in **Figure 8-7**.

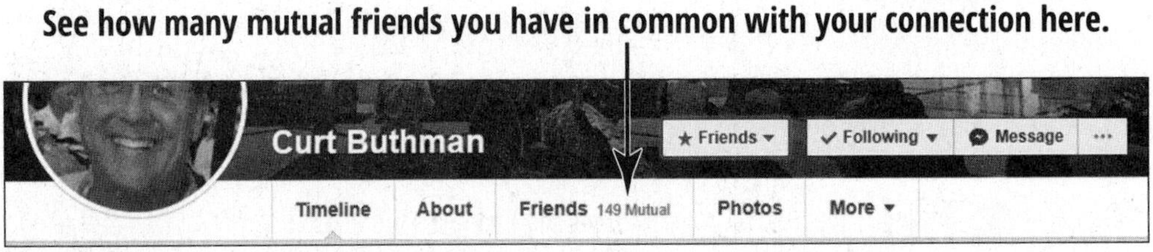

See how many mutual friends you have in common with your connection here.

FIGURE 8-7

2. By clicking the box, you can view all of a particular friend's connections in a new window (see **Figure 8-8**). And you also see links to your Mutual Friends.

3. You can search through the list (looking for a specific person) in two ways: by typing the person's name in the Search Friends box and clicking the magnifying glass, or by scrolling down the list and viewing each friend individually. As you type, names that match your search appear (as in **Figure 8-9)**. When someone is not already your friend on Facebook, an Add Friend link appears to the right of each entry that you can click to send a friend request.

FIGURE 8-8

FIGURE 8-9

Respond to a Friend Request

1. When people know you're a Facebook member, someone is going to want to be your friend on Facebook. There are two ways you will be notified of a friend request: You get a notification via email, or you find out when you log in to Facebook. If you receive your notification via email, just click the link contained in the message and it takes you directly to the request.

TIP

If, for security's sake, you prefer not to click links in email (I don't, ever) just go to Facebook and click the Friend Request notification on the top navigation bar. Your friend's request will be there.

2. When you log in to Facebook, any page offers you a notification area to see your friend requests. The place to check is at the top right of your page in your navigation bar. The button to click resembles the silhouette of two people. If you have a new friend request, you'll see a small red box with a number in it, overlapping the icon. To access your requests, click the icon.

3. When you access your Friend Requests icon, you see your potential friend's photo and name. You also see whether you have any mutual friends with this person (and how many). By clicking the Mutual Friends link next to the potential friend's name, you can see the friends you have in common.

4. To respond to a friend request, you have two choices. One is to click one of the two buttons to the right of your potential friend's name. One button reads *Confirm* and one reads *Delete*. Click one of those buttons and (respectively) you add a friend or ignore the request quietly.

TIP

When you ignore a friend request, an email isn't sent to the person who placed the request. That person will not know that you chose to ignore him or her, except for the fact that you didn't accept the request. Oops? Sometimes I just leave the request hanging there, just in case this is someone I may meet soon. Then "oops" is a graceful explanation.

5. If you'd prefer, you can click the person's name and go directly to his or her Timeline page. I do this myself, and often click the member's About link to jog my memory if I don't recognize the person right away. Once on that page, you see a couple of boxes: at the top of the page, *Confirm request,* and on the person's cover photo, *Respond to Friend Request*. Clicking in this lower box gives you the option to Confirm or Delete Request, as shown in **Figure 8-10.**

![Respond to Friend Request button with Follow and Message buttons; a dropdown showing Confirm and Delete Request options, and a More button]

FIGURE 8-10

Make Facebook Lists

1. Facebook gives you the chance to divvy up your ever-growing groups of friends into lists. The more your number of "friends" grows, the more posts you see in your News Feed. Quite frankly, even if you accepted a friendship from someone, you may not want to be burdened with every step-by-step description of daily activities. Quite aside from unfriending or banning the person (or "Hiding Friends' Posts," described further on), you can classify him or her as an Acquaintance.

2. Visit an offending friend's Facebook page and click the word *Friends*, as I've done in **Figure 8-11**. You have several options to build lists here:

FIGURE 8-11

- **Close Friends:** Use this selection for close friends and family members you really like and they show up with a star next to their name. Once you've indicated this status, all their posts always show up in your News Feed.

TIP

The people you designate on these lists will not be aware of your choices. Only when stating that someone is a direct relation in your family will Facebook send them a message to confirm the relationship.

- **Acquaintances:** The posts from friends in your Acquaintances list show up rarely in your News Feed, if ever.

- **Add to another list:** Facebook automatically sets up lists for you, based on information you've shared in your bio or put in your timeline. There may be a list from your high school, university, place of work, or family.

3. Now, when you post a status update on Facebook, you have a lot more control over who sees your post. For example, in **Figure 8-12**, when I post only to my small group of close friends, no one else on Facebook sees that post.

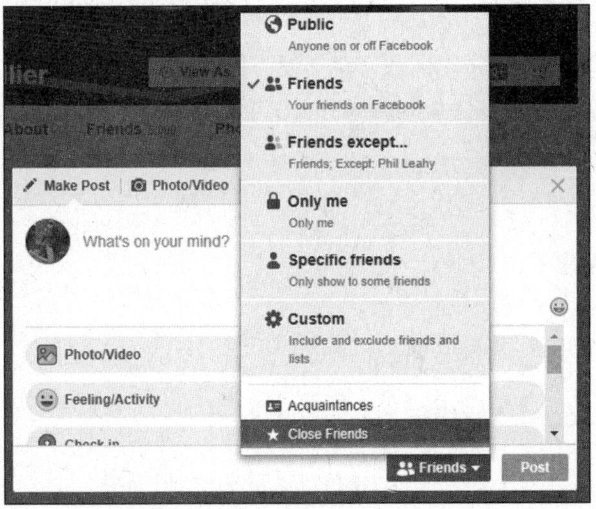

FIGURE 8-12

Hide a Friend's Posts

Once you've been on Facebook for a while, you may connect with people from your past, friends and family, and some folks you've met on Facebook through other friends. This is a good thing.

When you go to your News Feed to read posts, however, you may find that some of those folks have wildly varied views that (ahem) diverge from yours (some of which you may never have known about). Facebook operates in a conversational tone; many folks feel comfortable discussing their deepest feelings online, which may include opinions (political or religious) that differ from yours. You may choose to engage them in a discussion online (which may end up being a fruitless annoyance), shrug, and go on (another way of saying, "Live and let live"), or you can try to ignore the irritating posts as you scroll the page. It may not seem politically correct or courteous to unfriend (say) your cousin, just because you don't subscribe to views like his, but to avoid such postings altogether

1. Go to your friends' page, and in the cover photo, you will see a box entitled Following (refer to **Figure 8-13**). You automatically follow someone's feed when you become his or her friend. Consider whether it's time to stop following this person. You can also Unfollow a friend from one of their posts on the News Feed page, also shown in **Figure 8-13** (right).

FIGURE 8-13

2. Click the word *Following* and it toggles to Follow. If you're not following someone on Facebook, you won't see his or her updates in your news feed.

3. If the preceding seems too drastic and permanent, click on the three dots on the top of one of that person's posts. Select one of the options in **Figure 8-13** (left) to temporarily Snooze their posts for 30 days.

Send Direct Messages to Friends

1. Facebook has a feature, Messenger, which enables you to send direct messages to your friends. One way to send a message to a friend is to click the Messenger link on the left side of your home page. Facebook takes you to your Messenger page.

2. Click the New Message button in the lower right corner of any web page, next to the word *Chat*, and a blank message form opens on your screen.

3. In the blank message form, address the message by typing your friend's name into the To box. Facebook begins to autofill names from your friend list as you type. When you find the correct friend, select the name by clicking it or highlighting it, and then press Enter.

   For these messages, fill in the Message text box as you would for a text message. When you've completed your message, simply click the arrow to the right corner of the New Message form (or click the X at the top of the box if you've changed your mind).

   You have options to attach files, photos, videos, and links to your message, as well as a variety of items — depending on whether you subscribe to any Facebook applications.

   TIP

4. Alternatively, you can click a friend's name in one of their posts or visit a friend's Timeline page. Click Message at the bottom of the cover photo, as shown in **Figure 8-14**, or click the Message option when you click on their name in a post. A window opens at the bottom of the screen; just type in your message.

   You can share a post or a video in Messenger (also known as "messages" or chat).

   TIP

FIGURE 8-14

Retrieve a Private Message

1. More than likely, once you send a message, you'll get a reply. Retrieving and answering private messages is simple. Facebook sends you an email with the message. You can respond by going to Facebook (or the Messenger app) and clicking the Respond link on the message.

2. As with most Facebook tasks, you have a choice — in this case, two places on the site where you can retrieve a private message:

- In the navigation bar on the top right of your home page, click the button that resembles a bubble with a lightning bolt. A drop-down list with a snapshot of your current messages opens. Click to select the message you want to read from the list and you see the full message.

- Click the Messenger link on the left side of your home page, and Facebook takes you to your Messenger page. It's like your email Inbox. To read a message, simply click it and the full message opens.

You can also open the Messenger app on your phone to send or retrieve messages.

TIP

Chat with Friends or Video Call

1. Chat is the desktop interactive version of the Messenger app. When you're spending time using your devices, you may be reading friends' posts on your desktop. By the same token, they may be on Facebook at the same time you are. You might as well find out. On the bottom of your Facebook page is a chat option; in the lower right corner, you'll see a Chat box. Clicking there opens a vertical box that you can scroll to see your friends who are logged on to Facebook (see **Figure 8-15**).

FIGURE 8-15

2. It allows you to chat with friends who are online at the same time you are. To see the friends you have online, you can check in two places:

   - On the right side of your home page, beneath your messages, you see a chat area. An icon appears next to each of your friends' names (refer to **Figure 8-15**). If the icon is green, they may be open to a chat.

   - Click your friend's name and a small Message window opens. You can type a message to your friend and wait for an answer to show up.

3. If you see someone online you'd like to speak to, and find you want to start a chat session, click the name of the friend. A Message box opens at the bottom of your screen. After the box opens, type in your message and press Enter. Your message then pops up in the chat box and your session has begun.

4. You can also be on the receiving end of a chat session. If you hear a soft popping noise and a small window opens, someone is requesting to chat with you. To respond, type in your message and press Enter. Your message pops up in the chat box.

5. If you see a small video camera next to your friend's name in a chat box, this means your friend is open to having a video chat. If you have a webcam on your computer, click the video camera to initiate a video call. A window pops up on your friend's computer.

TIP

If you're just breezing through Facebook and have things to do, you may not want to get involved in a chat session. If this is the case, merely click the Chat link. Then click the cog icon in the right corner and select Turn Off Active Status from the drop-down menu in the box that opens (see **Figure 8-16**). You become "invisible" to all, and you'll be free to go about your Facebook chores undisturbed.

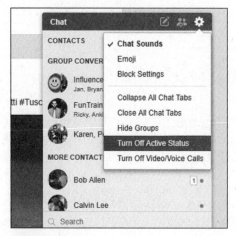

FIGURE 8-16

Post Updates on a Friend's Wall

1. On your Facebook home page, you'll see notations from your friends' walls — whether as status updates from the person whose wall it is, or by messages posted by their friends. To post a message directly on a friend's wall, go to your friend's Facebook Timeline page. The text box is filled with a prompt that reads *Write something* in grayed-out letters.

2. To post your message, simply type it in the text box. If you'd like to add a picture or video to your message, click the Photo link and add it. (Find more about attachments in Chapter 9.)

3. When you're done with your message and attachments, hit your Return (or Enter) key. Voilà! Your message is now on display for your friend (and potentially all visitors to your friend's page) to read.

TIP

If you want to refer to another friend in your posted message, before you type in his or her name, type the @ sign (the symbol for *at*). Then begin to type in the person's name. When the name pops up in the drop-down menu of friends' names that appears, click it to create a link to that friend in your post. You can also click the silhouette next to a + mark in the corner of the message box to add a friend. Your post then also appears on the linked friend's Timeline page.

Comment on a Friend's Status

1. If you see a status message that your friend has posted and you'd like to comment on it, it's as simple as 1, 2, 3. Click the Comment bubble under the status post. A window opens with a blank box in which you can type your comment.

2. Type your comment in the Write a Comment box and press the Return (or Enter) key when you're finished. Your response is posted below your friend's posting for all to see.

Remove Messages from Your Wall

1. There may be a time when someone posts a message on your wall that might be too personal, or you don't want others to see. Facebook gives you the option to hide the post. (Your friend may never know that's happened unless he or she comes back to your Profile page.) To remove a post from your timeline, find the post. Move your cursor over the right side of the post and click the three dots. This opens a menu, as shown in **Figure 8-17**.

FIGURE 8-17

2. When you click Hide from Timeline, a window opens to remind you that it can still be seen on the News Feed and perhaps other places. If you're cool with that, just click. Nobody will be the wiser. If you're really offended by the post, click the Report/Remove Tag and the post will be entirely removed from Facebook if deemed inappropriate.

» **Create a Photo Album**

» **Tag Photos**

» **Untag Yourself in a Photo**

» **Delete a Photo**

» **Upload a Video to Facebook**

» **Broadcast Live Video on Facebook**

Chapter **9**

Adding Photos and Videos to Facebook

Since Facebook is all about sharing, it's up to you to share! Putting up photos of you, your friends, and your family (that includes pets) is fun — and it gives your Facebook friends a chance to interact with you.

I figure you've uploaded a picture for your profile image already, but what I'm talking about in this chapter is setting up online photo albums.

So let's get started!

Upload a Photo to Your Account

1. As with most Facebook tasks, you have more than one way to post a photo. Start by signing in to your Facebook account if you're not already signed in.

   • If you took the photo with your phone or tablet, open the Facebook app and tap the What's On Your Mind text box at the top of the page to create a post. Tap the words Photo/Video shown in **Figure 9-1**. (Your Photo gallery appears, from which you can select an image to post.) Once you select the photo, you will be brought back to a Status Update text box.

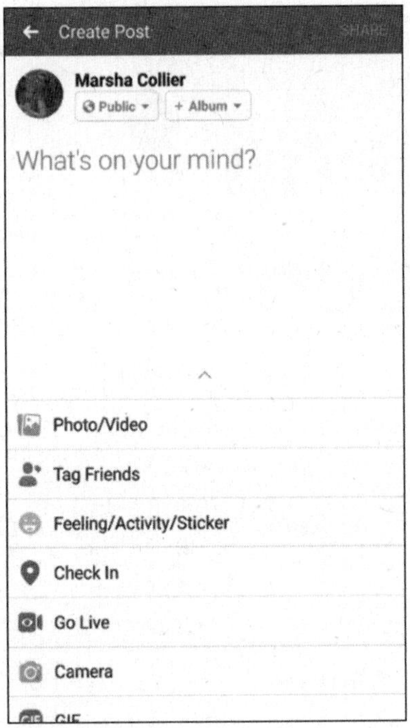

FIGURE 9-1

   • If you're at your computer, an easy choice is to post the image directly to your Home feed or Timeline page. Click your name in the upper right corner and you'll arrive on your timeline.

   • A status-update box appears on the top of your Home (News Feed) page where you can also upload pictures.

2. Type a message about the photo in the Wall posting box that says *What's on your mind?*

3. Below your message, find the icon for uploading a photo (it looks like a little photo of a landscape) with the words *Photo/Video,* as I show from a computer in **Figure 9-2**. Clicking the text area changes the status box.

Click here to add a photo

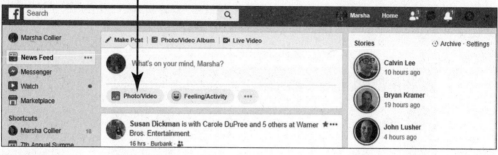

FIGURE 9-2

4. The new view gives you lots of choices: Upload Photo/Video from your computer or create Photo/Video Album out of many photos (shown in **Figure 9-3**). Here's how those choices work:

   a. *To use a single photo already on your computer,* click the Photo/Video bar. Your window changes to enable you to select a photo from your computer's hard drive. From the dialog box that opens, you can look for a photo on your computer's hard drive. Find the photo you want to upload and double-click it to select it. Click Open. The photo opens and uploads while the dialog box closes, and you see a thumbnail version of your photo in the text box. To post the photo, type a description and click Post.

TIP

   Before clicking Post when you're uploading photos to Facebook, you may want to change your default privacy settings. **Figure 9-4** shows the options that appear when you click the arrow in the box next to the Post button. Click the appropriate privacy option, and then click Post.

FIGURE 9-3

FIGURE 9-4

b. *To upload multiple photos,* click an image in the dialog box and hold down your Ctrl (Control) key on a Windows PC or the Command key (⌘) on an Apple machine. While holding down the key, click additional photos. You will see them line up in the File Name bar, as shown in **Figure 9-5**. When you are done, click Open to upload them to Facebook. After selecting your privacy setting (I allow everyone to see), click Share.

Four items selected

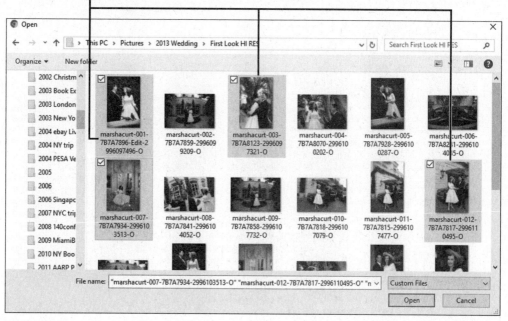

FIGURE 9-5

> c. *If you're ready to work with a batch of photos on Facebook,* click Create an Album and the multiple photos you upload will all be placed in a single album.

Create a Photo Album

1. You may have uploaded photos from your mobile device and later some from your computer and you'd like them all to appear in a single photo album. Facebook has many ways to get to the page where you can edit photo albums. Here are the two easiest:

   - *Click the word Photos below your cover photo on your Timeline page.* The resulting page, shown in **Figure 9-6**, brings you to all the photos of you that are posted on Facebook.

   - *Select the Albums link above the photos on your Timeline page.* At the top right, click the + Create Album link.

Click here to create a photo album

FIGURE 9-6

TIP

2. In either case, a window opens, showing you the contents of your computer. You can navigate around your computer by clicking the folders to find where your photos reside.

3. After you find the proper folder, you can begin selecting photos for your album. If you want to select just a few, click the check boxes for individual thumbnails, one at a time, to select them for upload.

   You do not have to select all the photos just now; you can go back to the album and add them one by one by clicking Add More Photos.

4. After you've finished picking the images, click Open. This brings you back to the Untitled Album page (see **Figure 9-7**).

5. On the Untitled Album page, give your album a title, add comments about the album, and type the location where the photos were taken in the Location box. Also, choose to *Use date from photos* or manually add the date.

6. Below each photo, if you want, type a description in the text box and tag friends who appear in the photos (more on tagging later). You may also set an individual privacy setting for a photo which will override the default setting.

Add where the photos were taken here

Click here to create a photo album

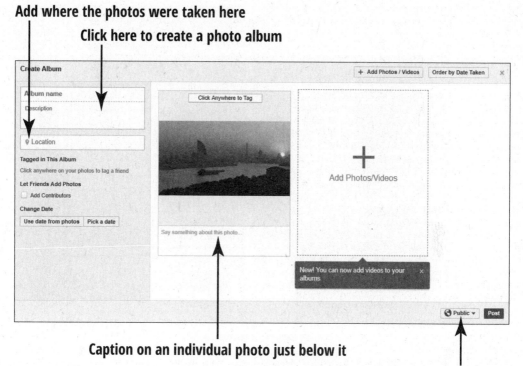

Caption on an individual photo just below it

Select the privacy setting for your album

FIGURE 9-7

7. Before clicking Post, you may select a general default privacy setting (for who can see the album) for the entire album.

8. You can edit the album by going to your timeline and clicking the Photos box, then Albums. Scroll down the page and you'll see your album (or albums), as in **Figure 9-8**.

9. Click the album you want to edit and you'll be brought to a page with thumbnail versions of your pictures. Click Edit in the upper right corner. **Figure 9-9** shows you the Edit Album page. Go through the photos, tag the pictures, write captions, and delete any photos you'd rather not use. When you're done, go to the top of the page and click Done.

10. Your photos will now show up on your Timeline page; if you've tagged friends in the photos, those pictures appear on your friends' Timeline pages.

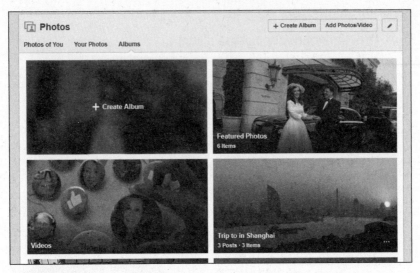

FIGURE 9-8

FIGURE 9-9

Tag Photos

1. No matter where you find photos of you or one of your friends on Facebook, you can tag them. *Tagging* is the Facebook phrase for adding the names of friends to photo information. Tagging a friend makes his or her name appear when someone puts a mouse pointer over the tagged friend's image. Tagging also links the photo to the appropriate profile. Whenever friends are tagged in a photo, that photo appears on their individual walls and becomes a permanent part of their Photos areas.

TIP

When you or anyone on Facebook is tagged, the *tagee* receives a notification letting him or her know of this newfound fame. Then the tagee can get online and look at the picture. If they have Privacy set up in their Timeline Settings (see Chapter 7), they can approve for the photo to appear on Facebook.

2. When you see a photo of you or one of your friends on Facebook, click it and you arrive at the photo's page. If no one has been tagged in the picture, no linkable names will appear beside it.

3. On the right, next to the photo, click the Tag Photo box, shown in **Figure 9-10**. After you've clicked this box, tag your friend and when you're done, click the Done Tagging box on the right.

4. Move your cursor, and click it on the face of one of your friends. A box will appear for you to type in the person's name.

TIP

Try not to freak out if, when you click someone's face, Facebook says, "Would you like to tag" — and has already filled in the person's name. According to a recent paper, Facebook's DeepFace technology can accurately recognize faces 97.25 percent of the time. Google also uses a similar intelligence; **Figure 9-11** shows you what this looks like. Unfortunately, this is part of the 2.75 percent or my husband has turned off Facial Recognition in his settings (more on Privacy settings in Chapter 7).

FIGURE 9-10

FIGURE 9-11

5. Start typing your friend's name (or your name if the photo is of you), and a list of your friends pops up. Facebook narrows the selection as you type. I've found my friend's name in **Figure 9-12**.

FIGURE 9-12

6. When you've found the person in the photo, click his or her name; then — bingo! The name of the person you tagged becomes part of the photo — and the photo is posted to your tagged friend's Timeline page.

7. If you have more than one friend in the picture, repeat Steps 1–6 given here until you've tagged everyone. When you've tagged all the friends in the picture, click the Done Tagging button to the right of the picture.

TIP

You must be friends with someone on Facebook to tag him or her in a photo. If you see a photo with a person you know — but aren't Facebook friends with him or her (yet) — send that person a Friend invitation. After your friend accepts, you can add a tag to the photo.

8. As people view the photo, they'll see the tagged names. If they move their mouse pointers over the picture, the person's name pops up (as in **Figure 9-13**).

FIGURE 9-13

Untag Yourself in a Photo

1. You may get a notification that one of your friends has tagged you in a photo on Facebook. Excited, you log on to your Timeline page . . . and groan. Have no fear. If you find a photo that a friend has taken of you that doesn't quite meet your standards, you can do something about it. Click the photo, and Facebook takes you to the photo's page. At the right corner above the photo, (as in **Figure 9-14**), is three dots. Click them to see a drop-down menu of options.

2. You now have all sorts of options for this photo. The Remove Tag link appears. When you click it, Facebook will ask whether you want to Remove or Report the tag. Click Remove and the photo goes into the Facebook ether and will never be associated with your profile again. The photo does remain in your friend's album, but someone would have to view the album to see that picture of you. Once you've untagged yourself in a photo, no one but you can tag you in that particular photo again.

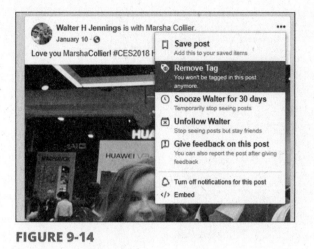

FIGURE 9-14

Delete a Photo

TIP

1. If you upload a photo by mistake — or simply decide you'd rather remove that photo-taken-with-your-ex — you can remove it. You can delete only the photos that you, personally, have uploaded. Facebook has to have a reason to remove photos others have posted of you.

If you want to dissociate yourself from a photo that someone else uploaded, you'll have to settle for untagging yourself (see the previous task in this chapter).

2. Mouse over the upper right corner of the photo and click the three dots. Click Delete as shown in **Figure 9-15**, and (poof) the photo is gone from your Facebook page.

3. If the photo wasn't posted by you, click the three dots. Then select Give Feedback on This Post. You will then see a box like the one in **Figure 9-16**. Use it to tell Facebook why you want the photo removed from the page. Personally, I find it easier just to remove my tag and move along.

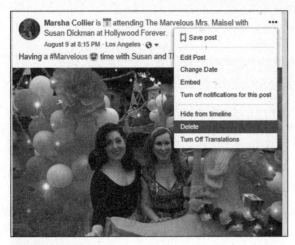

FIGURE 9-15

FIGURE 9-16

Upload a Video to Facebook

 This isn't rocket science. If you've uploaded a photo, you can upload a video. Go to your Timeline page and click the Photo/Video icon in the status-update box; you're given the option to upload a video.

2. You can also click Photos under your cover photo. Posted photos of you appear on the resulting page. When you're through admiring them, look at the top right, and next to the + Create Album button, you should see an Add Video button.

3. Click the button, and a window will pop up, offering a button you can use to choose a video file to upload from your computer. This link works similarly to Upload a Photo. When you click it, a standard search window opens on your computer.

4. Browse your computer's folders, find the video file you want to upload, and click to select it — be sure to select your Privacy Options. The upload begins immediately.

5. After the upload finishes, the video will be on your Facebook page, ready for you to tag and caption.

Broadcast Live Video on Facebook

Lots of marketers post live video on Facebook with the goal of selling something. Regular folks like us would broadcast live on video if we wanted to share a special event or a news story. You can even give a tour of your garden to your friends or in a group. This can be accomplished in front of your webcam, but I feel this is much more of a mobile-device activity.

1. Way back in **Figure 9-1** I show you what your phone looks like when you start a post. Only this time, click on the words *Go Live*.

2. Things start to happen quickly now, so I recommend not clicking Go Live until you're ready to . . . go live. The first time you want to live broadcast, Facebook asks your permission to access your camera and microphone. **Figure 9-17** shows you what it looks like. After that, Facebook asks your permission to record.

3. Once you've given Facebook access (you can always remove this access in your smartphone's app settings), the camera allows you to start filming.

FIGURE 9-17

4. First, set the privacy of the video broadcast. Note that in **Figure 9-18**, I've set it to *Only me* (I'm not quite ready to broadcast a tour of my garden to everyone or even to just my Facebook friends; I do draw a line). You can click there for a drop-down menu that lists Facebook's standard audiences.

5. Type a short description for your video so that people will want to watch it.

6. Tag friends who will be in the video with you, also a location if that's important (like for a tour of your local botanical gardens).

7. Line up your camera and select the selfie mode if you're going to be broadcasting yourself. If not, your regular camera takes over.

TIP

On Facebook, your video will appear square, so it doesn't matter if you hold your phone vertically or horizontally. If you're including images of written words, you might want to click the magic wand icon to mirror or flip your video.

FIGURE 9-18

8. When you're all ready, click the Go Live box. You know when your video is live because a red icon appears at the top left corner next to the word *LIVE*.

9. While you are broadcasting, you will see when your friends are watching. You can speak directly to them to engage your audience. They can comment or give you likes, hearts, and laughs.

10. Click Finish when you're done and you will be prompted to post it to your page for eternity (or until you delete it). You will see the broadcast on your page (and those you have selected in the Privacy settings can see it too). Also, tap the Download button so that you can save a copy of your broadcast on your phone.

11. As with all posts, photos, and videos on Facebook, you can edit the description, change the audience, or delete it altogether at any time.

Just remember, **some things can't be unseen** — even if you delete them. Someone could take a screenshot of an embarrassing photo before you have a chance to delete it.

TIP

Facebook

» Join a Facebook Group

» Start a Facebook Group

» Communicate with Group Members

» Create an Event Invitation

» Review Upcoming Events and Birthdays

» Watch Facebook TV

Chapter **10**

Exploring the Extras: Groups, Events, Watch, and Games

I f you thought your teen years were a busy time, just wait. Being a member of Facebook means that you're about to have a whole new group of friends to combine with your old ones. Best of all? You'll meet people who have interests just like yours. You'll have the opportunity to attend chats and join groups — and you don't even have to get out of your pajamas.

Is there something you really like? A series of books, films, or products? Look for a related page on Facebook; many businesses are joining up on Facebook. Even my local deli has a Facebook page. (I visit their page to check out the specials.)

And here are some other instances of Facebook member involvement:

>> When Kashi products stopped manufacturing a popular (my favorite!) shake mix, unhappy customers started a Facebook group to protest!

>> Someone came up with the idea that Betty White should host *Saturday Night Live* and started a Facebook group. They had a great idea. After spreading the word through wall posts and messages, over 500,000 people joined. The then eighty-eight-year-old Betty hosted the 2010 Mother's Day show, and SNL had the highest ratings in over 18 months! All because of a Facebook group.

Other ways to enjoy community action are to join special interest groups. To many members, these are the best parts of Facebook. Be advised: Groups can burn a lot of time, but they are a lot of fun.

Find Your Favorite Things on Facebook

1. If you're planning on navigating your way around Facebook, you're going to be up close and personal with that little search box at the top of the page. To look at some of the magic it can perform, type a *keyword* (a word that best describes the topic you're looking for) in that Search box. For this example, I'm looking for others who enjoy vintage cars (in this case, a Corvette); to find them, I typed **Corvette**.

Facebook finds all kinds of things with *Corvette* in the name and presents you with a busy page. The top bar and left column of the page (as **Figure 10-1** shows) provides all kinds of options, and the top results are shown. If you want to check out any of the results at this point, just click the name, and you're brought to that page.

2. Facebook has many types of "pages," and to confuse the issue even more, they all have different themes and are listed in the bar at the top of the search results. Here's the short story:

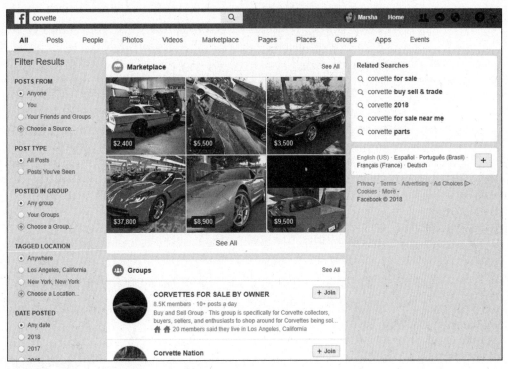

FIGURE 10-1

- **Pages:** The most basic are pages set up for celebrities (or authors), organizations, or businesses to communicate with their fans or customers. This is different from a Facebook profile; you don't make friends with a page, you use it to get information on the topic they're related to. Mine is at www.facebook.com/MarshaCollierFanPage if you'd like to visit or ask a question. Once you find a page you like, just click the Like button.

- **Groups:** These are pages and communities that any Facebook user (even you) can set up and start. They're put up to foster discussions about specific topics.

- **Posts:** Clicking to see Posts gives you recent Facebook posts that include your topic. These may be from friends or public posts from brands. It's a good way to find new connections by clicking, reading, and liking the posts.

- **Marketplace:** This can be a dangerous link when you are searching for Corvette. Here you'll find ads from people selling the object of your keyword.

- **Events:** Facebook has become the default place to find fun get-togethers that are in your area or are of interest to you (more on events further on). I often use Facebook as a social calendar, to find places to go over the weekends.

If you look at the Filter Results links on the left, there will be navigation links to further pare down your search.

TIP

3. Scroll down this page to also see a box that lists all pages that match your search (refer to **Figure 10-1**). Clicking there brings you to a list of Facebook pages related to your topic.

4. You'll find also a link to Groups, as shown in **Figure 10-2**, where you can see the many groups and whether they are open to public viewing or closed.

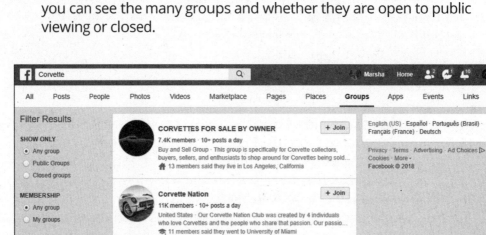

FIGURE 10-2

Don't jump willy-nilly into just any group or community that has a nice title and a cute picture. Click the title of a page and check it out before you choose to join; that way, you see what the page is really all about and who's behind it and what their rules are, if any.

TIP

(I clicked a couple in the example just given, and they weren't my cup of tea at all.)

My search for Corvette netted me way too many tantalizing pages to visit.

If you'd rather not confine your attention to the top results (but don't want to trudge through thousands), add some more keywords in the search box. Typing another keyword can help you refine your search.

Join a Facebook Group

As a member of Facebook, you'll no doubt want to connect with people who have common likes — and doing that through groups is quick and easy! Here's how:

1. Find a group through search. To find a group you're interested in, you can search for your keywords as I describe in the preceding section.

Click a group title that suits your fancy to check it out. If you think you've found one that you'd like to join, click the Join Group link on the group's page. After looking at many pages, I could see one I liked enough that it was worth joining.

2. Facebook groups come in three types:

- **Public:** Anyone who happens upon your group on Facebook or finds it in a search can join the group and read your posts.

- **Closed:** The group name will appear in search results. When viewing the page, its members and people invited to join the group are visible, but only members can see posts in the group.

For Closed (private) groups, you must click the Join Group link on the Group page and await confirmation, which you'll receive through Facebook messages. Some groups require an invitation to join. The only way you can join those groups is if a group administrator invites you and gives you access.

- **Secret:** A Secret Group won't appear in search, and the only way people can join is if the administrator (or one of the members — if this option is set up) invites them. No one other than the members will even know that a Secret Group exists.

Your friends may add you to a group of which they are members (or have just started). You will receive a notification that shows up in the Notifications area (globe icon) in the top navigation bar, and the group may show up in a list after you click the word *Groups* in the link found on the left side of your home page. It's up to you if you want to stay or go.

TIP

If you have a lot of friends who start groups, you will see a list of Pending Invites in the Groups area. You will have automatically become a member of these groups or pages just by your friends adding you. On that page, you do have the option to Join or Decline. (I just generally ignore them so that there are no hurt feelings.)

3. Click the name of the group to get a better look at it. If, after you visit the page, you find the group isn't something in which you're interested in participating — no sweat. You can remove yourself quietly. So (say) you're really not a morning person and don't want to join your neighbor's "Good Morning Coffee" group, you can always say you never saw the group. You can manually remove yourself, but there are other ways of ignoring it.

- Just click the word *Joined* to see the menu in **Figure 10-3** and click Unfollow Group. You'll still be a member but it won't show up in your news feed or notifications.

| Joined ▾ | ✓ Notifications | ➤ Share | ⋯ More |

Unfollow Group
Leave Group   Add Photo/Video   Live Video   More

FIGURE 10-3

- Alternatively, click Notifications and from the drop-down menu, select Off as in **Figure 10-4**. This way, you can still see the page posts in your news feed, but won't get notifications every time someone posts to the group or page.

FIGURE 10-4

- To really leave, click Leave Group (**Figure 10-3**) and a window pops up to confirm that you want to leave the group. The action of leaving a group prevents members from re-adding you. Should you wish to rejoin, you'll have to visit the group page and click Join Group again. But, at this point, you're sure you want to leave, click Leave Group.

TIP

I started a group specifically for readers of this book. It's a closed group so I will approve the members. Only members of this group can read or respond to the comments. The link to join is www. facebook.com/groups/SocialMediaForSeniors.

Start a Facebook Group

Groups can work as a substitute for mass emails you might otherwise send out to your family, friends, or any group you're a member of in the real world.

1. Want to plan a family reunion? Perhaps you might be interested in starting a new group on Facebook based on your hobby? You can do it. Start by clicking the Groups link found in the navigation bar on the left side of your home page. (You may have to click the More link first.) You'll be brought to your Groups page.

TIP

If you'd like, you can set up your Group so that you get an automatic email any time a member posts a comment or status update.

2. Click the Create Group after clicking on the grayed-out triangle (next to the question mark) in the navigation bar of your page (see **Figure 10-5**). The Create New Group pop-up window appears as shown in **Figure 10-6**.

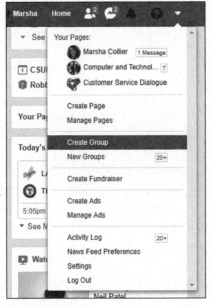

FIGURE 10-5

3. Give your group a name by typing it in the Name Your Group text box.

4. Add the initial members by typing their names in the Add Some People text box. A drop-down menu appears while you type, showing matching Facebook friends. After you see an entry with the correct person's name and photo, click it, and that friend becomes part of your list in the People box. Continue to type in names until you've invited all the folks you want in the group. Facebook will suggest new members, based on your relationships with the members whose names you enter.

FIGURE 10-6

5. Click the drop-down menu and select the appropriate option (below the Select Privacy setting) you want for your group. There are three options, as described in the previous section.

TIP

You can change your privacy setting later on if you want — as long as the total membership of your group remains under 250.

6. Click the Create button at the bottom of the Create New Group pop-up window when you're finished.

7. A new window opens, asking you to select a Group Type from an assortment of fanciful icons, shown in **Figure 10-7**, to identify with your group (the default icon is boring, so pick something appropriate). This icon shows up next to the name of your group in search results. After you've selected your icon, click Confirm and your group will be live on Facebook.

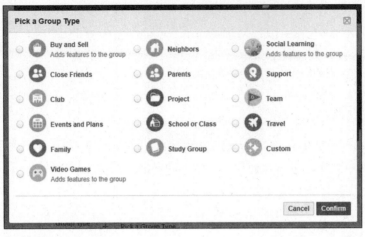

FIGURE 10-7

8. You will be transported to your brand-spanking-new group home page on Facebook.

TIP

Be aware! Facebook has a very important rule about online group behavior: "Groups that attack a specific person or group of people (e.g. racist, sexist, or other hate groups) will not be tolerated. Creating such a group will result in the immediate termination of your Facebook account."

9. You can edit your page and settings at any time by clicking the More box next to the word *Share*, shown in **Figure 10-8**, that appears (only to you) on the sections of your group page.

FIGURE 10-8

Communicate with Group Members

When you set up a group on Facebook, you're usually the group administrator (*admin*, for short) by default. Everyone else in the group constitutes its members; they can post to the wall and share with the group as well. As the group administrator, you can adjust the privacy settings, edit information, and add a group profile photo. It's just like setting up your own Facebook page. Think of your group page as much the same as your regular Profile page; it's not any different, with the following exceptions:

> » If you're the admin of your group (the Big Kahuna, the person who created the group and runs it), you decide who can join the group, and can ban or remove any member who does not play well with others.

> » A very handy feature of groups is that you can share files with other members of the group. You can upload files from your computer, or from those hosted on Dropbox.com, the file storage and sharing site. If you make changes to a file, all group members get an update.

Below the group photo is an area of links where Facebook allows you unique controls. Only admins can see these options:

> » **Add Members.** This opens a box where you can type in a Facebook member's name and add the person to your group's member roster, as shown in **Figure 10-9**.

> » **Create Event.** Want to have a meeting? A party? Admins only can click here and go to the Create an Event page. **Figure 10-10** shows you how this procedure differs from a regular Facebook event invitation. You have two options. You can invite all members of the group or just select ones.

> » **Email the group.** A great feature of groups is that the group has its own email address to send communications to post on the page.

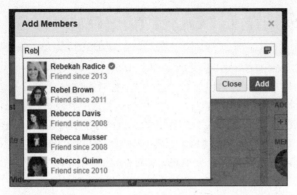

FIGURE 10-9

FIGURE 10-10

» **Edit Group Settings.** This takes you to an Administration page where you decide about privacy settings, page setup, and general information. In this area, you may also set up a group email address (as shown in **Figure 10-11**). Perhaps some group members rarely visit the Facebook site. By setting up a group exclusive email address, members can send posts via email to appear on the wall.

Web and Email Address   **Web:** https://www.facebook.com/groups/SocialMediaForSeniors/
Share this link to help people find your group.

Email: SocialMediaForSeniors@groups.facebook.com
Emails sent to this address will appear as posts in the group.

[Change Address]

FIGURE 10-11

Create an Event Invitation

1. Are you planning a party? Facebook is a good way to send out invitations. Any Facebook member can create an event and invite all their friends; you don't need to have a group. Start by going to your Facebook home page and clicking the Events tab found in the toolbar on the left side of the screen. On the left side of your Events page (as shown in **Figure 10-12**), you'll see the Create Event button.

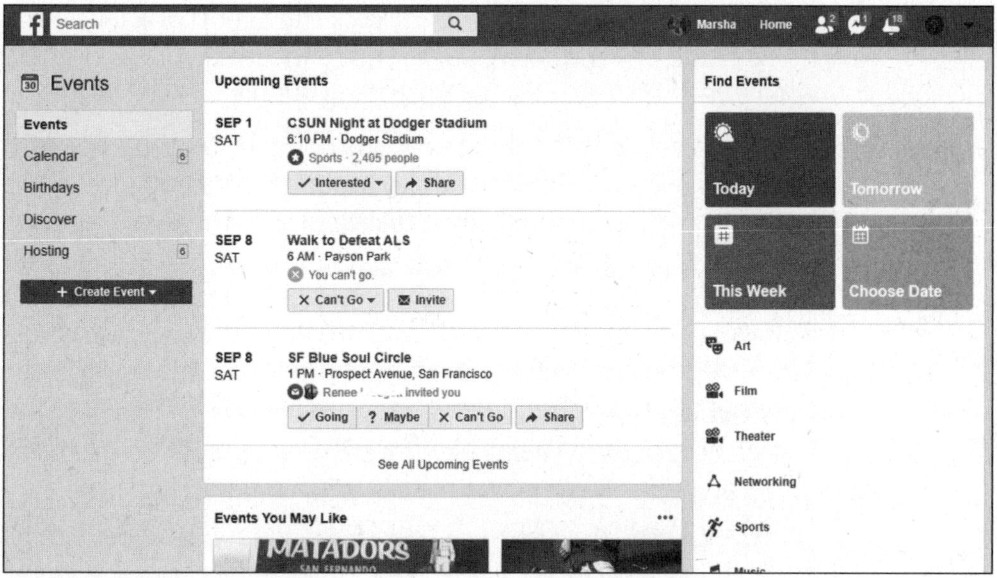

FIGURE 10-12

2. Clicking the Create Event button opens a pop-up window to create either a Private or Public Event. Click the appropriate box, fill out the when, what, and where of the event, and decide whether you want to allow guests to invite other guests or to make the guest list visible to all invitees. Check your work, and click the Create Event button.

3. On the new Event page, click Invite Friends to prepare your guest list from your Facebook friends list by placing a check in the circle next to your friend's name and photo. When you're through selecting folks, click Send Invites.

4. After clicking Create, you will be brought to the Event page where you can upload a cover photo to doll up the page. Your event, if Public, will appear on Facebook, and invitations will be sent to the friends you selected.

TIP As the event administrator, you can adjust the event's privacy settings, invite more people, edit the guest list, cancel the event, edit the event, and send messages to your guests.

Review Upcoming Events and Birthdays

1. To review your upcoming events, click the Events link in the links on the left side of your home page. You're taken to your Events page, where you can view all your upcoming events.

   You'll also see events that are recommended to you either by friends or ones in which Facebook thinks you are interested in your neighborhood. You have the chance to respond to the event right there. I always recommend that you take a moment and click the title of the event so you can find out exactly what's planned and where the event is. If you know all those details and are in a hurry, you can click the Interested button below the event and review it later. Under the word *Events* at the top of the page, you can select to view the upcoming events in a list or in a calendar format.

2. Click to view in Calendar mode and everything will be in chronological order. You'll also see your friend's upcoming birthdays so you can post a "Happy Birthday" message to their pages.

3. The best-laid plans often change, and you can also change your mind at any time (assuming it's okay with the host). Change your RSVP on the Event page by clicking your RSVP and selecting Not Going from the drop-down menu.

Watch Facebook TV

Facebook recently started encouraging people to upload home-produced videos. There are professional ones on the site too, ones from major studios and news outlets. To find them, from your home feed page, click Watch in the left-hand links and the page shown in **Figure 10-13** appears. You can search for topics, or see the latest episodes. Fair warning, its addicting!

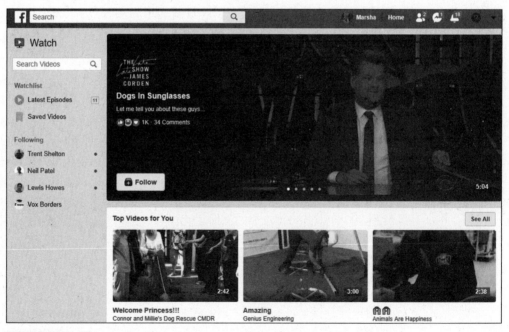

FIGURE 10-13

3

And Now, It's Twitter Time

IN THIS PART . . .

A guide to Twitter for beginners

Talking to friends, family, and strangers on Twitter

Twitter tools and how to use them

» **Adjust Your Account Settings**

» **Take Charge of Your Privacy**

» **Set Up Notifications on Web and Mobile**

» **Review Terms and Privacy Policy**

» **Find People to Follow**

» **Tour Your New Twitter Profile**

Chapter **11**

A Beginner's Guide to Twitter

I really enjoy the time I spend on Twitter, and I'm on there every day. I can visit the site at any hour and find links to interesting posts to read or a friend to respond to. It may not be someone I've met in real life, but someone I've met on Twitter with whom I respect and have common interests. The reason I enjoy Twitter more than Facebook is that I have the opportunity to meet people from all over the world — even their pets! Twitter is active 24 hours a day, and you can respond to (or just read) Tweets without worrying about a timeline. People on Twitter come from all backgrounds, and you can meet people of all ages.

Keep in mind that Twitter is not just about posting pithy thoughts online; it's all about sharing and having conversations. The second-best part of Twitter is that by listening (reading other people's posts, or *Tweets*, as they're nicknamed), you learn all sorts of interesting things. Almost all news events appear on Twitter before you hear about them on radio or television because people in the area share live photos and local news updates.

Twitter users love to spread information of all sorts (some are spam, but I ignore them). When you find your niche, you'll see what fun participating on the site can be.

Your posts on Twitter are limited to 280 characters. (When you send text messages on your phone, you're allowed 160 characters.) Figuring out how to abbreviate your thoughts and get your message into a short sentence will definitely exercise your brain; it can take a bit of thinking!

In this chapter, I help you get started with Twitter — by registering, setting up an account and Profile page, deciding what notifications you want to receive, and getting familiar with Twitter shorthand and emoji. Are you ready? Let's sign up and start making new friends!

TIP

Because social media platforms are updated almost daily as they try to improve the experience for the users, the registration process I show you may change order. You'll no doubt have to answer all the same questions. Just know that anything you input is editable, and you can make changes when you're more secure with the platform.

Register with Twitter

1. As with all interactive websites, you can't play until you sign up and agree to the rules. So type www.twitter.com in your browser's address bar, press Enter, and you'll come to a page similar to the one in **Figure 11-1**.

2. To start your Twitter adventure, begin here:

    a. *Click Sign Up to go to the registration page.*

    b. *On the next page, type your full, real name so that your friends can find you if they look for you in Twitter search. (Chapter 12 tells you more about searching on Twitter.)*

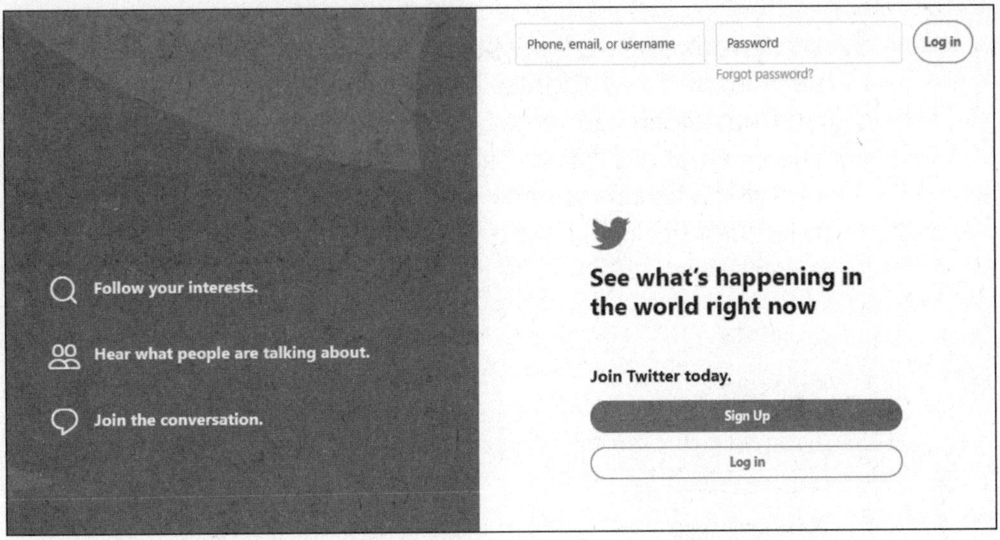

FIGURE 11-1

c. *Type your mobile phone number (or click the option to use your email address instead).*

d. *Select a password and type it in the Password text box.*

Make your password at least 6 characters. Twitter lets you know the security strength of your password after you type it. I recommend you select one considered *Strong. Okay* isn't quite good enough. You can change any of the above steps later if you want.

Why not check out the information on picking a password in Chapter 3 to make sure you select a secure one.

TIP

e. *Next, Twitter asks you to upload a selfie.*

You can upload a picture now, or click Skip for Now and do it later.

f. *Twitter presents you with a scrollable box of interests (move the slider up and down with your mouse to see all the options).*

Tap on boxes to select things that interest you. Scroll all the way to the bottom and select as many as you want. If you don't find all your interests, you can type them in the search box. Or you can click Skip for Now.

3. While you've been doing all this following, Twitter sent an email message to the email address you provided when you filled out the sign-up form. Open your email program and look for the message. You'll see an email like the one shown in **Figure 11-2**. Or you may have received a text on your smartphone to confirm your identity. You must click Confirm Now to prove you are you.

Final Step...

Confirm your email address to complete your Twitter account @ClaireC58682554. It's easy - just click the button below.

Confirm now

FIGURE 11-2

TIP

Be sure to check your Junk or Spam mailbox, especially if it's a bit overzealous in designating such emails — that's where my Twitter emails often show up!

You are now an official member of Twitter and are brought to your first Twitter page. From here you can find more people to follow, browse categories, or find more friends.

4. After you click through the confirmation email, you'll land on your new (empty) Twitter Profile page shown in **Figure 11-3**. Scroll down this page and you'll see what's trending on Twitter based on the interests you previously input. If you skipped that page, they will be based on the location of your computer. Now comes the work.

a. *Click the Add a Photo box and upload a selfie — or a picture of your dog, or a flower, for now.* When you tap the box, you will be prompted to upload a photo. People want to see a picture when they go to follow someone new, so they have some idea of who they're becoming friends with. Some people use pictures caricatures, their dogs or the logos for their businesses as avatars, but if you're on Twitter to make friends, I suggest posting a flattering image of yourself when you are ready to start using the platform.

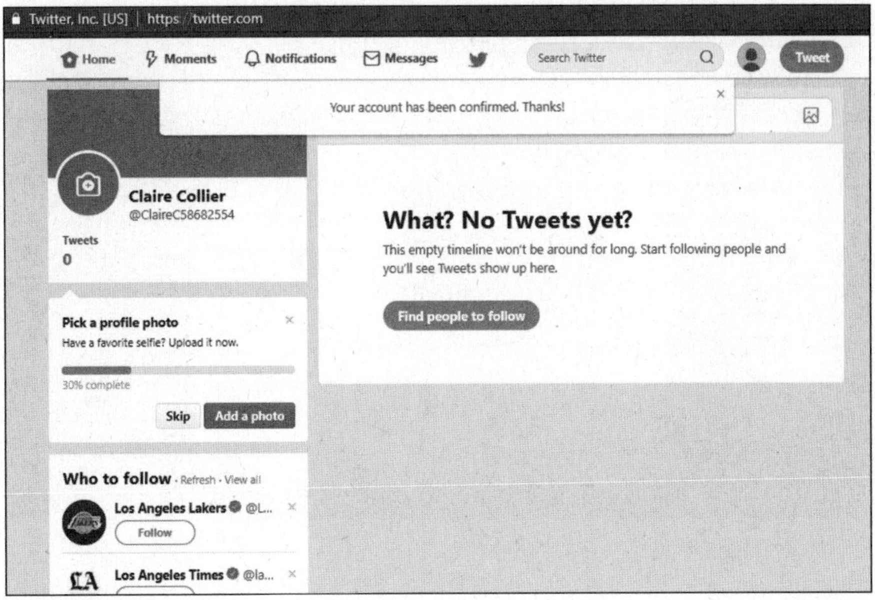

FIGURE 11-3

b. *To upload your photo, click the Upload Image button to open a dialog box where you can look for a photo on your computer.*

c. *In the dialog box, find the folder on your computer where you store your photos and select a photo by clicking it so that the name of the photo appears in the File Name box.* Click Open after you select your picture, and you return to the Twitter profile setup. The photo file you select can be in jpg, gif, or png format and will appear as 400 x 400 pixels, so select a small square image. The picture box that appears lists the filename and location of your photo on your computer. If you select the wrong photo accidentally, don't fret. Just go through the upload process again by repeating the steps.

d. *Once you select the photo, it will appear on the page with a circle around it, as shown in* **Figure 11-4**. You may move your picture by grabbing it with your mouse and resize it by using the slider below, so you center it to get the best image. Then click Apply. Your picture will appear on the Profile page.

FIGURE 11-4

5. Twitter asks you to describe who you are — to appear as your profile bio. In keeping with the brevity of the site, you have 160 characters to describe yourself. You can change this description at any time, so just put in a little information about yourself for now. You can compare your bio to those of the people you meet on Twitter and refine it as you go.

You can also add emoji to your bio (or anything else) on Twitter. (Emoji are small pictures used within text to express an idea, object, or an emotion). To find an appropriate one, click the smiley face in the corner of the Introduce Yourself box and search for an emoji in the text box. In **Figure 11-5**, I added a dog and clicked Save. For more on the fun of using emoji, see Chapter 14.

6. Twitter now wants to know your birthday so they know more about you. You can skip this for now and add it later.

7. It helps Twitter to know where you live so that you read local posts and find people in your area to follow (if you want). I suggest you type in your metropolitan area. I live in a suburb of Los Angeles, so that's what I have on my page. I try not to give away private information as to where I actually live.

Once you've put in your location, Twitter will congratulate you and prompt you to see your filled out Profile page by clicking See My Profile button shown in **Figure 11-6**.

FIGURE 11-5

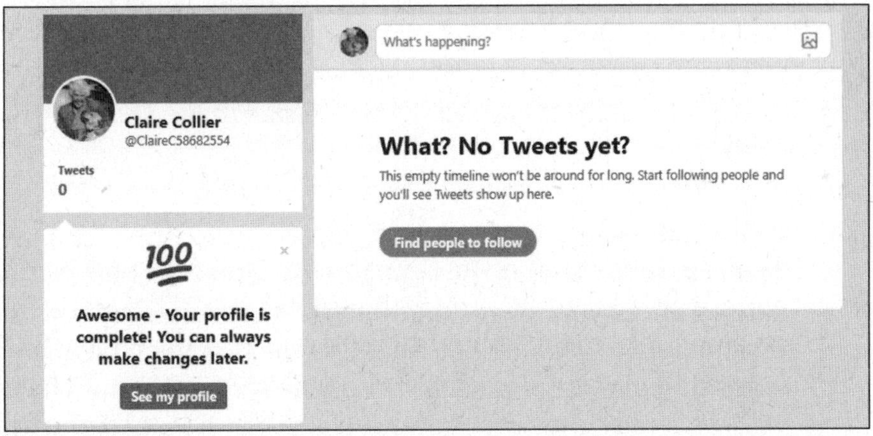

FIGURE 11-6

8. When you view your new page, you'll see that Twitter assigned a username for you that appears under your name. As you can see in **Figure 11-6**, their suggestions are generally not terribly engaging. Twitter usernames can be changed later so you can come up with a catchier one.

Its time to make your page look more inviting. To do this, click the box called Edit Profile, shown in **Figure 11-7**, to get started. You'll notice that you can add a header picture; edit your name, bio, and city; add a website; change your theme color; and add your birthday.

FIGURE 11-7

- **Add a header photo.** A header photo makes your page look like you've given this some thought and tells other users that you are serious about your page. Your header photo covers the entire top of your Twitter Profile page, so it'll be the first thing people notice when they visit your page. Select one that reflects your lifestyle or your interests. Click Change Your Header and upload one that is around 1500 x 500 pixels. Perhaps choose one of a beach from a vacation? Or of your garden?

  Click to grab the picture and move it within the space. Use the slider (like you did with the profile picture) to make the image larger or smaller. When you're happy with the image, click Apply, then Save changes.

- **Adding a website** isn't a bad idea. Your website link will add more to your story. If you don't have a website or a blog, you might want to include a link to your Facebook page or your LinkedIn page (if you have one). Just go to that page, copy the URL, and paste it into the text box on your Profile page that says *Website*.

- **Change your theme color.** Now it's time to gussy up and add a little character to your page. Twitter gives you a choice of 10 theme colors you can use on your page. As you click each color, you will see that the shading on the page changes. Settle on a color, then click Theme Color to save it.

- **Add your birthday.** If you put your birthdate in when you registered, you will see it here. If you skipped over it, here's your chance to add it, and I think you should. People on Twitter love to congratulate each other. The platform isn't intrusive like Facebook. They don't put announcements on your timeline. So when you wish someone a Happy Birthday, it means a lot to them. People enjoy seeing your birthdate (anyone else a Sagittarius?). To keep the year of your birth private, click the small lock icon (shown in **Figure 11-8**) to set Visibility Settings and a menu will appear. Select Only You on the menu — and then it's a secret only you will see on your page.

FIGURE 11-8

9. When you're done, click the Save Changes box near the top of the page and Twitter will ask that you confirm your birthdate. If you typed it in right, click Confirm.

TIP

On your birthday, Twitter adds a cute animated graphic with balloons and confetti, so that whoever lands on your page knows it's your birthday. Remember you have full control as to whether the year shows publically, or even if you want it to appear at all.

Adjust Your Account Settings

On your Twitter Profile page, mouse over the circle in the upper right that has the photo you uploaded, in the top right corner of the page, and from the drop-down menu that appears, click the Settings and Privacy link, shown in **Figure 11-9**. Your Account Settings page appears as in **Figure 11-10**.

1. **Sign up information.** The information you provided when you signed up is filled in on this page.

FIGURE 11-9

2. **Twitter username.** If you'd like to change your Twitter username, now might be a good time. You can always come back to do this, but once you invest time on the site, people will get to know you by your ID. So stop and think; you are allowed 15 characters. If your name fits and isn't

taken, then I'd use that! Twitter will alert you as you type as to whether the User ID you've selected is taken. **Figure 11-10** shows some of the options on this page.

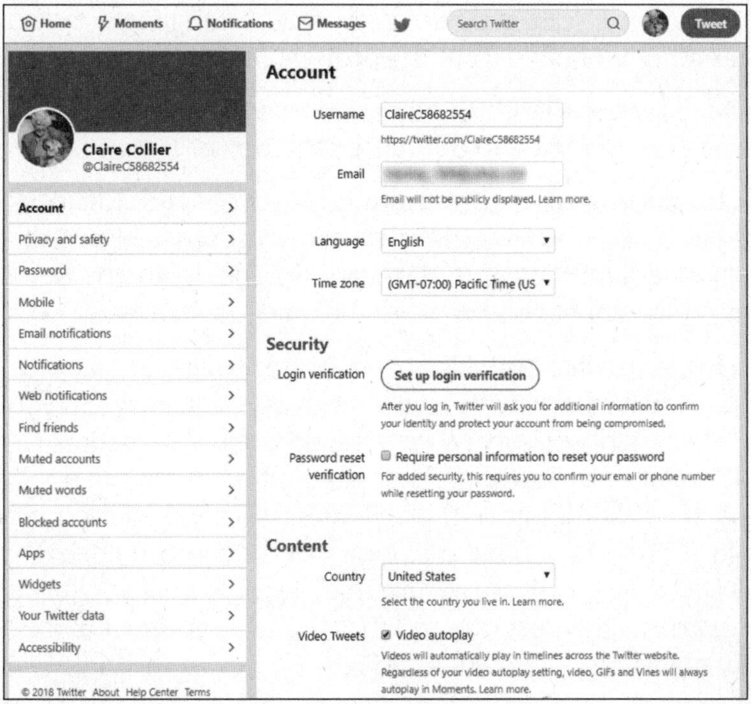

FIGURE 11-10

TIP

Your username can be a nickname or your real name, whichever you prefer. If you choose a nickname, it can be a name that reflects one of your hobbies, or a special interest you may have. Get creative! But remember: Your username cannot have any spaces or symbols, just letters, underscores, and/or numbers.

To change your temporary User ID, just type the new name in the Username text box.

TIP

Because Twitter has been around since 2006 and has over 335 million users, there's an excellent chance your name (to use as an ID) is already taken. If that's the case, get creative and try putting an under-score between your first and last name, put the word *Real* or *Im* in front of your name, or abbreviate to a nickname. Your registered name will always be searchable in Twitter search, so don't fret if you have a unique ID.

3. **Choose a language.** English is filled in as the default (and I assume you speak English since you're reading this book). If you'd prefer a different language, click the down arrow on the Language text box and select another language from the drop-down menu.

If you have Twitter friends in other countries, Tweets are translated into English within the app or on the desktop.

4. **Check for your correct time zone.** GMT (Greenwich Mean Time) will be filled in. If you don't live in the United Kingdom (where Greenwich is, the last I looked), I suggest that you click the down arrow and select the time zone where you live from the drop-down menu.

5. **Set up login verification.** Note that Twitter suggests that you associate your mobile phone with your Twitter account. Why? So you can set up a very tight security scheme called Login Verification. (This is the two-factor authentication I wrote about earlier in the book.) Once you register your mobile number, Twitter will send your phone a code via SMS (text). You need to type this code into Twitter. This way, your account is even more secure than it would be if you just used a password. I highly recommend that you avail yourself of this extra security measure.

6. **Password reset verification.** If you've forgotten your password, click the Forgot Your Password link; for added security, Twitter sends you a reminder by email so you can reset your password. Click the link in the email message or copy the link into your browser. You arrive at a page where you can change your password. Type in your new password twice (the second time is to verify your typing) and click the Change button.

To change your password at any time, just click your profile at the top right of your Twitter home page and, on the resulting Settings page, click the Password link in the left-side navigation.

7. **Video autoplay settings** are next and allow you to decide whether videos will automatically play in your timeline. I personally prefer *not* to watch each video as I scroll the timeline, but this is a personal choice. You can always come back here and change your setting.

8. **Settings for your timeline.** Further down the page, you can adjust these by clicking here and telling Twitter to put Tweets you are likely to care about at the top of your timeline. I do not click this option. No matter how smart artificial intelligence is, it won't know what I am in the mood to see. I prefer my Tweets to appear in the order they were posted. Your call.

9. **Archive.** Below the Timeline settings, you'll be able to access a file with all your Tweets. Once you've been on Twitter for a while, you might want to download this. Just click Request Your Archive.

10. If you're happy with what you've completed so far, click Save Changes.

Take Charge of Your Privacy

On the left side of the Account page, you'll notice lots of links (shown back in **Figure 11-10**). Each one of those links has settings that can improve the time you spend on the Twitter platform. Here's a short overview of some of what you can set in each of the sections.

1. **Privacy and Safety** is the best area for being sure you have a pleasant time on the site. Here you can make decisions as to how much contact you want from Twitter and from those with whom you connect on the site. I don't go over every option in this book; just be sure to read anything you are agreeing to before you give permission. Here's a few things I recommend:

   Don't protect your Tweets; this makes them visible only to those whom you follow. If you set this, someone (perhaps an old friend) will find you through search, but can't see what you're sharing. People get to know you and about you by reading your Tweets.

TIP

   Twitter is a public forum, so be careful what you say (or are willing to defend or argue). Never post anything on Twitter that you wouldn't want to see printed in your local newspaper. More than one celebrity has done this at one time or another and regretted it. You can delete Tweets, but they stay in the public timeline from the time you post until the time you delete them, and someone might take a screen shot. See Chapter 12 for more advice on how to enjoy the Twitter community safely.

A MOST IMPORTANT SETTING

Buried subtly below the *very* prominent Manage Your Contacts bar is an innocent-looking category called Personalization and Data shown in the following figure.

Remember when I mentioned that there's no free lunch on the Internet? If you followed any of the very public brou-ha-ha over the Facebook Cambridge Analytics scandal, this is where those permissions can leave you open.

Next to the bold phrase *Allow Some*, click the word *Edit*. The page that opens here transparently shows you where and how your data might be shared. (This advice is relevant on other platforms as well.)

- **Personalized Ads.** This means that the ads you see on Twitter would be based on your interests. Twitter knows your interests because of the words you share on the platform. For example, if you talk about dogs, you might see pet food ads; talk about a garden and you could see ads from florists or gardening suppliers; talk about politicians and you may see political ads. Get it? You can opt in or not right here.

- **Personalize based on your devices.** This option gets a bit trickier. When you're on Twitter, they obviously can see what you comment on and how you feel about things. Know this about your devices, this is one thing you can't control: Every browser or app you use on any device accesses the web via its own IP address set by the Internet provider. The IP address doesn't expose you personally, but it would indicate that, say, someone from Atlanta, Georgia is visiting a website at a certain time, on an iPhone using the iOS operating system (and what version). What you can control with this setting is whether you give Twitter permission to follow you around the web for further information on your interests.

- **Personalize on the places you've been.** This permission allows Twitter to serve you ads that may be relevant when you are away from home. This can be a good thing when you're traveling, like getting an ad from a local restaurant. Remember that because when you are on a mobile device, websites can tell where you are anyway.

- **Track where you see Twitter content across the web.** Data (not personalized — meaning they don't know your name, Twitter ID, email address, or phone number) will be used when you browse the Internet to serve up ads on websites that match your interests.

- **Share your data with Twitter's business partners.** This generally means they sell. (A business needs to make money, right?) Twitter might "share" device-level data (like that IP address), demographics about you, your interests, and what ads you've viewed (and/or taken action on). Again, as in the paragraph prior, your actual personal information will not be "shared."

Revisit these permissions occasionally on all platforms to see what changes have been made. To keep up on any changes in Twitter Privacy, visit

`https://help.twitter.com/en/safety-and-security`

2. **Why add a location to your Tweets?** Unless you want the public to know every place you are, leave this option blank.

3. **Address book.** I have never opened up and given access to my address book to any platform. My contacts are private. Although if you uploaded every contact you have, you might find some on Twitter, but why compromise your friends' privacy?

4. **Direct Messages are private messages that you access in a different area from the public timeline.** There's a lot of strangers out there. You can opt to receive Direct Messages from anyone, but I don't. I only accept private messages from people that I follow.

5. **Send/Receive read receipts.** If you read a private, Direct Message and choose not to respond, it could be considered a breach of etiquette. So I turn this option off. I want to answer messages in my own time.

6. **The Safety area.** This covers sensitive content and Tweet media settings, which allow you to label your media for the appropriate viewers, and select whose media appears on your Twitter home page. If you prefer not to see possibly offensive images, leave Display Media That May Contain Sensitive Content unselected. If you plan on posting some racy pictures, select the Mark My Media as Containing Sensitive Content check box — to protect the innocent.

Set Up Notifications for Web and Mobile

1. On the left of your Twitter Settings page, you see an Email Notifications link. Click there, and you find an area where you can customize how you'd like to be notified when a particular action occurs on your Twitter account, as well as whether you'd like to get news from Twitter.

2. Read the descriptions and click only the check boxes that correspond to the notices you want to receive. Twitter will send you an email communication when certain actions occur:

   - **Someone marks one of your Tweets as a favorite.** On Twitter, you have the option to save Tweets for posterity. They show up on the Favorites link from your Profile page. This lets you know when you're sharing content of value.

- **You get Retweeted!** If someone likes one of your Tweets, he or she can *Retweet* it (pass it on). This is a great compliment and it's always nice to thank someone for doing so. You can also thank them by Retweeting one of the Tweets from their feed.

- **Someone starts following you.** If someone finds you and decides to follow you (I explain how all that happens in Chapter 12), Twitter sends you an email telling you so. If you don't want this email notification, be sure there is no check mark in the box next to New Follower Emails.

- **You receive a new direct message (DM).** Click here so you won't miss a thing. The fun of Twitter, though, is that all the conversation happens in real time and you're going to have to go back to Twitter to respond. Unless you're checking your email regularly, you won't be in on the immediacy of the experience.

- **Updates from Twitter.** Occasionally, Twitter's founders and bigwigs like to reach out to users to explain new features on the site, or to let you know about changes in the rules (the Terms of Service, or TOS for short). You really need to know about this stuff, so leave the check in the box next to Email Newsletter.

3. Set up mobile notifications. Click the Mobile link on the left if you agree to receive notifications on your smartphone or tablet. If you don't want the text messages (especially if you don't have an unlimited data plan), deselect the Direct Text Emails check box.

TIP

If you have to pay an additional fee for text messages on your mobile-phone plan, then sending and receiving too many direct messages could get expensive. Be sure you have a full data plan on your smartphone if you want to get these messages.

Review Terms and Privacy Policy

1. When you have a moment, click on the Terms link next to the copyright date on the left side of the page. Read and agree to both of this as well as the Privacy policy (see next steps). Every website has Terms of Service (TOS), which are basically the rules that everyone

participating on the site has to follow. Read them and print them out if you want. Even if you don't do that, know that opening your account on Twitter means you agree to abide by their rules. To follow future updates of these policies, go to

```
https://twitter.com/en/tos
```

2. Also next to the copyright date is the all-important Privacy policy. On the page, Twitter states:

"We believe you should always know what data we collect from you and how we use it, and that you should have meaningful control over both. We want to empower you to make the best decisions about the information that you share with us."

I've talked to them about this and they mean it. Everything is clearly laid out for you to read, and they want you to understand.

Be sure to read it and check here occasionally for updates:

```
https://twitter.com/en/privacy
```

Find People to Follow

At this point, I need to explain the workings of Twitter. For the whole experience to work, you need to find people to *follow*. These would be people you might want to hear from — your Twitter friends, your online community. You can follow or unfollow anyone at any time and as often as you like. When you follow someone:

» Each time that person posts a comment (Tweet), you'll see it on your Twitter home page.

» The folks you follow may follow you back, and if they do, they'll see *your* comments on *their* pages.

» When they direct a comment to you (as @yourname), you will see it in your notifications.

» You can send a Direct Message (or DM) to someone you're following (or anyone, but that's not considered proper etiquette on Twitter). A DM is like a text message that you send on your cellphone. It's a private message between you and the recipient. It does not appear in the public stream of Tweets. In the "Set Up Notifications" section earlier in this chapter, I show you how you can have these messages sent directly to your cellphone if you want. That way, you can respond to a DM without having to go back to your computer.

Here is how to find people to follow:

1. Clicking the Home link (with the small house icon) at the top left of the page brings you to where your Home Twitter stream would be (if you were following someone). This page would be populated by the person's Tweets.

2. On the left, under your picture and ID, you'll also see suggestions of accounts to follow, probably from your city or state. They may also suggest some celebrities or business moguls to follow. Just click the Follow button next to their name and their Tweets will appear on your home page. Once you click to follow one, more suggestions will appear.

3. On this same page, you'll see the Find People to Follow button. Clicking there will help you begin finding people to follow by suggesting some famous people and brands. If you want to follow any of these accounts, click the Follow button after their name. **Figure 11-11** shows you some of the suggestions I was offered. Be sure to scroll down the right column so you see the full list; you can click More at the bottom to see more. Select topics and find people to follow, or click Skip.

Why not search for someone's name on Twitter so you can get followed back? Remember, this is all about conversing. If you find really no one of interest, you can pick a favorite brand (how about your favorite airline?), or — if you prefer to learn more about Twitter first — you may click Skip at the bottom of the list.

Know that you can always search for more people, by Twitter ID or by name, to add to your Follow list after you're fully set up on the site — so don't feel pressured to keep looking for people to follow as you're getting started.

FIGURE 11-11

4. Next, Twitter suggests some topics and those accounts that specialize in them. Click a topic that interests you from the list on the left, which suggests Twitter users (or sources) you might like to follow.

5. At this point, type a friend's name in the Search box at the top, and click Search Twitter. I typed in my husband's name and when his Twitter result came up onscreen, I clicked the Follow button, and presto! We were connected. Please feel free to follow me at **@MarshaCollier** and Tweet or DM me to say "Hi" once we're connected. (I show you how to do that in Chapter 12.) Note that after you follow someone and go back to the previous page by clicking your browser's back arrow, the Who to Follow column changes. It will be filled with people in your new follower's community.

6. On the left side of the Home page, there's a link to Find People you know. There, Twitter asks you to import your email contacts. It lists two web-based email services, Gmail and Outlook (which also encompasses Hotmail). You can use these to find (and follow) people from your email lists who are already on Twitter. If you use one of these services and want to search Twitter for your email buddies, you can click the name of the email service and type your user ID and password when prompted.

TIP

I personally skipped Step 6. You might want to be a bit more settled and secure with your participation on Twitter before you involve your outer circle of real-world friends. (The point of this book is to make you the expert!)

7. At this point, your pals at Twitter are so revved up to have you aboard that they send you a welcoming email message, as shown in **Figure 11-12**.

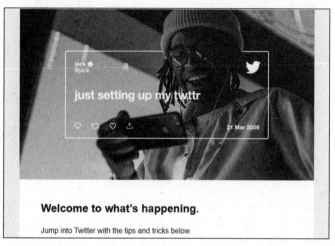

Welcome to what's happening.

Jump into Twitter with the tips and tricks below.

FIGURE 11-12

Read your email. On it, you find that Twitter gives you a rousing pep talk about how much fun your Twitter experience can be (and they're right). They provide a couple of suggestions of people for you to follow, along with a link you can use to check out more fun Twitter accounts.

TIP

While you've been busy setting up your Twitter account, Twitter has been busy too. Click the picture of yourself in a circle at the top of the page, then Profile. You'll see that your Twitter profile is ready to go — and your first Tweet is awaiting. Click one of the Tweet buttons shown in **Figure 11-13** and you will have launched your very first Tweet. Your Tweets (like the two on the page) will appear on your Profile page. They'll also be visible in your personal feed, as well as the home timelines of people who follow you.

FIGURE 11-13

Tour Your New Twitter Profile

When you've set up your profile and have Tweeted and followed a few people, the page will begin to look like the one I set up, @Twiter4Seniors, for the last edition of this book (see **Figure 11-14**). To find your way around this page, you'll have to click a few icons.

1. **Tweets.** In this column, you have a complete history of everything you have Tweeted on Twitter. When you click it, you see that it's divided into two categories:

- **Tweets.** Here you see a list of everything you've Tweeted.

- **Tweets and replies.** Here you see everything you have Tweeted out, and the replies you have answered.

FIGURE 11-14

2. **Following.** Here you see the people you've followed and their bios. Note that if someone is following you back, you see the word *Follow* next to the person's ID, as shown in **Figure 11-15**.

FIGURE 11-15

3. **Followers.** Here's the number of people following you; clicking there reveals names, pictures, and bios (as it does in the Following area).

4. **Likes.** When you click a heart at the bottom of a Tweet to Favorite it (more on this in Chapter 12), the post shows up as depicted in **Figure 11-16**. You may see a number next to the Tweet, representing the number of folks who also Favorited the post. Clicking that number shows you who found this Tweet to be a Favorite!

FIGURE 11-16

TIP

When you're on Twitter, you see web notifications pop up on the top of your page letting you know people have mentioned you. **Figure 11-17** shows you what they look like (and ooops, I have 99).

5. When someone Tweets to you (many people do so once you follow them), you'll see a number in your notifications. Since I followed someone with our test account, she Tweeted back, welcoming me to Twitter (see **Figure 11-18**)!

6. If you ever want to edit your profile, you can do that right from your Twitter page by clicking Edit Profile.

FIGURE 11-17

Welcome Tweet

FIGURE 11-18

Twitter has a hidden tool that allows you to Pin one of your Tweets to the top of your Profile page so it will be the first thing people see when they arrive. Click the downward-facing arrow at the top right of any of your Tweets, and then select Pin to Your Profile Page; **Figure 11-19** shows you how that works.

FIGURE 11-19

Conversing

» Pass Along a Chosen Tweet

» Like Your Favorite Tweets

» Search for Tweeted Topics

» Know What to Tweet About

Chapter **12**

Conversing on Twitter with Friends, Family, and Even Strangers

When you register on Twitter, you get all sorts of suggestions about how to connect with people. As I suggest in Chapter 11, I think it's best to get familiar with the basic ideas of a new site before inviting all your friends to the party. I mean, after all, what kind of host can you be if you barely know the lay of the land yourself?

I hope you've checked out Twitter a bit. I must confess, it took me quite a while to really "get" it. Once I did, I wanted to invite all my friends — and if they weren't already on Twitter, I wanted them to join so I could share my new shiny toy! There's a lot to be learned on Twitter, so that's where I spend most of my time.

In this chapter, I talk a little more about the finer details of communicating on Twitter. I give you guidelines about Tweeting, show you how to Retweet and accumulate favorite Tweets, and give you some advice on what to Tweet about.

Follow Basic Guidelines for Conversing

1. We're all adults here. I'm not going to tell you who to be friends with on Twitter, and I'm certainly not going to tell you what to Tweet. There are a few conventions and standards that make Twitter interesting, so read on and you'll be Tweeting like a pro in no time.

   - **Don't just broadcast your ideologies.** When you're on Twitter, you'll see that some people just continually broadcast their thoughts over the stream. *Broadcast media is so yesterday!* In 21st-century new media, it's all about sharing, conversation, and engaging others. Your interaction is with real people — talk to them!

   - **Do Tweet out ideas and comments.** Since it's all about conversation, give people something to reply to you about. Did you ruin a batch of cookies in the oven? If you're following other people who might be baking cookies, they'll commiserate with you. You have to buy new tires, and you're going through sticker shock? Certainly, in this economy, someone out there can relate. (If you share something controversial, be prepared to politely defend your stance.)

   - **Reply to others.** When someone makes a comment that you're interested in, make a comment back! In **Figure 12-1**, I'm about to reply to the user @craignewmark (founder of craigslist and Craig Newmark Philanthropies). He's an avid bird watcher and often shares birding photos. In the text box in the figure you can see my typed response. Once I click the Reply button, my words will be launched onto the platform.

2. Starting any posting with the at-sign (@), followed by the name of the person you're sending it to, is like putting an address on the Tweet:

@craignewmark means this Tweet is addressed to @craignewmark, as if we were in a conversation. Here's how to reply:

FIGURE 12-1

a. *In a Tweet on a Twitter page, look for the Cartoon balloon at the bottom of the box.* When you mouse over this, the word Reply appears. Once you click it, the Twitter member's ID appears above the Reply text box with an at-sign (@) in front of it — for example, @craignewmark. These are called @ *(at) replies*; they're visible to the person you addressed them to, and to the people who follow both of you.

TIP

If more than one person is mentioned in the Tweet you're responding to, all their IDs appear above the response text box. In the case of many names, you may respond to one or all. Just click on the line of names and deselect (by clicking the check box) any names you don't want in your response Tweet. (See the example in **Figure 12-2**.)

Replying to ×

Marsha Collier ✔ @MarshaCollier
Over 1 million 📚 sold Author: Social Media, eCommerce,
eBay, Customer Service. Founder #CustServ chat, #techradio
Podcast, marketing futurist. StarTrek nerd

Others in this conversation ✓

MissFitBit 👕 🍸 🎤 🍷 @Irish_IreneB
#SocialMedia Enthusiast ! Alas my Passion is my family❤️ |
#Fitness 🏋️ #GymBunny 👕 | #fashion 👠 |#bookworm 📖 | Oh
& 👟 👟 | Healthy lifestyle 99% 😜 ✓

#WinnieSun ⭐ ☀️ ⚪ @winniesun
Wealth Whisperer | @CNBC @Forbes @Cheddar Contributor |
Top Social 💰 Fin Advisor | Podcast | 🏆 Brands | Join
#WinnieSun chat Wed 11a PT | ✈️ #Travel #Speaker #TV ✓

Deirdre Breakenridge ✔ @dbreakenridge
CEO of Pure Performance, Speaker, Author of Answers for
Modern Communicators, LinkedIn Learning Video Instructor,
Podcaster & #PRStudChat Co-Founder. ✓

Robyn Stevens @robynstevensPR
Publicist w/ TV experts - finance, tech, nutrition, millennial,
fitness, fashion, lifestyle & beauty | brands @todayshow
@huffpost @qvc @cnn @gma @msn @aol ✓

FOX Business ✔ @FoxBusiness
The official Twitter page of FOX Business Network: Capitalism
lives here. Ask your cable provider for FOX Business in your
neighborhood. ✓

Apple ✔ @Apple
Apple.com ✓

FIGURE 12-2

b. *If you want all the people who follow you to see an @ reply, type the name(s) of the intended recipient(s) within the text of your Tweet.* You can also type a period (.) at the start of the @ reply if you want the Twitter user's ID to lead your statement.

> Remember that @ replies are not private; the private messages you can send are called *Direct Messages*.

TIP

c. *In* **Figure 12-3,** *notice how the message looks as I respond to @RebekahRadice and click the Reply button.* When you send a Tweet like this, the recipient will definitely recognize it as a conversation, and most likely will respond to you.

3. To see all your interactions and mentions, click the link on the top of your Twitter home page that has the bell icon and the word *Notifications* next to it.

FIGURE 12-3

4. In the Notifications area, you can toggle your view between *All* (every detail of your Twitter stream) or only the *Mentions* (@ replies) directed at you. **Figure 12-4** shows you the Mentions.

5. In your Notifications, All column, you may see a red heart (♥) or something that looks like a squarish recycle symbol next to a notification. The heart symbol means that person has liked your Tweet and the recycle symbol means they have Retweeted one of your Tweets. (More on Retweets and likes further on.) If more than one person engaged with your Tweet, you will see a teeny circle with their profile picture. Mouse over one and a mini version of their profile pops up. **Figure 12-5** shows you when the CEO of T-Mobile, John Legere, liked my Tweet.

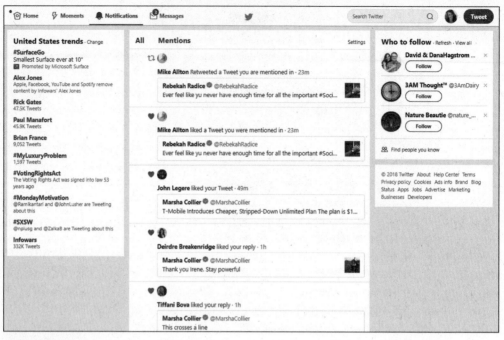

FIGURE 12-4

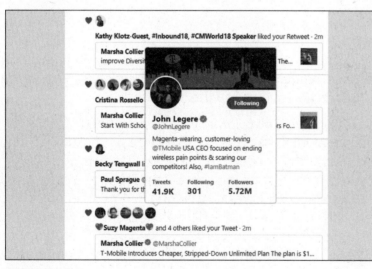

FIGURE 12-5

Pass Along a Chosen Tweet

1. To make a statement on Twitter is to *Tweet,* so to repeat a statement on Twitter is to *RE-Tweet,* right? If you see a comment from someone you're following, you can Retweet what they said to all your followers. That way, your followers who aren't following the person who made the pithy comment can have the chance to see it, too. (Twitter is all about sharing.)

2. You can Retweet (RT) in two ways. You accomplish the classic RT when you copy and paste the original Tweet in the text box; then type the letters RT before @ and the username of the original tweeter.

3. The second way to Retweet is to find a Tweet in your Tweet stream (just as you did with the @ reply) that you want to share. Hover your mouse pointer over the recycling icon, below the Tweet, and the word *Retweet* will show up next to the symbol. **Figure 12-6** shows Stan's Tweet that was Retweeted to the people who follow Susan.

FIGURE 12-6

TIP

If you want to see how many (and who) Retweeted an individual Tweet, click the Profile link at the top and go to your page. On one of your Tweets, click anywhere on your Tweet, and you see information similar to what's in **Figure 12-7** below your Tweet. Mouse over the avatars until you find the Twitter ID of the person who RTed your Tweet.

FIGURE 12-7

Like Your Favorite Tweets

1. When you see a Tweet that strikes your fancy, or a Tweet sent to you that makes you smile, Twitter lets you give it a Like. You can like any Tweet (except a private Direct Message). If you guide your mouse pointer over the Tweet, just next to where the Reply and Retweet symbols appear on the bottom, you see a small outline of a heart. Click the heart, and it turns red. After you click it, the Tweet is saved to your Likes page.

2. To find the Tweets you've liked, click your profile picture in the upper right of the page and click the link to go to your Profile page. A link to your likes can be found under your cover photo. When you click there, you arrive at the page that lists all the Tweets you've selected as your favorites. Check out **Figure 12-8**, and you'll see my recent likes. Notice that each of these Tweets has a little red heart next to it.

FIGURE 12-8

Search for Tweeted Topics

1. You can use *hashtags* — words with the pound sign (#) in front of them — in your Tweets to simply identify single-word topics or abbreviations of events. And you can search to find Tweets about the topics or events that are identified this way. For example, if you regularly watch *American Idol* and want to find all Tweets about the show, you can search for them by typing **#americanidol** in the search box (with the magnifying glass) at the top of your Twitter page and pressing Enter.

TIP

Because a search is not case-sensitive, you could also type #AmericanIdol or #AMERICANIDOL and get the same results. What you won't get in your search results are Tweets such as "*American* actress Morgan Fairchild is the *idol* of many" because the words aren't together and preceded by the hashtag.

2. You can append your Tweets with hashtags to join in Twitter chats that take place on a planned, regular basis. I participate in a weekly Twitter chat about customer service. (Yes, I tell you all about how to participate in chats in Chapter 13.) Because participants have only 280 characters per Tweet, we shorten *customer service* to *#custserv* so the hashtag takes up less space. (Hashtags get a message across in a much more concise manner.) In **Figure 12-9**, I typed **#custserv** into the Search box and all Tweets with #custserv showed up.

TIP

Notice on the top of the search results page, you can click to see Top Tweets that match your search, or Latest Tweets, People, Photos, Videos, News, Broadcasts (videos), and the option to perform an advanced search using filters.

FIGURE 12-9

Know What to Tweet About

I know that when you're new on Twitter (you're called a *newbie*), you want to join in the fun but maybe you can't think of anything to Tweet about. It's a frustrating feeling — know that I feel your pain. Even now, I often face the blank What's Happening text box with nothing in my head.

Check out this bullet list for some good ideas about common ways to start a Twitter conversation:

>> **Share quotes.** People on Twitter just love to read quotes by famous people. The quotes can be funny or inspirational. If you can't think of any off the top of your head, just search Google for the word *quote* and the name of your favorite smart person. For example, search *quote Lucille Ball* or *quote Eleanor Roosevelt*. (Searching for quotes from either of these women will no doubt

net you some doozies!) When you Tweet a good quote, people will no doubt Retweet it to their followers. When more people see how interesting you are, they may follow you, too. Personally, I share a quote at least once a week on Twitter (see **Figure 12-10**).

FIGURE 12-10

» **Start a poll.** If you're curious about something or just want to know what other people think about a subject, post a poll. To start a poll, click the button to Tweet, and tap on the third icon at the bottom of the text box that looks like a bar graph, like I did in **Figure 12-11**, and indicate how many days you want the poll to receive votes. (Below the initial poll Tweet are the results — in case you were interested.) Polls are a great way to stimulate a conversation on Twitter. To invite lots of folks to answer a question, you may use the word *Poll* and a hashtag preceding it. You don't have to use either. People will know what a question is!

» **Share videos.** Isn't it much more fun when you watch movies with your friends? I enjoy going to movies, but I also have fun on YouTube. When you find a video on the Internet that you like, why not share it? Once you're signed in to both Twitter and YouTube, anytime you "like" a movie, you can share it on Twitter. In **Figure 12-12**, I liked one of my favorite YouTube accounts, Lucas the Spider. When you Tweet a video, people can view it right on Twitter. In Chapter 16, I show you how to find and link to videos.

FIGURE 12-11

FIGURE 12-12

>> **Live-Tweet an event.** Okay, some people think this comes under the heading of *oversharing* (as in, "too much information" or "I really didn't need to know that"), but when you're participating in something interesting, other people find it fascinating. Perhaps it is a bit like voyeurism, but nonetheless, people love it. I Live-Tweeted my wedding (with the hashtag #marshaandcurtwedding).

In 2014, Twitter employee @Claire did one even better: She Live-Tweeted her labor and delivery of her baby! Those of us on Twitter at the time felt very included! **Figure 12-13** shows you how the event unfolded, and **Figure 12-14** ties it all together.

Claire Díaz-Ortiz @Claire · 5 Apr 2014
Taxi found. Checked in at hospital. Screaming women abound. **#inlabor**
12   18   43

Claire Díaz-Ortiz @Claire · 5 Apr 2014
Can't find taxi. Is this a joke?!? **#inlabor**
22   18   20

Claire Díaz-Ortiz @Claire · 5 Apr 2014
Car now broken down. On side of road. Need taxi. **#inlabor**
10   21   17

Claire Díaz-Ortiz @Claire · 5 Apr 2014
Car overheating again. Another gas station. Woe is me. **#inlabor**
1   7   12

Claire Díaz-Ortiz @Claire · 5 Apr 2014
Filled tank with water. Back on highway. **#inlabor**
7   8   14

FIGURE 12-13

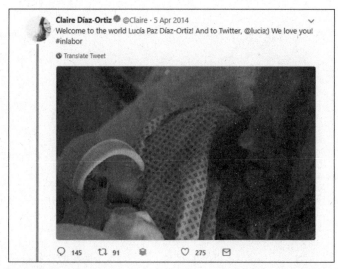

Claire Díaz-Ortiz @Claire · 5 Apr 2014
Welcome to the world Lucía Paz Díaz-Ortiz! And to Twitter, @lucia:) We love you! #inlabor
Translate Tweet

145   91   275

FIGURE 12-14

» **Pass on a news story.** There are so many great articles on the Internet, and news stories come to mind almost immediately. Why not send out an interesting article to your friends? To share a news story, copy the title and the URL from the story on the Internet and paste it into a Tweet text box like I've done in **Figure 12-15**. Add a comment or tag the author, and click Tweet. If there is a picture in the post, it most often will show up in your published Tweet, like it did on mine (see **Figure 12-16**).

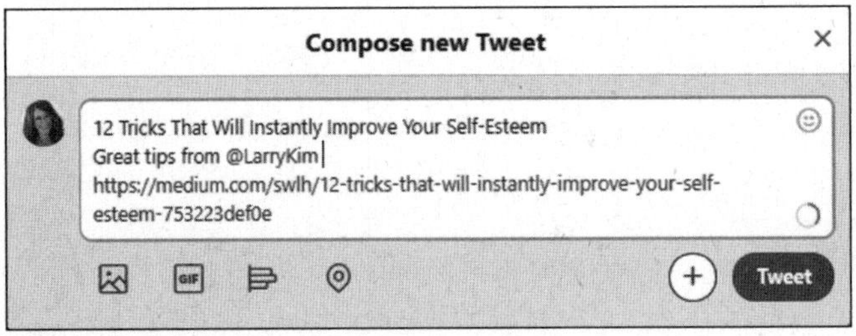

Compose new Tweet ✕

12 Tricks That Will Instantly Improve Your Self-Esteem
Great tips from @LarryKim
https://medium.com/swlh/12-tricks-that-will-instantly-improve-your-self-esteem-753223def0e

Tweet

FIGURE 12-15

Marsha Collier @MarshaCollier · now
12 Tricks That Will Instantly Improve Your Self-Esteem
Great tips from @LarryKim

12 Tricks That Will Instantly Improve Your Self-Esteem
On the bus to work, during your walk to Starbucks, as you lay awake in bed, unable to fall asleep, he sneaks onto your shoulder. The...
medium.com

FIGURE 12-16

» **Share a meme.** The Internet is full of memes. Search Google for a topic and the word *meme,* then look at the image results. You'll find fun ones to share like the one in **Figure 12-17** (that my husband posted while I was writing this chapter).

TIP

In some cases, you'll notice that a link to a web page may look a little like gibberish. That's because the web address for the story was shortened for brevity by Twitter.

» **Show off your pictures.** Everyone on Twitter loves to share photos. You can also share images from Instagram, but they don't appear live on the site. Viewers must click a link to see them, so it's best to post them directly on Twitter. (I tell you about Instagram in Chapter 13.) Click the tiny icon of a landscape image to open a dialog window that allows you to select a photo from your computer or your mobile device, as I've done in **Figure 12-18**.

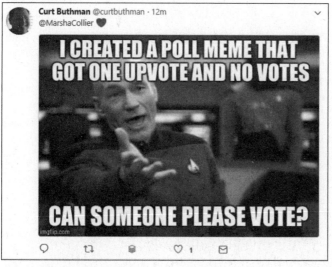

FIGURE 12-17

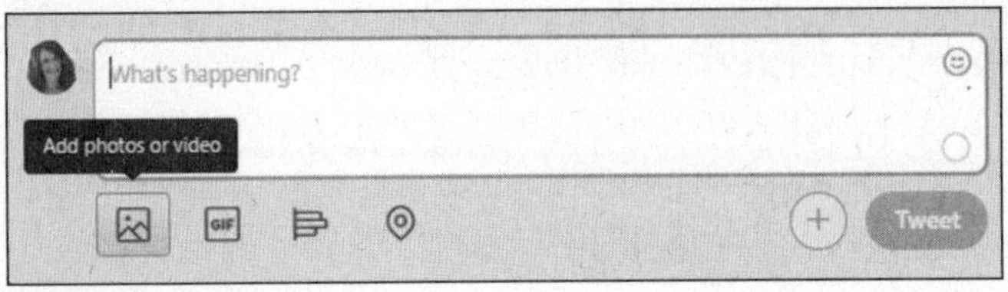

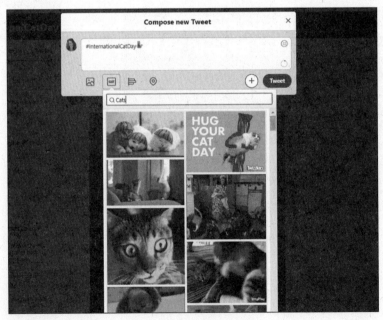

FIGURE 12-18

» **Punctuate your Tweets with GIFs.** Everything looks better with a picture, right? Well, GIFs (Graphic Interchange Format) come in animated form, and Twitter makes it easy to add them to your Tweets. Today is #InternationalCatDay and the topic is trending on Twitter (more on trending topics in Chapter 12). In **Figure 12-19**, you can see that I am preparing a Tweet. By clicking the small GIF box at the bottom of the text box, I see available GIFs. I type **cats** into the GIF search box and a multitude of funny (animated) GIFs show up. Clicking on one of the small animations puts that GIF into my Tweet.

FIGURE 12-19

Figure 12-20 shows you the final Tweet (but you can't see the animation). Find it on Twitter: `https://twitter.com/MarshaCollier/status/1027290649576407041`.

FIGURE 12-20

» Twitter Lite

» **Enhance Your Tweets with Emoji**

» **Read and Follow Foreign Language Accounts with Translate**

» **Find Topics with Twitter Search**

» **Discover What Is Trending**

» **FollowFriday, FF, and Other Hashtags**

» **Connect and Chat with People**

» **Solve Customer Service Issues Online**

» **Keep Track of Hundreds, Thousands of Friends?**

» **View Your Friend Lists**

Chapter **13**

Gathering Tools of the Twitter Trade

N ow that you're on Twitter and you're building up a small group of friends and followers, you'll see that you want to do even more. I'll bet you'd enjoy following more people, right?

Some people feel that if they have a small group of friends, they can manage conversing easily — but it's okay to branch out and meet more folks because not everyone is on Twitter all the time. Twitter is less of an immediate-response platform than Facebook. In this chapter, I show you how to make groups (lists) of different people so you can focus certain Twitter conversations on certain friends.

Let's really call this chapter *Twitter — the Advanced Course*. But don't let that scare you. I show you some simple ways to enhance your Tweeting experience. And you needn't spend any money on extra tools; I explain how to do just about anything you can on Twitter.

Save Data on Mobile with Twitter Lite

I think it's safe to say that, in general, computers are more powerful than tablets; and tablets are probably more powerful than smartphones. It's also safe to say that the size of the screen goes down incrementally when you're doing social media from a smartphone. This brings about a few issues:

1. If you're using Twitter fervently to follow a breaking news trend, or are spending hours without closing the app, Twitter may drop Tweets and chug slower.

2. If you're using Twitter on your mobile provider's connection, you're burning though lots of possibly expensive data. (It's always best to connect to Wi-Fi when you're near a trusted signal, like at home.)

3. Adding apps to your smartphone takes up space. The iPhone app takes more than 178MB, and that takes a big chunk out of your smartphone's storage.

Your solution? Try Twitter Lite. Twitter Lite is a special version of Twitter developed for use in places where Internet may be unreliable or slow. According to GSMA (Global System for Mobile Communications) the amount of global connections worldwide are 7.8 billion, and people in all countries are going online. Many of those connections are only on a 2G network. So, naturally, Twitter wants their platform to be accessible in every corner of the world.

Twitter Lite is a mobile web experience (you don't have to download an app) accessed through the browser on your smartphone. It provides all the key features, your timeline, Tweets, direct messages, trends, profiles, media uploads, notifications, and more.

It only takes up 1MB of memory on your phone and is 30 percent faster than the app. By using the data-saving mode in settings to download only the images or videos you want to see, you can reduce the data usage by 70 percent.

1. Type the URL **mobile.twitter.com** into your browser.

2. You have to sign in, or, if you have two-factor authentication on your account, you are texted a security code.

3. When the code arrives via text, type it into the code box, as I'm about to do in **Figure 13-1**.

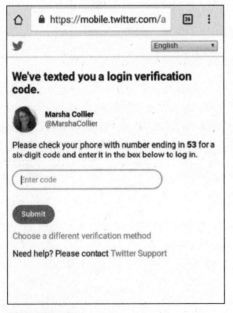

FIGURE 13-1

4. Twitter appears, and it is very similar to the experience you would have on the mobile app. A comparison is shown in **Figure 13-2**.

Mobile version of Twitter   **App version of Twitter**

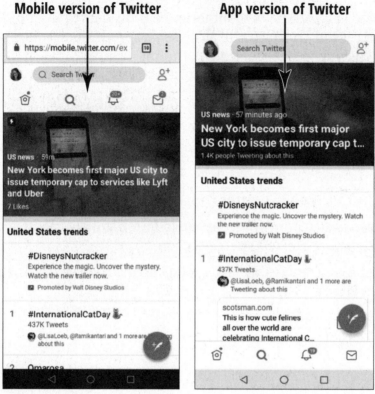

FIGURE 13-2

5. You'll see a bar at the bottom that suggests you click it to send an icon to your phone's home page. On your phone's home page, you'll have a new icon that is in reverse colors of the Twitter app icon. **Figure 13-3** shows what these look like.

Add Twitter to Home Screen   **Twitter App icons**

FIGURE 13-3

Enhance Your Tweets with Emoji

Emoji, the small text-size pictographs that you see just about every-where, are the hieroglyphs of the 21st century. They were first created in 1999. They were preceded by emoticons typed with the keyboard in 1982 — you may remember them? :-)

It is said their name is derived from the Japanese for "picture" and "moji" for character. I say they are emojis because with one tiny picture, you can communicate all kinds of emotions and things. You see emoji everywhere: on clothes and even in interior decorating. I've found them to be fun to use and have to keep myself from using them too much. Have you ever wondered about their how and why?

1. There are thousands of emoji. The same emoji will look a bit differ-ent on Apple, Android, Microsoft Windows, Chrome OS, and Twitter.

Twitter converts emoji from your device to its own design of Twemoji. Twitter also often combines unique emoji with seasonal or sponsored hashtags.

2. Reading Tweets with emoji is definitely more fun. **Figure 13-4** shows a Tweet from my friend Diana Adams (she admits she's a bit of an emoji-holic).

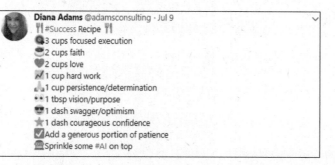

Diana Adams @adamsconsulting · Jul 9
🍴#Success Recipe 🍴
🔴3 cups focused execution
☕2 cups faith
❤2 cups love
🙏1 cup hard work
👏1 cup persistence/determination
✦✦1 tbsp vision/purpose
😎1 dash swagger/optimism
⭐1 dash courageous confidence
✅Add a generous portion of patience
🤖Sprinkle some #AI on top

FIGURE 13-4

3. When you are communicating through words in a short-format SMS or Tweet, there's a good chance your words may be misconstrued. Innuendo is difficult to read in 280 characters. By inserting a "wink" or a "smile," people will know that you're just kidding (or JK).

4. Emojis have been evolving and the industry behind them updates the number of emoji, which regularly grows. The June 2018 Unicode update added 157 new ones, giving you a total of 2,823 possible emojis to use in your Tweets.

5. If you come across an emoji that you can't figure out, Tweet it to the @botmoji Twitter account. I questioned one. If you are on a smartphone, they are very tiny (at least to me) and I often wonder, what is this? **Figure 13-5** shows a question I sent to @botmoji and their response. You can also go to their website (`www.emojipedia.org`) and look them up by description.

6. According to the website EmojiTracker (which counts emoji usage on social media in real time) the most popular emoji used on Twitter are (**Table 13-1**).

FIGURE 13-5

TABLE 13-1 ## Most Popular Twitter Emojis

Emoji	Meaning
	Face with tears of joy
	Heavy black heart (red heart)
	Smiling face with heart-shaped eyes
	Black heart suit (from deck of cards)
	Smiling face with smiling eyes
	Universal recycling symbol

(continued)

TABLE 13-1 *(continued)*

Emoji	Meaning
	Unamused face
	Two hearts
	Face blowing a kiss
	Weary face

Table 13-2 has a few of my personal favorites:

TABLE 13-2 **Emoji Personal Favorites**

Emoji	Meaning
	Face with tears of joy (replaces ROFL for me)
	Thinking face
	Prayers folded hands
	Grinning face with smiling eyes

7. It's easy to insert an emoji into a Tweet on the web interface; **Figure 13-6** shows you how it's done.

a. *Compose your Tweet and place the cursor where you want the emoji to appear.*

b. *Point your cursor to the little smiley face in the upper right-hand corner of the text box and click.*

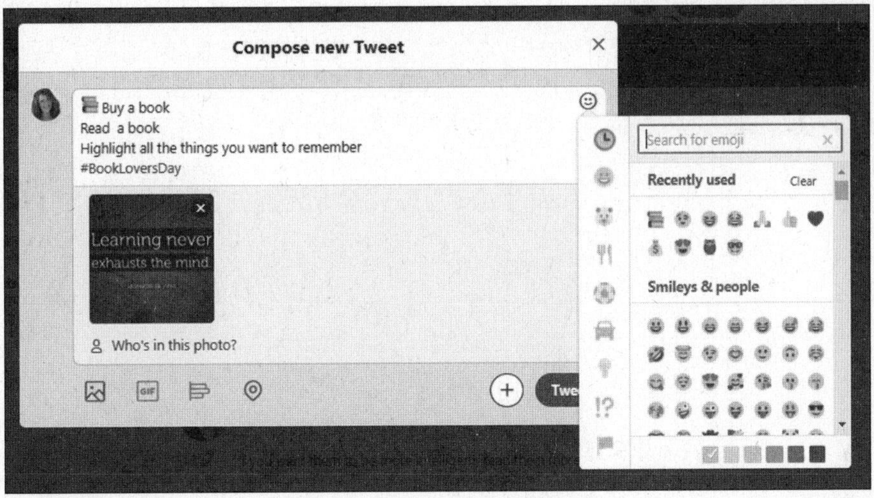

FIGURE 13-6

   c. *If you see the emoji you want to use, click it and it will appear in the text area.*

   d. *When you're not sure which emoji to use, type a descriptive word in the text box and the matching emoji will appear.*

8. To insert an emoji in a Tweet from a mobile device, take a look at **Figure 13-7**.

   a. *Tap the quill in a circle on your screen to begin a Tweet.*

   b. *Type your comment into the text box.*

   c. *Tap the smiley face on your mobile keyboard on your device to make the emoji keyboard appear.*

   d. *Select your desired emoji by tapping and it will appear in the text box.*

   e. *On devices (Apple or Android) with the GBoard app (available in the Play or App Store) installed, you can search for an emoji by keyword in the Google text box above the emoji keyboard.*

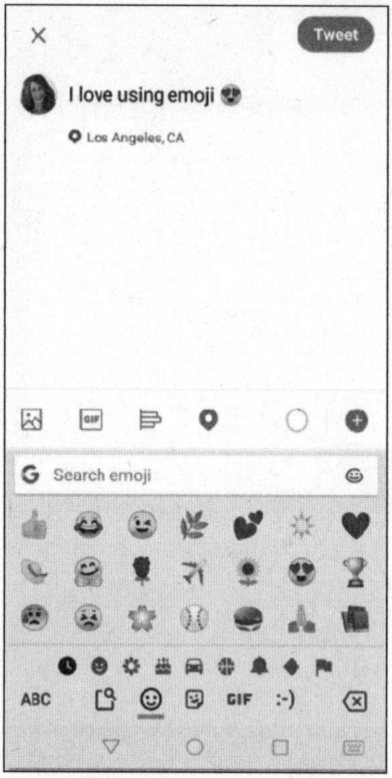

FIGURE 13-7

Read and Follow Foreign Language Accounts

With 335 million users on Twitter, you've got to realize there are accounts from other countries, and many of them Tweet in their native language. Personally, I have friends from all over the world who Tweet in two languages. Sometimes I'm curious to see what they have to say. Twitter partnered with Microsoft's Bing-powered translation to make this easy on the web or on mobile devices. **Figure 13-8** shows it in action.

1. When you see a Tweet in a foreign language, look for the globe icon in the Tweet. Click to expand the Tweet.

2. Next to the globe, you'll see the words *Translate tweet*.

> **Koichi Hagiwara**
> @KoichiHagiwara
>
> Replying to @MarshaCollier
>
> こんばんはマーシャ。このツイートに気づいたのが今日でそのため返事が遅れてしまいました。SNSを通じてお友達になってからもうだいぶ経ちましたね。大事にしていた愛犬 Lana ちゃんが居なくなってしまいましたが、これからも良い友達でいて下さい。よろしくお願いいたします。
>
> Translated by ⊞ Microsoft
>
> Good evening Marcia. I noticed this tweet today, so I'm late for the reply. It has been quite a while since I became a friend through SNS. The dog Lana-chan that I was taking care of has disappeared, but please be a good friend in the future. Best regards.
>
> 5:28 AM · 14 Aug 18 from Meguro-ku, Tokyo

FIGURE 13-8

3. Tap on the Translate Tweet link and you'll get a translation to your native language.

TIP

Twitter bios do not have the translate option. When I want to know more about someone from another country, I go to Google and request it to translate. **Figure 13-9** shows how it works.

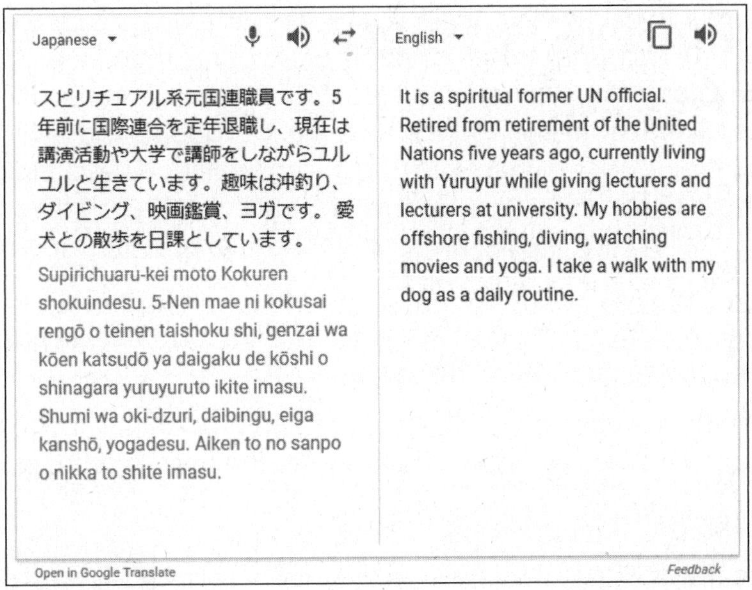

Japanese ▾ 🎤 🔊 ⇄	English ▾ ⧉ 🔊
スピリチュアル系元国連職員です。5年前に国際連合を定年退職し、現在は講演活動や大学で講師をしながらユルユルと生きています。趣味は沖釣り、ダイビング、映画鑑賞、ヨガです。愛犬との散歩を日課としています。 Supirichuaru-kei moto Kokuren shokuindesu. 5-Nen mae ni kokusai rengō o teinen taishoku shi, genzai wa kōen katsudō ya daigaku de kōshi o shinagara yuruyuruto ikite imasu. Shumi wa oki-dzuri, daibingu, eiga kanshō, yogadesu. Aiken to no sanpo o nikka to shite imasu.	It is a spiritual former UN official. Retired from retirement of the United Nations five years ago, currently living with Yuruyur while giving lecturers and lecturers at university. My hobbies are offshore fishing, diving, watching movies and yoga. I take a walk with my dog as a daily routine.
Open in Google Translate	Feedback

FIGURE 13-9

TIP

When you become friends with people from other countries, it's handy (and fun) to go to Google Translate to wish them a Happy Birthday or Happy Holidays in their native language.

Find Trends and Friends with Twitter Search

1. Twitter's own search capability is pretty intense. You can perform search after search directly from your Twitter home page or from the magnifying glass at the bottom of a Twitter mobile page. On your computer, type `www.twitter.com` into your web browser and press Enter.

2. Type a subject that intrigues you into the search text box at the top of the page and click Search. For example, I often type in *recipe* because it's Sunday and I feel like getting creative in the kitchen.

3. You arrive at the search results page and see all the current Tweets that have the word you typed in them.

TIP

I love dogs and enjoy following the accounts their owners set up (and some Tweet *as* their dogs), so I type in different breeds to see if they have accounts. Here's a couple of accounts that I've enjoyed following for years, who have posted their dogs adventures daily. **Figure 13-10** features @samsBellabob the greyhound and her charming sidekick Charlie. Note that @samsBellabob has a blog. **Figure 13-11** shows @KoichiHagiwara's inimitable Frenchie, Lana chan. Lana recently passed away and hundreds of Twitter members shared Koichi's grief (I did as well).

4. You can click any ID and a snapshot of that person's Twitter profile appears. (More on profiles further on.)

5. Then, if this new person's Tweets interest you, go ahead and follow the person on Twitter (it's not just okay, it's the expected thing).

FIGURE 13-10

FIGURE 13-11

6. Notice below the top of the search results page you see the following sections:

- **Top:** These are the top Tweets, the Tweets from the cool kids — the most popular on the site at that moment.

- **Latest:** Here your results show everything Tweeted, in whatever media, about your search query.

- **People:** These results show only the people whose Twitter bios have the keyword you specified in your search query.

- **Photos:** This view shows all the Tweets in your search results that have photos attached to them.

- **Videos:** Yes, when people post videos, those videos appear in these results. Just click to watch them!

- **News:** These results open Tweets with links to news stories that contain your keyword.

- **Broadcasts:** People live-Tweet videos on Twitter, too. Here's where you can see and interact with them.

7. On the top of the left side of your search results, there's a link to show Search Filters (see **Figure 13-12**). By clicking there, you can add filters to narrow down your search with more specificity.

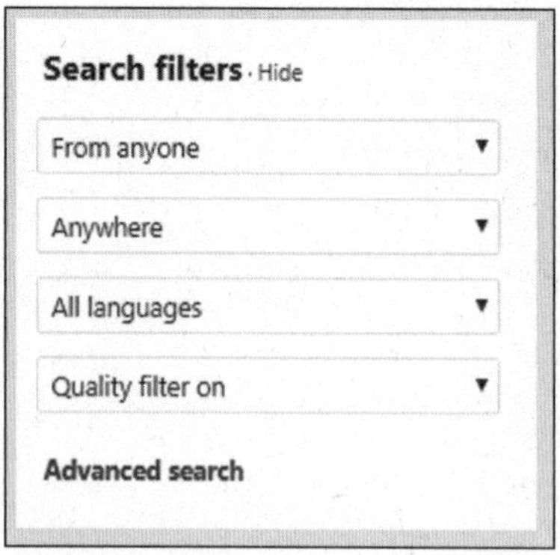

FIGURE 13-12

Discover What Is Trending

We hear on the news that, more and more, Twitter is the go-to source for breaking news. Tweets are even quoted on the news networks, and they are at your fingertips, too — so why not get the news first? It's not just news, but silly, made-up holidays. Why not click one and check them out?

TIP

I must confess that I'm not always on top of these trending topics. I'll often have to click on them to see exactly what they are referring to. Many Twitter users get a sick feeling in their stomachs when they see the name of a beloved older celebrity appear, for fear that person has passed away. Believe it or not, you get a great feeling of relief when you learn they've just done something kooky.

1. On the side column of almost every Twitter page, you'll see Trends (what topics are *trending* and attracting a lot of online interest) that Twitter has curated for you. **Figure 13-13** shows my up-to-the-minute results.

> **United States trends** · Change
>
> **#NationalSmoresDay**
> Celebrate with your favorite Hershey's classic!
> ▣ · Promoted by HERSHEY'S
>
> **Nicki**
> 504K Tweets
>
> **#Queen**
> Nicki Minaj drops new album Queen
>
> **Barbie Dreams**
> 147K Tweets
>
> **Derrius Guice**
> 18.5K Tweets
>
> **Pogba**
> 92.6K Tweets
>
> **#NationalLazyDay**
> @DannyShookNews, @jandis_price and 4 more are Tweeting about this
>
> **Justin Bour**
> 3,367 Tweets
>
> **Omarosa**
> 93.2K Tweets
>
> **#FridayFeeling**
> @Kugey, @ShiCooks and 4 more are Tweeting about this

FIGURE 13-13

2. In **Figure 13-14**, I clicked on #NationalLazyDay (which seems to be a trend that I could get behind). Scrolling the results will definitely bring me lots of chuckles.

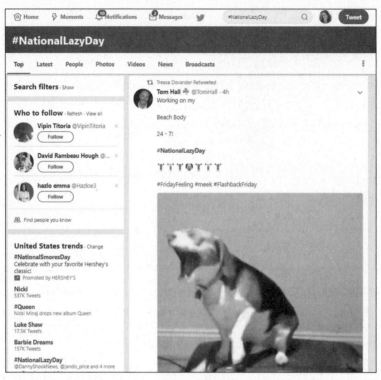

FIGURE 13-14

3. When it comes to local or national news stories, even if they are not trending (yet), you can type a descriptive keyword into the Search box to see all the tweets that will give you an up-to-the-minute report. Many brands live-stream their product launches on Twitter, as well as news events of interest to many. **Figure 13-15** shows a link to the live stream on YouTube of the late Aretha Franklin's funeral. Over a million people watched the various streams of this sad event.

FIGURE 13-15

FollowFriday, FF, and Other Hashtags

1. When you've been on Twitter long enough, you'll see Tweets with hashtags (#) preceding them. The hashtag may be followed by strange abbreviations, `severalwords thatruntogether` (say what?), or single topics. Hashtags help to spread and organize information on Twitter.

TIP

Using hashtags makes subjects easier to search for and find. Conferences, major events, and even disasters (such as #swineflu) use hashtags to put specific Tweets in order and make it easier for you — and your followers — to follow. Chapter 12 gives you more information of finding topics through the use of hashtags.

2. Here's a list of some Twitter hashtags and what they refer to. After you look at the list, you'll get the drift. You can find more, along with their activity and the top members, at `www.hashtags.org` (shown in **Figure 13-16**), a user-editable dictionary for hashtags found on

Twitter. After that, I give you some conventions to follow when creating your own hashtags.

FIGURE 13-16

- **#sxsw:** A popular conference, South By Southwest, has a name too long to Tweet because Tweets are limited to 280 characters. People at the conference include #sxsw in their Tweets to show where they are and what they're doing there.

- **#CES:** Consumer Electronics Show. Again, too long to Tweet. Let your friends know you're talking about it by using #CES.

- **#MusicMonday:** On Mondays, Twitter users like to Tweet their favorite songs and music references. It's like sitting around a record player (remember?) with your friends. Tweets may have a link to a playable version of the song or contain videos of Twitter member's performances.

- **#ThrowbackThursday or #TBT:** Folks on Twitter like to post pictures from "the olden days" on Thursdays and tag them with this hashtag. I know you'll enjoy those Tweets.

- **#FF or #FollowFriday:** Do you have someone you really like to follow? Someone who often posts interesting Tweets? Recommend that person to your followers by Tweeting his or her ID, followed by the hashtag.

- **#earthquake:** When someone feels the ground shake, they usually just Tweet #EARTHQUAKE because they're too freaked to say anything else. People follow up with information on damage, provide brief news reports, and append their Tweets with this hashtag.

- **#tcot:** Top Conservatives on Twitter. This hashtag is used by a very vocal and interesting group. If you Tweet something with a politically conservative slant, add this hashtag to your Tweet. You're bound to get more like-minded followers.

- **#p2:** The #p2 hashtag stands for *Progressives 2.0*. Their official mission statement reads, "A resource for progressives using social media who prioritize diversity and empowerment, the 'progressive batchannel,' and an umbrella tag for information for progressives on Twitter."

- **#tlot:** Top Libertarians on Twitter. What more can I say?

- **#uniteblue:** The tag is used by liberal activists to show there's strength when people unite.

- **#custserv:** A hashtag for the Customer Service chat which I host every Tuesday at 9:00 p.m. ET. People participate in chats on Twitter at prescribed times each week. When they take part in the chat, they follow each Tweet with the #custserv tag.

- **#jobs:** Looking for a job? Search for Tweets with this hashtag.

- **#quote:** When you post a quote as a Tweet, follow it with the #quote hashtag for quote-lovers to find.

TIP

Rather than using search during chats, people use sites like Twubs (http://twubs.com), hashtags.org (http://hashtags.org), or TweetChat (http://tweetchat.com) where they can see the Tweets and respond to them in real time. These sites also insert the hashtag at the end of your Tweets automatically. **Figure 13-17** shows the Twubs page for our #custserv chat.

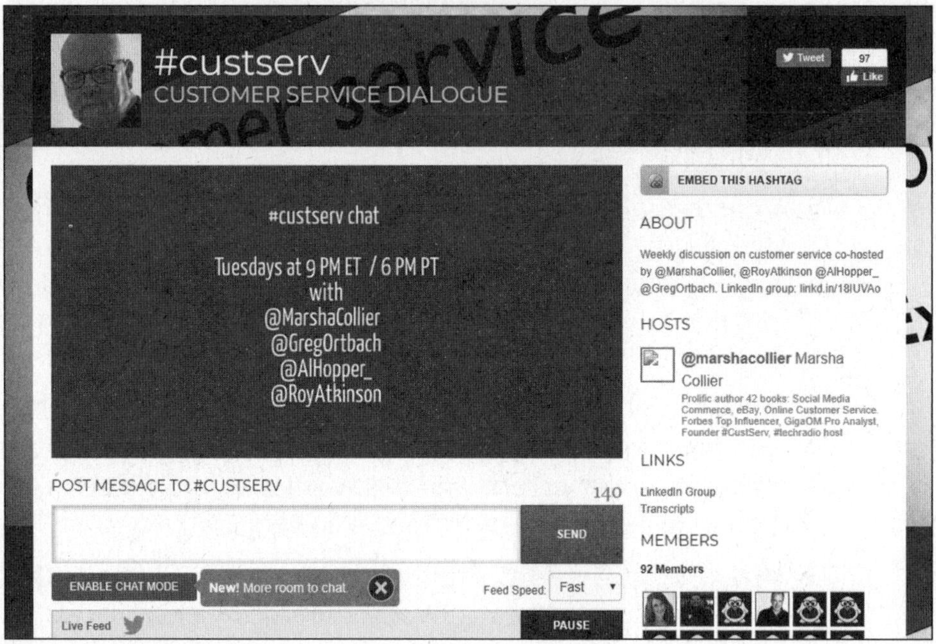

FIGURE 13-17

3. Twitter hosts many weekly chats, and you might find one you'd like to take part in by using Twitter's search feature. **Figure 13-18** shows a search for #gardenchat. Here are a few examples of chats:

- **#gardenchat:** Every Monday at 9:00 p.m. ET, @TheGardenChat hosts open conversation on all things gardening.

- **#petchat:** Share pet tips and discuss pet trends and issues on Monday nights at 8:00 p.m. ET, hosted by pet advocate Elly McGuire.

- **#NostalgiaChat:** Do you love remembering the good old days? We all do! Steve Case (@JoeBugBuster) looks back on our traditions every Sunday at 7:00 p.m. ET/4:00 p.m. PT.

- **#blogchat:** Starting a blog? Run by blogging expert @MackCollier, this chat is full of tips and ideas. Find them every Sunday at 8:00 p.m. CT.

- **#winechat:** If you can't resist a great bottle of wine, visit this chat held each Wednesday at 6:00 p.m. PT. Hosted by @ProtocolWine.

FIGURE 13-18

TIP

Here's a site with a massive directory where you can search Twitter chats by date, time, and subject:

`http://twubs.com/twitter-chats`

- **#americanidol:** Watching *American Idol* on TV by yourself? Want to make a comment and possibly get an answer? Incorporate the TV show name with a hash mark in front and look for others.

TIP

Keep in mind that hashtags should be used sparingly (unless you're in the middle of a live chat). They're kind of annoying to look at, and lose meaning when used superfluously.

Connect and Chat with People

Did someone @ reply to you, and you want to know more about that person? See a Tweet you like? Want to know whether you're following someone? Want to see who's following you? Twitter has a quick and easy tool you can use to find out more.

1. On your Twitter page, click the icon of the bell, followed by the word *Notifications.* The page opens to show interactions with your account: when people follow you, favorite your Tweets, or mention you. Click Mentions and you'll see a list of people who have mentioned you in their Tweets.

2. If you want to know more about someone, hover your mouse over his or her avatar. A profile summary like the one in **Figure 13-19** appears. If you're not following the person, you see a Follow button; if you *are* following, you see a box in red and the word *Following.* Clicking the ID will take you to the person's Twitter Profile page.

Shows whether you're being followed

FIGURE 13-19

TIP

Verified Accounts: You may notice that next to some Twitter user's name is a blue check mark badge. This means their account is of public interest and has been verified by Twitter. A verified badge is assigned by Twitter, but does not imply endorsement.

3. Before you follow someone you don't know, read the bio in the profile summary and see if they have a link to a website; the person's full Twitter information shows up in the small box (shown in **Figure 13-20**) along with a list of other people you follow who also follow that user. If you like what you see, go ahead and follow.

4. If you do follow this new person — and want to know if he or she is following you — notice the words *Follows You* in the profile summary (refer to **Figure 13-19**).

FIGURE 13-20

Solve Customer Service Issues Online

If you're anything like me, you feel that making customer service phone calls is a long and laborious process. Here's where Twitter comes to the rescue! Many of your favorite brands have agents online 24/7 to help you out when you have a problem. If they are not constantly there, they post the hours in which they will respond to your query. Just search for the brand on Twitter to contact the brand. I've made a short list of businesses that give customer service help on Twitter. You can find it at

```
https://twitter.com/MarshaCollier/lists/brands-on-twitter
```

Keep Track of Hundreds, Thousands of Friends?

It's a challenge, but you'll soon be following more people than you could possibly imagine at the moment (unless you're channeling Cecil B. DeMille). The more the merrier? Sometimes. You may want to monitor a smaller group of real-life or business friends, and if you follow hundreds of people, you may never see their Tweets.

1. Enter (behold!) *Twitter Lists*. You're allowed to make lists of as many people as you want. You can choose to make them public or private. If the lists are private, no one can find out that he or she is not on the list of your personal friends (which can be tactful). Start your lists by going to your Twitter page. Click your picture on the upper right of the page, and in the drop-down menu that appears you'll see the Lists heading.

2. Click the Lists link, and on the new page you'll see any lists you've subscribed to or are a member of. A box with a link to Create New List appears on the right side of this page. Click it and in the boxes shown in **Figure 13-21**, give your list a name and a short description. Typing a description for a private list isn't necessary (because you know what the list is about); doing so is optional in that case.

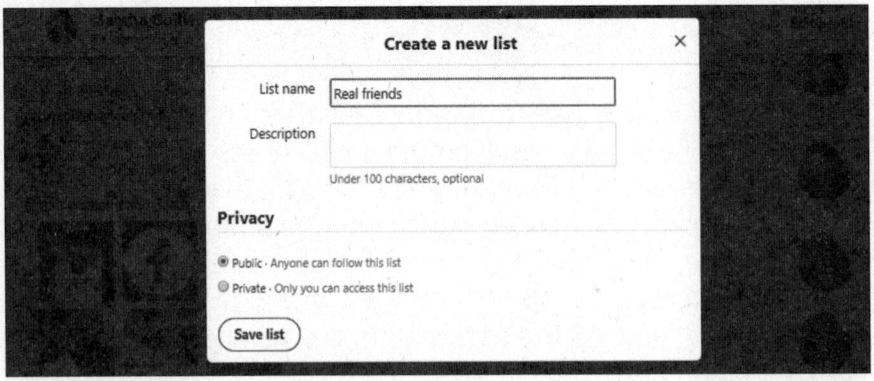

Create a new list ×

List name | Real friends

Description |

Under 100 characters, optional

Privacy

⦿ Public · Anyone can follow this list
○ Private · Only you can access this list

Save list

FIGURE 13-21

3. Selecting the Private option means only you can access the list (by clicking the link that appears under the Lists heading on the right side

of your Profile page). If you want to share your list with others — the way I do with my Funny-twits list — click the Public option. That way, other folks can follow the people on your list.

4. After you make a list, you'll want to add people to it. Here's the procedure:

   a. *You can either search for people by clicking* Who To Follow *for suggestions, or click a new person's ID when he or she comes up in the Twitter stream.* Clicking the ID opens the person's profile summary where you'll see a bio and other such information. You can stay on the profile summary or click the link to go directly to the user's Profile page.

   b. *At the right of the profile summary, next to the word* Follow *(or Following), click the three vertical dots to access a drop-down list.* An Add or Remove from Lists option appears (in **Figure 13-22**).

   c. *Click there and select the list to which you want to add this person — and click the small box next to the list's name.* A tiny lock icon will appear next to any list you've made Private, which means you can see the list but no one else can.

FIGURE 13-22

You'll also see that you can make a new list for the person you're adding; that option is available in the drop-down menu. This is very handy if you haven't set up a list yet.

d. *After you click the box, the menu will close.* When you go to your Twitter page, you'll see Lists below your page banner. Click there and you see Lists that you're subscribed to and the ones that you're a member of. Clicking one of your private subscribed lists (remember, each of those has a small padlock next to the name) shows (only to you) the Tweets from who is on your lists. Clicking the List Members link on the left shows you a list of the people you've put on a list.

View Your Friend Lists

1. Now that you've made your super-secret list of those you follow, you want to be able to watch your friends' Tweets, right? That's the easy part. You start on your Twitter home page, under the Lists heading, with the lists you've made. Clicking the name of a list shows you Tweets from just the friends you've selected to be on the list. Pretty cool, eh?

2. But (there's always a *but*) you can't see the Tweets from the other people you follow — *or* your direct messages *or* your @ replies! What to do? You're going to have to use a Twitter personal browser. But don't worry, those clients are *free* and safe and work in a web browser window. They allow you to see all your Tweets, all at once.

3. The most popular is TweetDeck. Here are a couple of features to note about Twitter clients:

   - Twitter clients update Tweets automatically and allow you to have separate columns for @ replies, direct messages (private messages), your lists, your followers, and your searches. You're limited only by the amount of space on your desktop (and how good your eyes are). They do allow you to scroll back and forth to view all the columns.

- You can send Tweets while you're using a personal browser window, and do anything you can do on Twitter — the only difference is that you can see everything you're doing all at once. Call it a bird's-eye view.

- TweetDeck (shown in **Figure 13-23**) shows columns for my @replies, my @MarshaCollier/Friends private list, and my Home list, which consists of everyone I follow. (You didn't really think I'd let you see my private direct messages, did you?) In settings, it has options to auto-shorten your links, change the theme of the page, and create keyboard shortcuts. You can add any of your lists to create a search column. Find the settings on the left side of the page.

FIGURE 13-23

4. You can find TweetDeck at www.tweetdeck.twitter.com for any browser. Twitter also has a mobile client that you can use in your device's mobile browser.

4
Instagramming with the Pros (Your Kids)

IN THIS PART . . .

Telling your story with photos

Editing your pictures artistically

Fine tuning Instagram to work for you

» **Complete Your Profile in a Browser**

» **Check Through the Privacy Settings**

» **Decide to Use Instagram on a Desktop or Mobile Device**

» **Find Friends and People to Follow**

Chapter **14**

Where Only Visuals Will Do . . . Instagram

How can I explain Instagram? If you think of Facebook as a place where you connect with friends and family, and Twitter as a place to learn the news and discuss topics with strangers from around the world, then Instagram is a place to view pictures in the comfort of your own home. These might be pictures of people or far-off locations, of food and recipes or pictures of new products. Instagram is my happy place. I often visit it right before I go to sleep and look at pictures of friends on vacations, puppies, and kittens; there are even short videos, as well. Instagram is for entertainment and sharing the joys of life in pictures.

Finding photos to enjoy on Instagram is easy. Of all the social media platforms, I think that Instagram is the most soul-satisfying. You have an almost unending stream of pictures to like and comment on. Instagram began as a mobile-only platform (smartphones and tablets), but you can now use it on a desktop or laptop PC. The only difference between the platforms is you cannot receive DMs (Direct Messages) on the desktop (which some would say is a blessing), and you can't check to verify if someone is still following you.

You can find many services for sharing your personal photos, but the most popular (especially for mobile uploads) is Instagram. I use Instagram from my phone and tablet, as a chronicling the fun things I see. You can also take short videos and post them to your Instagram page. I can, for example, share photographs or videos easily and directly to Facebook (which makes sense — the app is owned by Facebook), or through a shortened link to Twitter. This process gives the image a shortened URL that you can use anywhere.

In this chapter, I ease you into this world and show you how to sign up and make your first inroads.

Set Up Your Instagram Account

Because Instagram has two distinct platforms, I'll describe them both. Joining is easy. I encourage you also to download the app from the App Store or Google Play, and *join* Instagram before you have a photo to post; doing so will make your first upload move quicker. Here's how you sign up on a web browser (basically the same on a smartphone):

1. To set up from your desktop or laptop, type `www.instagram.com` into your URL web browser's address box, pictured in **Figure 14-1**, and press Enter.

TIP

You will notice an option to "Log In" with your Facebook account. If you have a Facebook account and are fine with this, go ahead. Just keep in mind that you may want to get the feel of Instagram first — before Instagram sends out a message to all your friends that you've joined. Trust me, because Instagram is owned by Facebook, the accounts will merge anyway soon enough. I just feel there's an additional security advantage to having two separate passwords.

FIGURE 14-1

2. In the text box provided, type your email address or mobile phone number.

TIP

If you plan on using Instagram on mobile as well as on desktop as I suggest you do, you might want to type in your mobile number.

3. Fill your full name in the text box, as well as your desired username (why not use your own name so your friends can easily find your account?).

If your desired username is already taken, a red X will appear next to the name you typed. Please keep trying to think of a good ID, because a user ID made up of letters and random numbers makes it look like you don't care.

TIP

In Internet circles, a User ID with a string of numbers is often suspected to be a bot or someone who is up to no good. Keep things honest and keep your guard up.

4. Decide the password you want to use. Type it in and — once again — if the password you select isn't good enough, a red X will appear next to it.

   Instagram wants your password to be a combination of at least six letters, numbers, and punctuation marks.

5. When you're finished inputting the required data, click Sign Up on the web form or tap Done on a smartphone.

   At this point, Instagram wants to confirm you are you and sends a six-digit code in the form of a text to your smartphone. **Figure 14-2** shows you what it looks like.

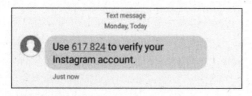

FIGURE 14-2

6. Now go back to Instagram and you'll see a request for the code. Type it in as I have in **Figure 14-3**.

Instagram

Just one more step: enter the 6-digit code
we sent to 212▓▓▓▓▓47.

######
617824

Confirm

Change Number | Request New Code

FIGURE 14-3

7. Once you have signed in to Instagram, because it is owned by Facebook, you are presented with a list of people you might want to follow.

8. You probably don't want to start following people quite yet. So on to the next step.

Complete Your Profile in a Browser

Your Profile page is the hub of all your Instagram activities. Navigating is slightly different on the web than from the mobile app. It's your choice as to whether you want to fill out your page and settings on the web or in the app.

1. If you're on the web interface in a web browser (versus the app), you'll find several navigation points at the top of the page. These icons, shown in **Figure 14-4**, are at the top of the Instagram web page. **Figure 14-5** shows you the location of the icons on the mobile app.

FIGURE 14-4

2. The icons you see on the web page do the following:

    -   **The Instagram logo:** This is a stylized camera on the left takes you to the home screen where you can view all the posts your friends have uploaded to the site.

        On the mobile app, tapping on the little house icon on the bottom of the screen takes you to the home screen.

FIGURE 14-5

- **A Search box:** In the middle of the page is a text box where you can search for people by name, username, topic, or hashtags (more on hashtags further on).

   Tapping the magnifying glass on the mobile app takes you to a Search text box.

- **The compass icon:** This helps you find new people to follow who have interests similar to yours. This feature becomes more accurate the more you Follow other people's accounts and after you begin to post pictures.

   The three bars on the top right of the mobile app take you to a place to Discover People and more options.

- **The heart icon:** Clicking this icon on either interface shows you a drop-down list that alerts you when someone has "liked" or commented on one of your posts.

- **The icon of a person:** Clicking this icon, in the shape of head and shoulders, takes you to your Profile page.

- **Edit Profile button:** Next to your username on the web version, you see a link to edit your profile and clicking the cog next to it takes you to links that go to your account and privacy settings, shown in **Figure 14-6**.

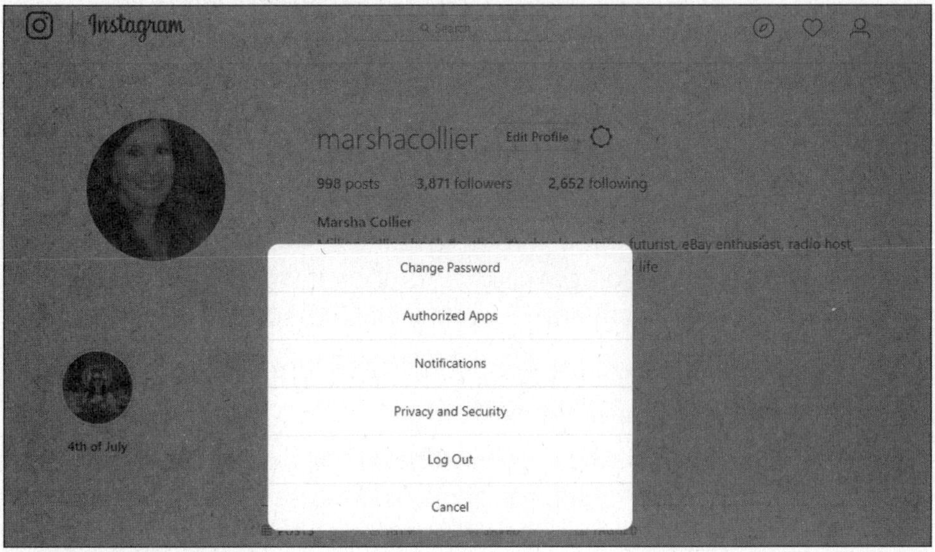

FIGURE 14-6

3. Click Edit Profile next to your username to buff up your profile. In this area you can make your account more distinctive . . . more you! On the Edit Profile page, it is time to

- **Upload a profile picture:** Click Change Profile Picture to upload a photo of you. Instagram is very personalized, so I suggest you dig out the best image you can find.

  Instagram profile photos are very forgiving. Most people use Instagram on their phones or tablets so they will never see your profile picture any larger than ½ inch tall.

- **Change your username:** If you didn't pay much attention and named yourself CookieMonster, you might want to personalize your account better at this point.

- **Website:** This is a useful place to link to your website, blog (if you have one), or even a Twitter account. People like to visit URL addresses so they can get to know a person better.

- **Bio:** You now have 150 characters to tell your life story . . . or not. How about just say a few words that give a surface description of you. (Inquiring minds want to know.) Don't give away any information that may expose you to bad actors.

- **Email:** If you didn't type in your email address upon initial registration, you can insert it here. Or not. Instagram keeps this information private.

TIP

Your email address will be needed if you ever forget your password and cannot get into your account.

- **Phone number:** Typing in your phone number is critical for security reasons if you want to use Instagram on your phone. If you initially signed up with the number, it will already appear in this box. It's private and not exposed to the public (or your Followers).

- **Gender:** Select the gender (male or female) you most identify with or leave this as Not Specified.

- **Similar Account Suggestions:** When you've been on the site for a while, your tastes, hobbies, and interests are noted by the platform. When someone follows someone similar to you, Instagram suggests other people to follow. I checked this option and have discovered many other interesting accounts.

When you've filled out the boxes, tap Submit to save them. Your profile should look pretty snappy now.

Check Through the Privacy Settings

There are many Instagram Privacy settings provided for your benefit. **Figure 14-6** shows you where to access them on a desktop. The options are the same, so now I will show you how to edit them on the Instagram mobile app. For my examples, I'm using the Android app (which isn't very different from the iOS version). The icons appear at the bottom of the screen, and on top there are a bit different as you see in **Figure 14-5**.

TIP

To activate (or deactivate) a setting on your mobile device, tap the slide bar (in **Figure 14-7** shows the "On" position) to either be grayed out (Off) or blue (On).

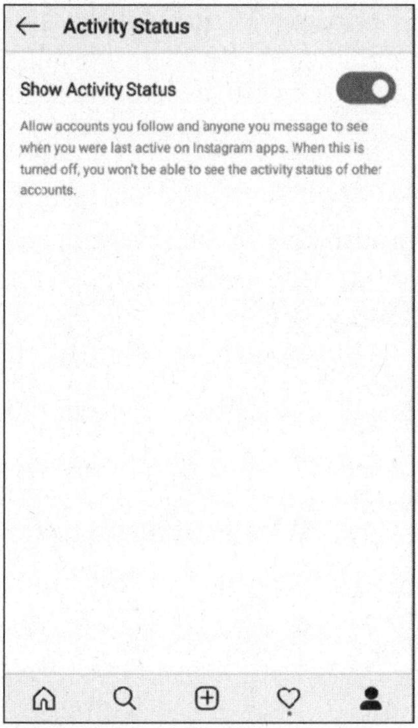

← **Activity Status**

Show Activity Status

Allow accounts you follow and anyone you message to see when you were last active on Instagram apps. When this is turned off, you won't be able to see the activity status of other accounts.

FIGURE 14-7

1. Tap the three horizontal lines at the top of the screen to get to your account settings.

2. The page slides aside. At the very bottom of the resulting page you'll see a cog next to the word *Settings*. Tap the word *Settings* and the Settings page will appear.

3. There's a plethora of settings to go over, so let me give you some of the most important.

- **Private Account:** See the sidebar for more information. I like to meet new people and see their photos, so my account is not private.

HAVING A PRIVATE INSTAGRAM ACCOUNT

You have the option of setting your account as Private. This setting means that folks who know you're on Instagram can find you by your ID, but must request permission to view (or *follow* in social parlance) your photostream.

This means that only people you've approved to Follow will see your posts on the site. In my opinion, this is an important tool for those who need to keep a tight rein on their privacy (and their children's).

I'm also of the opinion that being on a social platform means participating. If my account would have been private, I wouldn't have found friends from long ago; I also wouldn't have the breadth of photos to look at.

When your account is private, most people on the site won't know you are there and those you follow may not follow you back.

I never post anything (again) that I need to be ashamed of. I also won't follow any private account from a stranger because I have no idea who they are or what sort of pictures they post.

Social media is about sharing, commenting, and liking. It's way more fun to be able to participate fully on the site.

TIP

I will also not follow a private account from someone that I do not know. That's one important way to stay safe and avoid fraud online.

- **Show Activity Status:** If you'd like to see which of your friends are online at any moment, turn this on. I do not have this setting turned on because I like to browse Instagram at odd hours and don't want to be disturbed by direct messages.

- **Photos and Videos of You:** If someone posts a photo or video with you in it, they can tag the image with your username. If you'd rather be able to approve these images before they appear with your tag, don't allow automatic tags.

- **Link Social Accounts:** To share your posts on Facebook or Twitter, you need to give Instagram permission to integrate with your social accounts. Click each of your social media accounts and follow the prompts to connect them.

- **Two-Factor Authentication:** This is important for every app you own. If you (or someone else) attempts to log into your Instagram account from a device that is not known to the platform, a code is texted to your smartphone. Instagram requires you to type in that login code in order to access your account.

- **Story Controls:** Decide if you want anyone to be able to use your posts in their stories. (More on stories in the following chapter.) I want to control my content and who uses it, so I have this option turned off.

- **Contacts Syncing:** This gives Instagram access to all the contacts from your phone and gives permission for them to periodically sync them and store them on their servers. I don't think anyone should have access to my contacts, so this feature is disabled on my account.

- **Notifications:** If you want to be notified any time someone likes or follows you, Instagram will notify you. Be sure to go through the list of actions so that you can selectively decide on which ones you want to be notified. Instagram can notify you in three ways:

  a. *Push notifications:* This means your phone will directly get a notification through a popup or sound. You do not have to be active in the app to get a Push notification.

  b. *SMS:* This is an acronym for Short Message Service (or what we all call texts) that are sent direct to your phone.

  c. *Email:* You give Instagram permission to send you an email when the action occurs on your account.

Should You Use Instagram on a Desktop or Mobile Device?

Viewing Instagram on a smartphone or in a browser window are two completely different experiences, and many people have strong ideas about their preferences. **Figure 14-8** shows you the desktop view.

FIGURE 14-8

You'll notice that the picture of a beautiful Fancy Green Cheek Conure bird is from the famous pop and country singer B. J. Thomas (yes, you can follow him on Instagram at @thebjthomas — www.instagram.com/thebjthomas) and it takes up the entire screen.

To go to see the next image, you will need to scroll down with your mouse, somewhat like reading a magazine online. To see the entire collection of B. J.'s photos, you just click on his username at the top of the photo.

On a mobile device, you still see the same picture full screen in all its glory, but getting to the next picture is accomplished by a flick of your finger. A mobile device is far more time efficient, but you cannot see the detail in all its glory like you can on a desktop.

When you consume Instagram in a browser, you cannot send direct messages.

I must admit, I'm a fan of using Instagram on a mobile device. That's what it was designed for, and I find it easier to navigate.

Find Friends and People to Follow

Opening up Instagram for the very first time can be somewhat disheartening. Who you follow regulates what you see, and until you follow someone, you won't see any pictures. You may end up following people from across the world because you enjoy seeing the world through their eyes. I know I do.

You can follow celebrities, brands you like, or just plain people. The account for @Apple (see **Figure 14-9**) has over 8 million followers and posts some very beautiful images. They even ask their followers who post Instagram pictures on an iPhone to tag the picture with the hashtag #ShotoniPhone so they will be seen by the company.

Instagram (like Facebook and Twitter) verifies accounts with a pale blue check badge next to their username so you will know they are official accounts. In a statement, Instagram confirms, "The blue verified badge is an important way for you to know that the account you are interacting with is the authentic presence of a notable public figure, celebrity, global brand or entity."

Before you follow someone you don't know, be sure to scroll through their pictures to be sure there is nothing you find offensive.

FIGURE 14-9

Here's some of the most efficient ways to search and find people to follow:

1. Click the magnifying glass icon at the bottom of your Instagram app and you'll see a dazzling array of videos and images from people you don't know, as in **Figure 14-10**. Tap them to view and maybe discover someone new.

2. In the Search box, type the name of a friend of yours. As you type the name, Instagram will populate the bottom of the page.

    -   When you find your friend, tap their name, go to their page, and look at their pictures.

FIGURE 14-10

- If this is the account you want to follow, tap the word *Follow* at the top of the page.

TIP

Later, if you want to see if someone is following you back on Instagram, go to their profile and click on the word *Following*. When their list of followers opens, a search bar appears near the top of the screen. Type your name in the bar, and if they are following you, your profile picture and ID will appear.

3. Post on your Facebook page and tell your friends you've just joined Instagram and you'd like to follow them. People are generally very nice about sharing their Instagram IDs. Then follow the procedure described in Step 1.

4. Although I haven't discussed tags much (I will in the next chapter), put a keyword after a hashtag. In **Figure 14-11**, I put in the name of my favorite dog breed. Why not type in yours? #frenchies (French bull-dogs) are very popular!

FIGURE 14-11

5. Use the geotargeting feature and type in a city name. I typed Los Angeles as shown in **Figure 14-12** and found some great accounts to follow.

In the next chapter, I'll show you how to interact on the site.

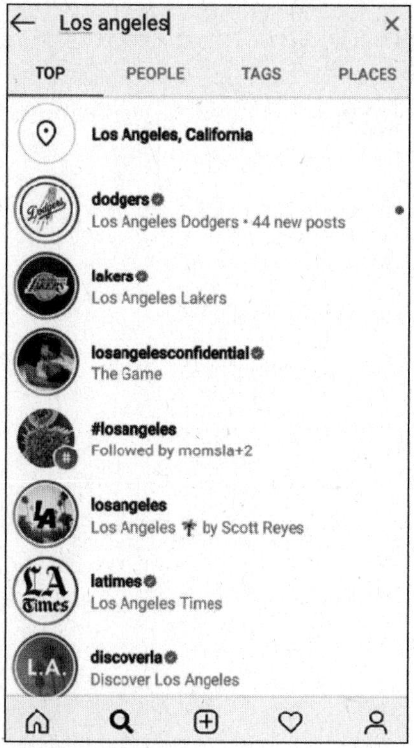
Los angeles
TOP
PEOPLE
TAGS
PLACES
Los Angeles, California
dodgers
Los Angeles Dodgers • 44 new posts
lakers
Los Angeles Lakers
losangelesconfidential
The Game
#losangeles
Followed by momsla+2
losangeles
Los Angeles by Scott Reyes
latimes
Los Angeles Times
discoverla
Discover Los Angeles

FIGURE 14-12

Photo Tips

» **Post Photos Taken on Your Phone**

» **Take Photos and Videos in the Instagram App**

» **Post Your Stories on Instagram**

» **Learn to Take a Selfie**

Chapter **15**

Posting and Perfecting Your Pictures

As of June 2018, there are over a billion active users on Instagram. It's even more popular than Twitter, mainly because of the visual content. So you are not alone in wanting to post photos on Instagram. You may not consider yourself to be a master photographer, but you might surprise yourself. Sharing pictures on Instagram is more about what they depict and if they make you smile. I have a friend who catalogs the progress in her garden every year, another friend who shares photos of new shoes . . . and of course everyone shares pictures of pets and babies.

Today's smartphones pack a bunch of power into their cameras, so you needn't be worried about quality. Finding photos to share isn't all that hard either. A friend of mine just shared a photo of a spider who had spun an interesting web in her garden. Think of this as an art form: Ever see a beautiful street scene? Stunning car? A beautiful flower? You get the idea. This is the place to put all those photos you take because you carry a camera in your pocket and see amazing things. Share what makes you happy and if your pictures make others happy, they will follow you and you will be pleased with the type of photos you will see in your home stream.

In this chapter, I show you how to post pictures and videos.

Make a Difference with Simple Photo Tips

I love taking photos with my smartphone. Although you can take pictures directly through the app, I like to see the pictures first (before I share with the world) and maybe do some on-phone editing first. The newer phones have such great tools that you can create almost any photo look great (more on that later).

Here's a couple of tips as to what to consider first:

1. Check the background of the photo; be sure there is no personally identifiable information.

2. Look for negative space, the area around the main focus of your picture, for distractions that draw the eye away.

3. Pay attention to the lighting of your pictures. Creative natural lighting can make or break a photo.

4. If your camera can accommodate it, using a bokeh effect (soft, out-of-focus) backgrounds make for stellar pictures if your smartphone has that setting. If your camera has pro settings, try a wide aperture and a very fast lens.

5. Pre-editing on your phone is easily performed in your camera app. Take a look at the before and after in **Figure 15-1**; I'm no expert either! I just applied one of the filters in my Samsung Galaxy Note 9.

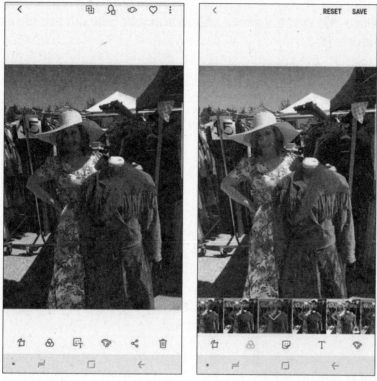

FIGURE 15-1

Post Photos Taken on Your Phone

After you have taken some photos at an event or just "because," wait until you have several images to choose from. After you have applied any filters or edits on your smartphone as I did in the preceding section, follow these steps:

1. Open the Instagram app.

2. Tap the Plus + on the bottom center of the screen.

This brings you to a screen that shows the photo gallery on your phone.

TIP

On the bottom of the screen you will see links to tap to go to Gallery (or Library on iPhone), Photo (where you can take a photo), and Video (to shoot a video in the app).

3. Tap on the photo you want to share, and it appears in the photo box as in **Figure 15-2**.

FIGURE 15-2

4. To select multiple photos in one post, tap the Select Multiple link and select additional photos. You can select up to 10 photos to tell your story. Why bother? Most users won't click through to see them all. I recommend you share only the best images.

TIP

The site is called Instagram as a combination of "Instant Camera" and "telegram." Your posts may not always be "instant," but keep them short like a telegram.

5. Tap the word *Next* and you'll see your photo in the Instagram square. From here you can perform more edits to your image. This square allows you to crop the image to the standard square format used in Instagram. You can move the square to position it on the image, or zoom in and select a portion of the image by pinching the selection.

When your picture is just right, tap the arrow at the top right of your screen to proceed to make even more magic with your image. Editing options for your photos:

- **Lux:** A sun icon appears at the top of the screen. This allows you to apply Lux to your picture (see **Figure 15-3**). Lux applies an effect that can lighten shadows and increase contrast. Tap the slider at the bottom to apply more or less. If you don't like what you see, tap Cancel and the effect is gone.

FIGURE 15-3

- **Filters:** Instagram gives you a bunch of very fancy filters that you can apply to your picture. Tap on the scrolling selections at the bottom of your screen (as in **Figure 15-4**) to see how your picture looks with each filter. You can press the filter and use the slider below your photo to apply only a percentage of it. If you don't want to add artistic license to your image, just leave the selection on the default Normal. When you're happy with the effect, tap the word *Next* in the upper right of your screen to open the posting page.

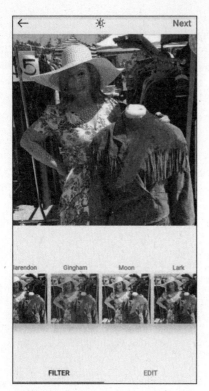

FIGURE 15-4

TIP

Depending on your photo subject (food, portrait, nature, architecture, fashion), the filters affect the picture differently. Don't be afraid to try them. In informal survey of my friends, these are the top filters used on Instagram:

1	Clarendon	5	Mayfair
2	Ludwig	6	Sierra
3	Juno	7	Valencia
4	Lark	8	Lo-fi

- **Editing tools:** There's also an option to use professional level-editing tools. I recommend you play around with them to see what they do and how they affect your image (as in **Figure 15-5**). Nothing is permanent. You can always click the back arrow at the top left of the screen to remove the effect.

FIGURE 15-5

6. Once you like what you're looking at, tap Next and you get to the posting screen (**Figure 15-6**).

7. Write a caption, in the box marked "Write a caption." You have 2,200 characters at your disposal, but to maximize engagement, use only 130 to 150 characters. Keep it short and concise (maybe even witty) and let the picture do the talking. You can also add hashtags to make your photos easy to find by other Instagram members (more on that in Chapter 16).

TIP

Before you click the word *Share* to post your image, decide whether you want the picture to immediately appear as a Tweet on Twitter or in a Facebook post with your text. If you don't want to share it everywhere, just ignore the boxes to share on other sites. You can always go back to one of your Instagram images and share at any time.

Share To   Share

Write a caption...

Add Location

Los Angeles, California   Los Angeles, California   San F

Tag People

Share To

Facebook

Twitter

Tumblr

Advanced Settings

FIGURE 15-6

8. Now you're ready to share your photo to your Instagram page and other social networks if you want. Select the social network (or networks) where you would like to share the photo.

- When you post to Twitter, the picture posts with your comment and shortened link that directs people off the site to your Instagram web page. Many people aren't a fan of doing this.

- Posting to Facebook is a far more satisfying event. Because Facebook owns Instagram, your full image is posted to your timeline, along with your comment. Note that images shared from Instagram to Facebook are visible only to your Facebook friends, and not to the general public. If you want the picture to be publicly viewable, you may go to Facebook and change the image's privacy status. (See Chapter 9 for more on photo privacy settings.)

Take Photos and Videos in the Instagram App

1. Launch the Instagram app on your smartphone and tap on the Plus + sign at the bottom of the screen.

2. Select Photo or Video, depending on which you want to capture.

   Center and focus on your picture.

3. Tap the circle (camera shutter) to capture the image.

4. Click Next in the upper right corner and proceed as you did in the previous instructions for setting filters (see **Figure 15-7**).

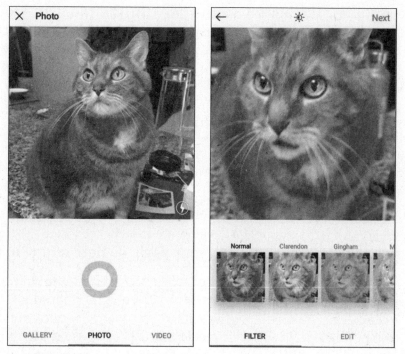

FIGURE 15-7

5. For video, tap and hold the shutter down as you film your video.

   - The maximum length for an Instagram video is 60 seconds.
   - You can also tap and hold to record multiple video clips for a single view.

6. Follow the process previously described to filter, edit, caption, and post your video.

Post Your Stories on Instagram

At the top of the Instagram home screen (when you open the app) you will see small, circled pictures with a red ring around them; they are *stories*. Instagram stories are "in the moment" shares on Instagram. They stay on the website for only 24 hours and are meant to be snapshot moments of your life. Tap on them to see stories from your friends in the form of ten-second increments of photos or video.

Your story, with a red circle around it, will appear:

» On your profile
» At the top of the main feed
» In the feed next to posts you share

You may want to post a story to your page, so here's how to do it.

1. Tap *Your Story* at the top left of the Instagram home feed, shown in **Figure 15-8**.

   The first time you do this, click the cog to go to the Story Controls page (shown in **Figure 15-9**) and select the options you want for this story. Then click the back arrow to take a picture.

Click here to start your own story

Red circles around profile photos mean these are stories

FIGURE 15-8

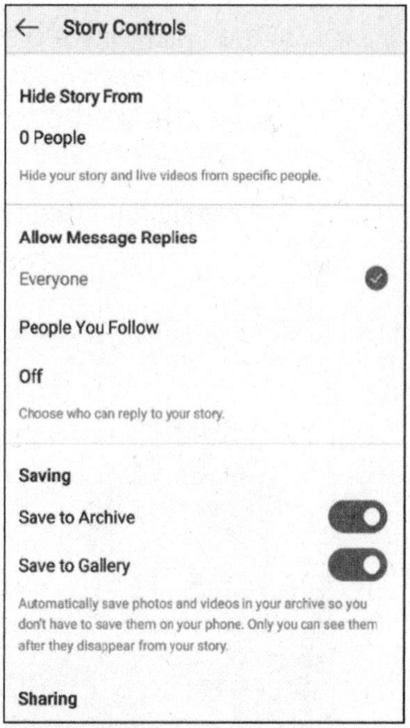

FIGURE 15-9

2. Share an existing photo or video, or take a new one within the Instagram app by tapping the circle at the bottom of the picture.

- When you take a picture, you can add special facial features by tapping in the far right face icon. The different facial features appear at the bottom of the screen. After selecting from a bunch of funny ears, my husband photobombed, and I selected the ones in **Figure 15-10**.

  Beware sending photos like **Figure 15-10** to your children; they may react bizarrely.

TIP

- To the left of the face icon are two arrows which let you switch from Selfie mode to Front Camera mode.

- As a reminder, the lightning bolt icon turns the flash on and off.

- You can also tap the word *Boomerang* to use video Boomerang mode. It films looping GIFs up to three seconds in length.

3. Once you take a picture you can save it to your story, save it to your camera roll or Gallery, or send it via private message; these options appear at the bottom of the screen in **Figure 15-11**.

...to apply fun facial features.

Click this face icon...

FIGURE 15-10

FIGURE 15-11

- Before you do that? Tap the first icon at the top left to superimpose a banner. You'll see suggestions like those in **Figure 15-12**.

- You can also tap the paintbrush icon to select a color and paint or add effects like fireworks in different styles on the image. **Figure 15-13** shows paint options at the top and color options at the bottom of the screen.

- I like to tap the letters icon on the top far right of **Figure 15-11** to superimpose a personal written message on my story.

FIGURE 15-12   **FIGURE 15-13**

Figure 15-14 is the result of a story I posted on the Fourth of July. Instagram took the three pictures and showed them over a period of 10 seconds.

FIGURE 15-14

TIP

The fun of Instagram is checking the *main feed* (the small Home icon on the app) to see the pictures your friends have posted. You can like their images by tapping the heart icon (or by double-tapping the picture), by tapping the cartoon text bubble you can type in a comment.

Learn to Take a Selfie

Selfies. All the kids do it and even some grownups. Do you want to do it? My very first selfie was taken in 2013 when I ran into Lionel Richie at a party (it's on my Instagram). There was no one else to take the picture, so it had to be a selfie. You never know when you might be caught without a photographer, so here are a few tips on how to get the best photos of yourself.

1. Never take a selfie facing harsh sunlight with shadows. Look for muted light (like when you are facing a window). Unlike using a flash, the right indirect lighting can smooth under eye circles and wrinkles. If the sun is strong, turn away and block the sun with your head. Bring the camera closer to your face. The sunlight can glint off of your hair.

TIP

You can carry your own lighting in the form of a selfie ring. See **Figure 15-15** for one that I use. (You can buy them on Amazon for under $10.)

FIGURE 15-15

2. It helps to hold your camera higher than your head and pose to shoot the picture downwards on your face. Chin down and camera up. Keeping the bottom of the phone level with your eyes improves your jawline and opens up your eyes (because you're looking up at the camera).

3. If you're taking a picture eating a snack or holding something in your hand, put your palm up. It helps the muscles in your forearm tighten up.

4. Test several poses so that you can draw attention to the angles of your face and the position of your shoulders. You'll be surprised at how moving just a smidge can make a big difference in how you photograph. Flattering photography is all about angles.

5. Use a newer version camera that has a built-in Artificial Intelligence for portrait mode. It automatically airbrushes your face lightly. Also, try out the filters that the newest cameras have on your selfie to enhance the look.

6. Try a selfie stick! I have a small one that telescopes out. It prevents the stretched arm look.

7. Maybe extend your neck forward? It might just remove a double chin (even if you feel silly doing it).

8. Double-check and see if your smartphone has a voice control setting where it snaps a picture when you use a keyword like "Cheese" or "Capture." This avoids the awkward pointing your finger at the camera angle.

9. Don't put your face in the center of the photo. Photographers understand the rule of thirds. Take in some background.

10. Go into Instagram and use their decorative filters (like the ones described previously to add ears, or a bow in your hair or a hat). They also gracefully smooth your skin and bug your eyes just a bit so you will look even more pleasant.

11. After you've taken a selfie, you can improve it even more! Go to the App Store and find an app called Facetune. It has a smoothing feature that removes almost all your wrinkles (don't go overboard) and one that whitens your teeth. If you like the app, you can pay for it so you don't see all the ads.

12. Practice, practice, practice. Kylie Jenner might take up to 500 before she finds one that she likes. (Maybe just take a few; you can always delete ones you don't post.)

Don't over-edit. No one is going to believe you are a high-schooler.

This all said, I don't take a lot of selfies. But I often do take photos of myself with friends. Now that you know some secrets, you can put forth your best face possible.

» Interact with Friends and Photos

» Comment on a Photo or Video

» Respond to Follows, Likes, and Comments

» Follow Those Who Have Followed You

» Send and Read Private Messages

Chapter **16**

Socializing and Fine Tuning Your Instagram

The previous two chapters covered the basics: setting up an account and showing how to post pictures. I'll bet you've even spent time browsing the site and enjoyed looking at the pictures. This chapter helps you fine-tune your Instagram experience: You'll discover how to view pictures from people you don't know and the proper etiquette for connecting with them online. The information here will help you grow your account.

Over 95 million photos are posted on Instagram a day. To make yours stand out, you might use a hashtag. *Hashtags* consist of a keyword preceded by a pound sign (#). Keywords online are single words that describe the core of a feeling, thing, or product. They are common on all social media platforms because they categorize content and make it more discoverable. You may have noticed that I've mentioned them in the sections on Twitter and on Facebook. They play an even more important part on Instagram; it's part of their success. It makes finding like-minded people on the site easier when keywords are used in bios. That's why I hashtag my city, #LosAngeles, in my bio. I've met a lot of interesting people from my city online and enjoy seeing their perspective of a city that I live in.

When you post a picture or video on Instagram, your friends or people who have similar interests can like (♥) or comment. This will encourage you to post more interesting pictures in a similar vein. One of my friends eats out a lot and every day posts a beautiful photo of the meal. I've discovered many interesting types of food by seeing his posts. Sometimes I like the posts and sometimes I comment. Interacting is what makes social media fun.

In this chapter, you'll learn how to become a master of hashtags, grow engagement on your pictures, and learn how to send private messages, pictures, and videos (even disappearing ones) to your friends.

Learn the Social Media Shorthand: Hashtags

Instagram permits the usage of hashtags in posts and bios. By including hashtags in your bio, you may connect with people of similar interests. Are you a #guitarlover, a #consultant? Perhaps you're into #coloring or #jewelry? Or, as I mentioned previously, are you from #MiamiBeach or #NewYork? Or are you a #Texan?

An enticing description of you in your bio helps your friends (and others) discover your Instagram photos. To buff up your profile:

1. Open the Instagram app.

2. From the home page, tap the head and shoulders icon on the far right to get to your Profile page.

3. Once on your Profile page, click the Edit Profile box, shown in **Figure 16-1**, next to your name.

FIGURE 16-1

TIP

Some features of Instagram are available on an iPhone but not on an Android device — and the other way around. Posting from an Android device or editing on the web allows you to insert hard returns (hard returns enable you to space out your bio and posts into sentences on separate lines) in your bio.

4. On the following page, the Edit Profile area appears.

Take a look at how I've laid out my bio in **Figure 16-2**. Rewrite your own bio using emoji (that describe the words you write) and insert hard returns if you can. Remember, you only have 150 characters (including emoji and spaces) to fill in your profile. You have 2,823 emoji on your emoji keyboard to choose from.

TIP

In the latest version of Google's Gboard app for iPhone or Android devices, you can search for emoji by name. The app replaces your current keyboard with a far more powerful one. Therefore, when you search emoji by name, you won't need to squint your eyes trying to figure out the exact emoji you need. **Figure 16-3** shows how I found the teeny palm tree to put next to #LosAngeles in my bio. Just tap the emoji key to open a search area over the keyboard, then type in the descriptive word for your desired emoji. You can download the new keyboard in Apple's App Store or in Google's Play Store. You'll find the descriptions on the web at:

```
https://itunes.apple.com/us/app/gboard-a-new-keyboard-
    from-google/id1091700242
https://play.google.com/store/apps/details?id=com.
    google.android.inputmethod.latin&hl=en
```

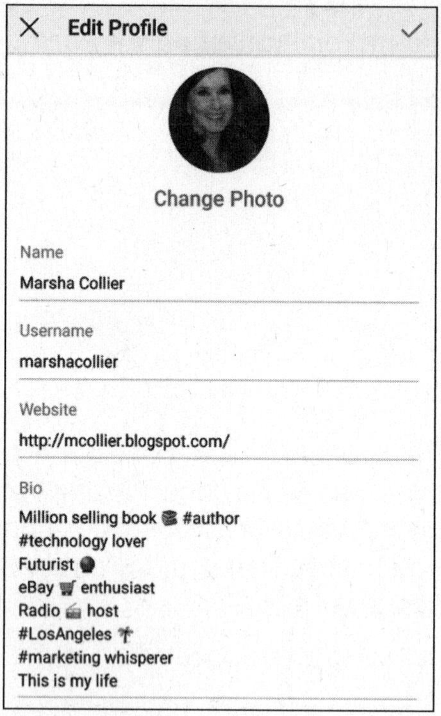

FIGURE 16-2

FIGURE 16-3

5. Once you've judiciously input just the right bio, tap the blue check mark at the top of the screen, or Done on an IOS device, and you'll return to your Profile page.

TOP HASHTAGS FOR POSTS ON INSTAGRAM

At the end of your Instagram post, you might want to add a few hashtags to focus on the topic of your image. Once you type the # and a few letters, a list of Instagram suggested hashtags opens automatically to the right that you can use. Next to each of the hashtags, you'll see the number of times they are used on the site. The bigger the number, the more popular the hashtag. People will who follow hashtags may follow other accounts that post with that hashtag.

The following are some popular hashtags. They are the ones many people tag and look for. Don't put too many hashtags in a post caption, or it looks spammy.

- **#love:** Because who doesn't like love?

- **#instagood:** Used in posts you are proud of.

- **#photooftheday:** Reserved for your finest photos.

- **#happy:** Everyone wants to see a picture that makes them smile.

- **#cute:** Perfect tag for a picture that's just plain . . . cute.

- **#TBT:** The Throwback Thursday tag is used on older photographs (and posted on Thursday).

- **#selfie:** Photos with faces get 38 percent more likes.

- **#foodporn:** When food is your porn, use this hashtag.

- **#caturday:** Saturday is #caturday. Post your cat pictures on Saturday and use this tag.

- **#travel:** Hashtag your travel pictures this way.

- **#avgeek:** Aviation geek. Pictures of airplanes and the like.

- **#dogsofinstagram:** Social media loves pictures of dogs. Use forms of this for your pet pictures: #catsofinstagram, #squirrelsofinstagram, and so on.

- **#nofilter:** Post a picture using no filters or edits; it means it is special.

Interact with Friends and Photos

Posting pictures and videos are just the tip of the iceberg. Seeing other's images makes the entire experience much more fun. Interacting with them builds your community online and makes other people happy. Just wait until one of your pictures starts to collect ♥'s and you'll know what I mean.

1. Open the Instagram app and you find yourself on the home page.

2. Flick (okay, maybe drag) your finger on the pictures you see to scroll to more images.

3. When you see one that you like, tap the (outline of a heart) ♡ (shown in **Figure 16-4**) at the bottom of the picture, to like the image.

FIGURE 16-4

4. The heart turns into a pretty red ♥ and a notification that you liked it appears in the photo's owner's notifications.

Comment on a Photo or Video

1. Scroll through the photos in the home stream and find one you'd like to comment on. (People love to receive comments — and compliments.)

2. Tap the cartoon bubble icon next to the ♡ below the picture, as in **Figure 16-5**, and type your comment in the line that says *Add a comment*.

FIGURE 16-5

3. When you're done, click the word *Post* on the right and your comment will accompany the post on Instagram.

4. The person who posted the picture gets a notification that you commented.

TIP

To send your comment in a personal message, tap the arrow next to the cartoon bubble.

Respond to Follows, Likes, and Comments

1. When you're in the Instagram app, you may see a red dot under the heart (♥) icon on the bottom of the app.

2. Tap the heart and you land on a page that shows where people have liked your posts, commented, or followed you (see **Figure 16-6**).

FIGURE 16-6

3. It's a nice gesture that when someone liked one of your pictures, that you tap on their name to see their Profile page. Tap on one of their pictures and like it.

Reciprocity is the key to enjoying social media in all forms.

4. For those who commented on one of your pictures, tap on the mini version of your picture on the far right. On the next screen

- Let them know you appreciated their comment by tapping the small heart to the right of their comment.

- You can also respond to their comment by tapping the word *Reply* (the person's name). A text box and keyboard opens up as shown in **Figure 16-7**, and you can post your comment to theirs.

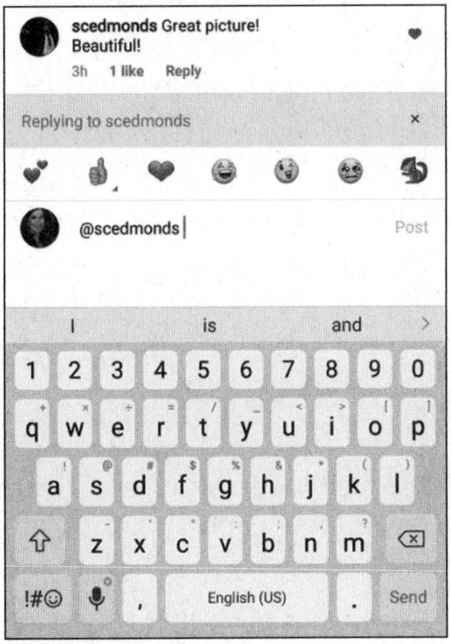

FIGURE 16-7

5. When you tap Post, your reply joins their comment on that photo's comment stream.

TIP

To remove a comment that you don't like or find offensive, on an Android, just press your finger on the post. On the iOS app, slide the comment left and press your finger on the trash can that appears. On the top of the screen you will see the words *One selected* and a trash can on the far right. Tap the trash can and the offending post is gone.

Follow Those Who Have Followed You

1. On the notifications, you may notice that next to a person's name there are the words *(name) started following you,* and there will be a Follow button on the far right. (Look back at **Figure 16-6**.)

2. Tap the name of the person that followed you, and take a look at the type of photos they post on their Profile page.

3. If you like the pictures you see and might like to see more, tap the Follow Back box at the top of their profile.

4. Their posts now will show up in your home stream.

Send and Read Private Messages

1. At the top right of your home feed is a blue arrow (this is a white arrow on the iOS app). If there is a number superimposed on it, it indicates that you have that many messages.

2. After tapping the arrow, you arrive at your messages screen.

3. Tap the message to read it.

4. If you want to respond, you can do so in several ways; **Figure 16-8** shows you how.

FIGURE 16-8

- Tap the heart to send back a like.

- Type a message in the message box to respond.

- Tap the GIF icon to send a GIF. A selection of fun animated pictures shows up for you to tap and send. If you send one in error, hold your finger on the GIF and tap the word *Unsend* (poof, it's gone).

- Select the landscape icon to upload a picture from your device in return.

Index

A

Acquaintances list (Facebook), 146

Acquaintances privacy setting (Facebook), 117

Ad Settings (Facebook), 121

admin (administrator) (Facebook groups), 183

Ads (Facebook), 119

Advertisers you've interacted with (Facebook), 121

AMA (Ask Me Anything) (slang expression), 82

Amazon

  Amazon OS, 13

  Amazon Prime Video, 71

  Android App Store, 13

  Fire Tablets, 13

  Fire TV Sticks, 30

  as source of devices, 19

#americanidol hashtag (Twitter), 255

Android phone, photo of, 16

animation, via GIFs in Twitter, 232–233

antenna, in network connections, 34

app

  defined, 12

  mini versions of on smartphones, 16

Apple

  App Store, 12, 266, 303

  Apple Store as source of devices, 19

  factory-refurbished equipment, 19

Apps and Websites (Facebook), 122

@ (at) replies (Twitter), 219, 220, 255

attachments, cautions in opening, 39

#avgeek hashtag (Instagram), 305

B

backward-compatible wireless format, 33

BAE (Before Anything Else) (slang expression), 82

Best Buy, as source of devices, 19

Bing (Microsoft), 244–246

Birthdays (Facebook), 124–125

bitly.com, 77, 78–82

Bitmarklet, 80

Blocking (Facebook), 123

blog, as shortened version of web-log, 67

#blogchat (Twitter), 254

Blogspot, 67

blue badge (verified)

  Instagram, 277

  Twitter, 256

Bluetooth, keyboard, 17

Boomerang mode (Instagram), 294

broadband connection

choosing, 29–30

as one of two basic types of connections, 25

quality of different types of, 26

types of, 27

browser

defined, 12, 20

selection of, 20–22

shortcuts in, 22–23

C

cable Internet connection, 26, 27

Captcha codes, 53

captions

Facebook, 161

Instagram, 289

#caturday hashtag (Instagram), 305

central processing unit (CPU) (a.k.a. chip)

defined, 17

recommended speed of, 17

#CES hashtag (Twitter), 252

Charlie Bit My Finger Again (YouTube movie), 85, 86

Chat (Facebook), 125, 150

Cheat Sheet, 6

Chromebook, 13

Clarendon filter (Instagram), 288

Close Friends list (Facebook), 145

Closed (Facebook group), 177

Coffee Bean and Tea Life, using Wi-Fi at, 28

Collier, Marsha (author)

blog, 6

Blogspot, 67

book Twitter ID, 212

closed Facebook group for readers, 179

daughter's LinkedIn Profile, 65

daughter's Rat Pack radio on Pandora, 70

eBay For Seniors For Dummies, 7

emoji personal favorites, 242

example of Photobomb, 83

Facebook "Fan" Page, 60, 61, 175

Facebook Profile page, 60, 61

list of businesses that give customer help on Twitter, 257

Pinterest Board, 89

search for Google Photos, 69

Twitter ID, 210

Twitter page, 21, 22

Twitter Profile page, 62

YouTube channel, 66

comments

on photos and video in Instagram, 307–308

responding to in Instagram, 308–310

community action, on Facebook, 173–174

Contacts Syncing (Instagram), 275

Contour Mouse (Contour Design), 18

Costco, as source of devices, 19

CPU (central processing unit) (a.k.a. chip)

  defined, 17

  recommended speed of, 17

Creative Commons, 75–76

#custserv hashtag (Twitter), 253, 254

Custom privacy setting (Facebook), 104, 117

customer service issues, solving of online with Twitter, 257

#cute hashtag (Instagram), 305

cyberspace, as slang for Internet, 59

D

Dell, factory-refurbished equipment, 19

desktop computers, 12

dial-up ISP, 26

Dickman, Susan (author's daughter)

  LinkedIn profile, 65

  Rat Pack radio on Pandora, 70

digital cable Internet connection, 27

DM (Direct Message)

  defined, 206, 208–209, 220

  not able to receive on desktop in Instagram, 266

  receipt of in Twitter, 207

  sending on Twitter, 208–209, 210

  as slang expression, 82

#dogsofinstagram hashtag (Instagram), 305

domain address, defined, 41

DSL (Digital Subscriber Line) connection, 25, 26, 27

DSL Reports, 26, 27

E

#earthquake hashtag (Twitter), 253

EarthLink ISP, 26

eBay For Seniors For Dummies (Collier), 7

Edge browser, 21, 22

Edge browser (Microsoft), 21, 22, 23

editing tools (Instagram), 288

Edmunds Chris (podcaster), 74, 75

802.11g format, 34

802.11n format, 34

802.acn format (Gigabit or 5G Wi-Fi), 34

ELI5 (Explain Like I'm 5) (slang expression), 82

email

  address, 41, 42

  caution in clicking links and opening attachments in, 39

  choosing web-based email provider, 44–48

  composing and sending, 55–57

  domain address, 41

  places to get email service, 43–44

  web-based email services, 43–44

Email Notifications (Twitter), 206

emoji
  defined, 239, 303
  enhancing tweets with, 239–244
  as looking different in different
    programs, 239–240
  most popular ones used on Twitter,
    241–242
  questioning ones you can't figure
    out, 240

encryption, WPA encryption, 35

Epic (slang expression), 82

equipment
  factory-refurbished models, 19–20
  knowing what options to look for,
    16–18
  to match your needs, 12–16
  shopping for, 19–20
  tech-lite economical solutions, 13
  used, 19

Ethernet, as type of home
    network, 29

Ethernet adapter, 31

Ethernet cable, 31, 32, 36

etiquette, for sharing what you find
    online, 74–76

Events (Facebook)
  checking on, 125
  creating event invitation, 185–186
  for finding favorite things, 176
  review upcoming events and
    birthdays, 186–187

events, live-tweeting of, 228–229

F

Face Recognition (Facebook),
    121–122

Facebook
  Acquaintances list, 146
  Acquaintances privacy setting, 117
  active users on, 60
  Ad Settings, 121
  adding life events to timeline,
    132–133
  adding photo to timeline, 132
  adding your personal information,
    103–104
  admin (administrator), 183
  Ads, 119
  Advertisers you've interacted
    with, 121
  Apps and Websites, 122
  benefit of over Twitter, 60
  Birthdays, 124–125
  Blocking, 123
  broadcasting live video on,
    169–171
  captions, 161
  Chat, 125, 150
  chatting with friends, 150–151
  Close Friends list, 145
  Closed group, 177
  commenting on friend's status, 152
  communicating with group
    members, 183–185
  community action on, 173–174
  confirming you are you, 104–105

connecting with friends and family, 135–153

creating event invitation, 185–186

creating photo album, 159–162

deleting photos, 167–168

deleting status update or other post, 131–132

editing your timeline later, 111

Events, 125, 176, 185–187

Face Recognition, 121–122

filling out other profile information, 106–110

finding favorite things on, 174–177

finding friends initially, 101–102

Friend Finder, 139

Friend Requests, 137, 141–144

Friends except privacy setting, 117

Friends of Friends privacy setting, 113

Friends privacy setting, 104, 113, 116

giving a little Facebook love, 75

Groups, 175–185

hiding friend's posts, 146–148

home page, 138, 139, 148, 149, 152, 178, 179, 185, 186

Home page (a.k.a. News Feed), 123–126

home-produced videos, 187

info page, 40

Instagram as owned by, 266

joining Facebook group, 177–179

likes, 128, 171

making lists on, 145–146

Marketplace, for finding favorite things, 176

Messages, 137

Messenger, 148–149

navigation bar, 136

Notifications, 122, 137, 141, 178, 179

Only me privacy setting, 104, 116

Other Friend's Lists, 142–143

Pages, for finding favorite things, 175

Photo gallery, 156

as place where you connect with friends and family, 265

posting updates on friend's wall, 152

Posts, for finding favorite things, 175

privacy settings, 104, 114–123

profile defined, 95

Public group, 177

Quick Help, 138

removing messages from your wall, 153

responding to Friend Request, 143–144

retrieving private message, 148–149

review upcoming events and birthdays, 186–187

Search, 139–141

Secret group, 177

Security and Login, 118–119

Facebook (*continued*)

  security controls, 40

  sending direct messages to friends, 148–149

  sending Friend Request, 141–142

  sharing video on, 87–88

  sharing YouTube video on, 133–134

  signing up and prepping your profile on, 95–111

  signing up for account on, 96–98

  Specific friends privacy setting, 117

  starting Facebook group, 179–182

  tagging photos, 163–166

  Timeline and Tagging, 119

  Timeline page, 125–129, 132–133

  two-factor authentication (2FA), 49, 118

  untagging yourself in photos, 166–167

  updating your status, 129–131

  uploading photos to, 156–159

  uploading video to, 168–169

  uploading your profile photo, 98–100

  use of, 60

  Video Call, 151

  wall, 119, 132, 133, 137, 138, 152, 153, 174, 183

  What's On Your Mind, 129, 132, 156, 157

  Your Interests, 119

Facepalm (slang expression), 82

factory-refurbished equipment

  on name brands, 19

  warranties on, 19

feedback, author's invitation for, 7

#FF or #FollowFriday hashtag (Twitter), 253

fiber Internet connection, 26, 27

filters (Instagram), 287–288

Firefox browser, 20–21, 22, 23

5 GHz band, 34

5G Wi-Fi, 34

follow

on Instagram, 277–281, 308–310

on Twitter, 208–212, 256–257

#foodporn hashtag (Instagram), 305

format bar (Gmail), 56

free advertising license, 76

Friend Finder (Facebook), 139

Friend Requests (Facebook)

  described, 137

  responding to, 143–144

  sending, 141–142

friends

  chatting with on Facebook, 150–151

  Facebook as place to connect with, 265

  finding of initially on Facebook, 101–102

  finding of to follow on Instagram, 277–281

  finding with Facebook Search, 139–141

  interacting with on Instagram, 306

sending direct messages to on Facebook, 148–149

Friends except privacy setting (Facebook), 117

Friends of Friends privacy level (Facebook), 113

Friends privacy setting (Facebook), 104, 113, 116

G

#gardenchat (Twitter), 254, 255

GBoard app, for searching for emoji by keyword, 243, 303

GIF (Graphic Interchange Format), punctuating tweets with, 232

Gigabit, 34

gigahertz (GHz), 33

Global System for Mobile Communications (GSMA), 236

Gmail

  adding your Contacts in, 54–55

  composing and sending, 55–57

  described, 46–48

  as free service from Google, 42

  signing up for, 50–53

Google

  Blogspot, 67

  Chrome browser, 20–21, 22

  Chrome Hot Keys, 23

  Chrome OS, 13

  GBoard app, 243, 303

  Google Calendar, 47–48, 50

  Google Docs, 50

  Google Hangouts, 46, 47

  Google Mail (Gmail), 42, 46–48, 54–57

  Google maps, 37

  Google Photos, 68–69

  Google Play, 266, 303

  Google Voice, 47

  Play Store, 12

  registering for any Google service, 66

  two-factor authentication (2FA), 49

Groups (Facebook)

  communicating with, 183–185

  for finding favorite things, 175, 176

  joining, 177–179

  leaving, 179

  starting, 179–182

GSMA (Global System for Mobile Communications), 236

H

#happy hashtag (Instagram), 305

hard drive, recommended size of, 16–17

hardware

  factory-refurbished models, 19–20

  knowing what options to look for, 16–18

  to match your needs, 12–16

  shopping for, 19–20

  tech-lite economical solutions, 13

  used equipment, 19

hashtags
   #americanidol hashtag
      (Twitter), 255
   #avgeek hashtag (Instagram), 305
   #caturday hashtag (Instagram),
      305
   #CES hashtag (Twitter), 252
   #custserv hashtag (Twitter),
      253, 254
   #cute hashtag (Instagram), 305
   defined, 225
   #dogsofinstagram hashtag
      (Instagram), 305
   #earthquake hashtag (Twitter), 253
   examples of in Twitter, 252–253
   #FF or #FollowFriday hashtag
      (Twitter), 253
   #foodporn hashtag (Instagram), 305
   #happy hashtag (Instagram), 305
   #instagood hashtag
      (Instagram), 305
   #jobs hashtag (Twitter), 253
   learning about in Instagram,
      302–305
   #love hashtag (Instagram), 305
   #MusicMonday hashtag
      (Twitter), 252
   #nofilter hashtag (Instagram), 305
   #ps hashtag (Twitter), 253
   #photooftheday hashtag
      (Instagram), 305
   #quote hashtag (Twitter), 253

   #selfie hashtag (Instagram), 305
   #sxsw hashtag (Twitter), 252
   #TBT hashtag (Instagram), 305
   #tcot hashtag (Twitter), 253
   #ThrowbackThursday or #TBT
      hashtag, 252
   #tlot hashtag (Twitter), 253
   top ones for Instagram posts, 305
   #travel hashtag (Instagram),
      305
   #uniteblue hashtag (Twitter), 253
   use of in Instagram, 301–302
   use of with Tweets, 251–255
hashtags.org, 253
home network, setting up, 29
home page
   Facebook, a.k.a. News Feed,
      123–126, 138, 139, 148, 149,
      152, 178, 179, 185, 186
   Instagram, 302, 306
   Twitter, 21, 202, 206, 208, 209, 210,
      220, 246, 260
Hotmail, 45, 46
HP, factory-refurbished
   equipment, 19
Huawei MediaPad M3, 14, 15
Hulu, streaming service, 71

I

icons, explained, 5
ICYMI (In Case You Missed It) (slang
   expression), 82

images
  adding photo to Facebook timeline, 132
  adding photo to Twitter profile, 194–195
  commenting on in Instagram, 307–308
  creating album for (Facebook), 159–162
  deleting (Facebook), 167
  posting of ones taken on your phone to Facebook, 290
  posting of ones taken on your phone to Instagram, 285–290
  showing off on Twitter, 231
  tagging (Facebook), 163–166
  taking of in Instagram app, 291–292
  tips for on Instagram, 284–285
  untagging yourself, 166–167
  uploading to Facebook, 156–159
  uploading your Facebook profile photo, 98–100
IMHO (In my humble opinion) (slang expression), 82
in the commons, defined, 75–76
#instagood hashtag (Instagram), 305
Instagram
  Boomerang mode, 294
  captions, 289
  Clarendon filter, 288
  commenting on photo or video, 307–308
  completing your profile in browser, 269–272
  Contacts Syncing, 275
  difference in using on desktop and mobile device, 276–277
  editing tools, 288
  filters, 287–288
  finding friends and people to follow, 277–281
  following on, 277–281, 308–310
  following those who have followed you, 310
  as having two distinct platforms, 266
  home page, 302, 306
  interacting with friends and photos on, 306
  Juno filter, 288
  Lark filter, 288
  learning to take selfie on, 297–299
  likes, 275, 305, 308–310
  Link Social Accounts, 275
  Lo-fi filter, 288
  Ludwig filter, 288
  main feed, 296
  Mayfair filter, 288
  as most popular service for sharing personal photos, 266
  Notifications, 275, 310
  number of photos posted on per day, 301
  as owned by Facebook, 266
  photo tips, 284–285

Instagram *(continued)*

  Photos and Videos of You, 274

  as place to view pictures, 265

  posting of stories on, 292–296

  posting photos taken on your phone, 285–290

  privacy settings, 272–275

  Private Account, 273–274

  Profile page, 269–272, 303

  responding to follows, likes, and comments, 308–310

  sending and reading private messages, 310–311

  setting up account on, 266–269

  Show Activity Status, 274

  Sierra filter, 288

  Story Controls, 275

  taking photos and videos in app, 291–292

  two-factor authentication (2FA), 49, 275

  Valencia filter, 288

Internet

  connecting to, 25–40

  nothing on Internet is free, 37

Internet service provider (ISP)

  getting email account with, 43

  selection of, 26–29

  types of connections with, 25

Internet slang, 82–84

interwebs, as slang for Internet, 59

IRL (In Real Life) (slang expression), 83

J

#jobs hashtag (Twitter), 253

JSYK (Just So You Know) (slang expression), 83

Juno filter (Instagram), 288

K

Kashi products, Facebook group protest, 174

keyboard

  on Apple's App Store or Google's Play Store, 303

  types of, 17

keyboard shortcuts, 22–24

keyword, defined, 174

L

laptop

  compared to desktop, 15

  compared to tablet, 13

  keyboards for, 13

  monitors on, 13

  photo of, 14

Lark filter (Instagram), 288

Lenovo, factory-refurbished equipment, 19, 20

library, using Wi-Fi at, 28

license rules/icons, for Creative Commons, 76

likes

  Facebook, 128, 171

  Instagram, 275, 305, 308–310

  Twitter, 207, 214, 218, 224, 227

Link Social Accounts (Instagram), 275

LinkedIn
  connections, 64–65
  users of, 64

links, caution in clicking on, 39

Lo-fi filter (Instagram), 288

Login Verification (Twitter), 202

LOL (Laughing Out Loud) (slang expression), 83

#love hashtag (Instagram), 305

"Lucas the Spider" (YouTube channel), 85

Ludwig filter (Instagram), 288

Lulz (For the laughs) (slang expression), 83

Lurker (slang expression), 83

M

mail transfer agent (MTA), defined, 42

main feed (Instagram), 296

Manage Your Contacts bar (Twitter), 204

manners, for sharing what you find online, 74–76

Marketplace (Facebook), for finding favorite things, 176

Mayfair filter (Instagram), 288

media-card reader, use of, 17–18

meme
  sharing of on Twitter, 231
  as slang expression, 83

messages
  DM (Direct Message), 82, 206, 207, 208–209, 210, 220, 266
  email messages, caution in clicking links and opening attachments, 39
  PM (Private Message), 82
  sending and reading private messages in Instagram, 310–311
  SMS (Short Message Service), 47, 62, 275
  text messages, 47

Messages (Facebook), 137

Messenger (Facebook), 148–149

Microsoft
  Bing, 244–246
  Edge browser, 21, 22, 23
  Office, 42, 46
  OneDrive, 46
  Outlook, 42, 45–46

modem, 30, 36

monitor
  cost of, 18
  recommended size of, 18

mouse, recommendations for, 18

mouse shortcuts, 22–24

multiple-output (MIMO) technology, 34

Music Genome Project, 70

music videos, on YouTube, 85

#MusicMonday hashtag (Twitter), 252

N

navigation bar (Facebook), 136

Netflix, streaming service, 71

network, defined, 29

news story, passing on via Twitter, 230

Nielsen

number of phone calls by mobile subscribers, 62

number of text messages by mobile subscribers, 62

#nofilter hashtag (Instagram), 305

#NostalgiaChat (Twitter), 254

Notifications

Facebook, 122, 137, 141, 178, 179

Instagram, 275, 310

Twitter, 206–207, 208, 214, 220, 221, 256

Twitter Lite, 237

NSFW (Not Safe For Work) (slang expression), 83

O

Office (Microsoft), 42, 46

One Drive (Microsoft), 46

One Six Right (YouTube video), 86, 87

online, as source of devices, 19

online bio, 39

Only me privacy setting (Facebook), 104, 116

Other Friend's Lists (Facebook), 142–143

Outlook (Microsoft), 42, 45–46

Overstock.com, as source of devices, 19

P

#ps hashtag (Twitter), 253

Pages (Facebook), for finding favorite things, 175

Pandora, 69–70

Panera Bread, using Wi-Fi at, 28

passphrase

example of, 48

for WPA, 35

password

defined, 48

as encrypted on Facebook, 96

picking pick-proof one, 48–50

reset verification on Twitter, 202

Personalization and Data category (Twitter), 204

#petchat (Twitter), 254

phishing emails, 39

photos

adding photo to Facebook timeline, 132

adding photo to Twitter profile, 194–195

commenting on in Instagram, 307–308

creating album for (Facebook), 159–162

deleting (Facebook), 167

posting of ones taken on your phone to Facebook, 290

posting of ones taken on your phone to Instagram, 285–290

showing off on Twitter, 231

tagging (Facebook), 163–166

taking of in Instagram app, 291–292

tips for on Instagram, 284–285

untagging yourself, 166–167

uploading to Facebook, 156–159

uploading your Facebook profile photo, 98–100

Photo gallery (Facebook), 156

#photooftheday hashtag (Instagram), 305

Photobomb (slang expression), 83

Photos and Videos of You (Instagram), 274

pictures

adding photo to Facebook timeline, 132

adding photo to Twitter profile, 194–195

commenting on in Instagram, 307–308

creating album for (Facebook), 159–162

deleting (Facebook), 167

posting of ones taken on your phone to Facebook, 290

posting of ones taken on your phone to Instagram, 285–290

showing off on Twitter, 231

tagging (Facebook), 163–166

taking of in Instagram app, 291–292

tips for on Instagram, 284–285

untagging yourself, 166–167

uploading to Facebook, 156–159

uploading your Facebook profile photo, 98–100

Pinterest, sharing on, 89–93

PM (Private Message) (slang expression), 82

poll, starting of on Twitter, 227

posting, defined, 129

Posts (Facebook), for finding favorite things, 175

powerline network

benefits of, 31

defined, 31

setting up, 31–33

as type of home network, 29, 30, 31

pre-shared key (PSK) mode, for security, 35

privacy, protection of, 36–40, 49

privacy laws, following of, 37

privacy policy

reading of, in general, 38

Twitter, 207–208

privacy settings

on Facebook, 104, 114–123

on Instagram, 272–275

on Twitter, 203–206

Private Account (Instagram), 273–274

Profile page
author's on Facebook, 60, 61
author's on Twitter, 62
Edit Profile box on Instagram, 303
Favorites link on on Twitter, 206
Instagram, 269–272
linking to others' Profile pages on Facebook, 108
pinning Tweet to on Twitter, 215
posting update from on Facebook, 129
posting video to Facebook Profile page, 87
posting your photo on on Facebook, 98
posting your photo on on Twitter, 195
removing current status update from on Facebook, 131
Twitter, 194, 197–203

PSK (pre-shared key) mode, for security, 35
Public (Facebook group), 177
Public privacy setting (Facebook), 104, 113, 116
PWNAGE (slang expression), 83
PWNED (slang expression), 83

Q
Quick Help (Facebook), 138
#quote hashtag (Twitter), 253

R
radio frequency band, 33
reciprocity, as key to enjoying social media, 309
Retweet (RT)
defined, 207
how to, 223
router, 30, 35, 36
rural areas, choice of Internet connections in, 26

S
Safari browser, 21, 22
safety, online, 36–40
Samsung, Galaxy Note 9, 14
Saturday Night Live (TV show), Facebook group campaign to get Betty White to host, 174
Search
Facebook, 139–141
Twitter, 246–248
Secret (Facebook group), 177
Security and Login (Facebook), 118–119
security questions, 53
selfie, learning to take on Instagram, 297–299
selfie ring, 297
selfie stick, 298
#selfie hashtag (Instagram), 305
sharing
given credit when, 74–76
making links short, 77–82

meme on Twitter, 231

photos on Twitter, 231

preparing to share info on Facebook, 113–134

uploading photo to Facebook, 156–159

uploading video to Facebook, 168–169

shipping costs, 20

Short Message Service (SMS), 47, 62, 275

shortcuts, in different browsers, 22–24

Show Activity Status (Instagram), 274

Sierra filter (Instagram), 288

Skype

  for making international phone calls, 63

  Messenger service, 46

  Video Chat, 46, 63–64

slang expressions

  AMA (Ask Me Anything), 82

  BAE (Before Anything Else), 82

  cyberspace, 59

  DM (Direct Message), 82

  ELI5 (Explain Like I'm 5), 82

  Epic, 82

  Facepalm, 82

  ICYMI (In Case You Missed It), 82

  IMHO (In my humble opinion), 82

  interwebs, 59

  IRL (In Real Life), 83

  JSYK (Just So You Know), 83

  LOL (Laughing Out Loud), 83

  Lulz (For the laughs), 83

  Lurker, 83

  NSFW (Not Safe For Work), 83

  PM (Private Message), 82

  PWNAGE, 83

  PWNED, 83

  SMH (Shaking My Head), 83

  TBT (Throwback Thursday), 83

  TL;DR (Too Long; Didn't Read), 83

  TROLL, 83

  Well played, 83

  YOLO (You Only Live Once), 83

smartphone

  defined, 16

  as giving up data about your location, 37

  photo of Android phone, 16

  tasks not performed by, 15

SMH (Shaking My Head) (slang expression), 83

SMS (Short Message Service), 47, 62, 275

social media

  examples of, 12

  fun of, 39

  reciprocity as key to enjoying, 309

social networking, speaking language of, 59–71

social security number, cautions with, 40

spam
  defined, 47
  filters for, 47
Specific friends privacy setting
    (Facebook), 117
Starbucks, using Wi-Fi at, 28, 38
status, defined, 129
stories, posting of on Instagram,
    292–296
Story Controls (Instagram), 275
streaming, TV and movies, 71
#sxsw hashtag (Twitter), 252
synchronizing (sync), with Gmail, 48

T
tablet
  compared to laptop, 15
  defined, 14
  tasks not performed by, 15
tagging
  defined, 163
  of photos (Facebook), 163–166
Target, as source of devices, 19
TBT (Throwback Thursday) (slang
    expression), 83
#TBT hashtag (Instagram), 305
#tcot hashtag (Twitter), 253
terabyte (TB), 17
text messages, 47
#ThrowbackThursday or #TBT
    hashtag, 252
Timeline and Tagging
    (Facebook), 119

Timeline page (Facebook), 125–129,
    132–133
TinyURL.com, 77
TL;DR (Too Long; Didn't Read) (slang
    expression), 83
#tlot hashtag (Twitter), 253
TOS (Terms of Service)
  Google's outline of, 53
  reading of, 38
  Twitter, 207–208
translation, of Tweets, 244–246
#travel hashtag (Instagram), 305
trending, discovering what is
    trending, 249–251
Trojan, defined, 39
TROLL (slang expression), 83
Tweet
  defined, 14, 62, 191
  enhancing of with emoji,
    239–240
  knowing what to tweet about,
    226–232
  liking favorite ones, 224
  passing along chosen one, 223
  punctuating of with GIFs, 232
  recommendation to not
    protect, 203
  searching for tweeted topics,
    225–226
  translation of, 244–246
  use of hashtags with, 251–255
TweetChat, 253
TweetDeck, 260–261

21st-century new media, as about sharing, conversation, and engaging others, not about broadcsting, 218

Twitter. *See also* Retweet (RT); Tweet
adjusting account settings, 200
archive, 203
@ (at) replies, 219, 220, 255
author's Profile page on, 62
basic guidelines for conversing on, 218–222
beginner's guide to, 191–215
blue badge (verified), 256
changing username, 200–202
checking for correct time zone, 202
choosing language on, 202
connecting and chatting with people, 255–257
discovering what is trending, 249–251
editing profile, 197–199
Email Notifications, 206
Favorites link on Profile page, 206
features about Twitter clients, 260–261
finding people to follow, 208–212
finding trends and friends with Twitter Search, 246–248
following on, 208–212, 256–257
hashtags, 225, 251–255
home page, 21, 206, 208, 209, 210, 220, 246, 260

as hosting weekly chats, 254
keeping track of friends on, 258–260
knowing what to tweet about, 226–232
liking favorite tweets, 224
as limited to 280 characters, 62, 77, 192, 225, 240, 252
live-tweeting event on, 228–229
Login Verification, 202
Manage Your Contacts bar, 204
most popular emoji used on, 241–242
Notifications, 206–207, 208, 214, 220, 221, 256
passing on news story via, 230
password reset verification on, 202
pasting URL into Tweet, 77
personal browser on, 260–261
Personalization and Data category, 204
personalize based on devices, 205
personalize on places you've been, 205
Personalized Ads, 205
pinning Tweet to Profile page, 215
as place to learn news and discuss topics with strangers, 265
posting your photo on Profile page, 195
privacy policy, 207–208
privacy settings, 203–206
profile page, 197–199, 200–203

Twitter *(continued)*

reading and following foreign language accounts, 244–246

registering with, 192–200

Retweet (RT), 207, 223

reviewing terms and privacy policy, 207–208

saving data on mobile with Twitter Lite, 236–239

Search, 246–248

searching for tweeted topics, 225–226

searching Twitter chats, 255

seeing what's trending on Profile page, 194

setting up login verification, 202

setting up notifications for web and mobile, 206–207

settings for timeline, 203

sharing data with Twitter's business partners, 205

sharing of mem on, 231

sharing video on, 88–89, 227

solving customer service issues online, 257

starting of poll on, 227

starting poll on, 227

TOS (Terms of Service), 207–208

touting your new profile on, 212–215

tracking where you see Twitter content, 205

Twitter Lists, 258–260

Twitter Privacy, 205

two-factor authentication (2FA), 49, 202, 237

updates from, 207

as variety of SMS (Short Message Service), 62–63

Verified Accounts, 256

video autoplay settings, 202

viewing friend lists, 260–261

Twitter Lite, 236–239

2.4 GHz band, 33

two-factor authentication (2FA), 49, 118, 202, 237, 275

Twubs, 253

U

#uniteblue hashtag (Twitter), 253

updates, 6

URL (Uniform Resource Loctor)

defined, 4, 21

every website as having, 42

shorteners, 77–78

USB (Universal Serial Bus) port/connection, recommended number of, 17

USB dongle, 34

USB flash drive, 17

V

Valencia filter (Instagram), 288

Verified Accounts (Twitter), 256

Verizon, Yahoo! Mail, 44–45

video
  Boomerang mode, 294
  broadcasting live on Facebook, 169–171
  commenting on in Instagram, 307–308
  sharing of on Twitter, 227
  taking of in Instagram app, 291–292
  uploading home-produced videos on Facebook, 187
  uploading to Facebook, 168–169
Video Call (Facebook), 151
Video Chat (Skype), 46, 63–64
virus, defined, 39
VOIP (voice over the Internet) client program, 63
VPN (Virtual Private Network), 37–38

W

wall (Facebook), 119, 132, 133, 137, 138, 152, 153, 174, 183
Walmart, as source of devices, 19
war-driving scammers, 35
Well played (slang expression), 83
WEP (Wired Equivalent Privacy), 35
What's On Your Mind (Facebook), 129, 132, 156, 157
White, Betty (actress), Facebook group campaign, 174

Wi-Fi
  apps for locating free Wi-Fi zones, 29
  hotspots, 28, 35, 38
  networking with, 33–36
  Wireless Fidelity, 28
#winechat (Twitter), 254
Wired Equivalent Privacy (WEP), 35
wireless network
  formats for, 34
  security on, 35
  setting up, 33–36
  as type of home network, 29, 30
worm, defined, 39
WPA (Wi-Fi Protected Access), 35

Y

Yahoo! Yahoo! Mail, 44–45
YOLO (You Only Live Once) (slang expression), 83
Your Interests (Facebook), 119
YouTube
  defined, 65
  finding and sharing videos on, 84–89
  linking to video on, 75
  monthly unique user visits to, 84
  setting up account on, 66
  sharing video from on Facebook, 133–134

About the Author

Marsha Collier spends a good deal of time online. As a blogger, the author of the best-selling *For Dummies* books on eBay, and a radio host, she shares her love of the online world with millions.

Marsha is one of the foremost eBay experts and educators in the world and the top-selling eBay author. In 1999, Marsha created the first edition of *eBay For Dummies*, the bestselling book for eBay beginners. She followed up the success of her first book with *Starting an eBay Business For Dummies*, a book targeting individuals interested in making e-commerce their full-time profession. These books are updated regularly to keep up with site and market changes.

Marsha's books have sold over one million copies (including the special editions in foreign countries — two in Australia, two in Canada, and two in the United Kingdom — as well as translations in Spanish, French, Italian, Chinese, and German).

Along with her writing, Marsha is an experienced e-commerce and customer service educator speaking at conferences all over the world. Embracing social media has earned Marsha awards as an influencer and author:

- Forbes: Must Follow Marketing Minds on Twitter
- Forbes: Top 10 Women Social Media Influencers
- 2012 Small Business Book Award Winner: *Starting an eBay Business For Dummies*
- Forbes: Top 50 Social Media Power Influencers
- The 100 Most Powerful Women on Twitter
- PeerIndex #1 Customer Experience Online Influencers
- MindTouch #1 Most Influential in Customer Services

Dedication

To all the future online citizens who have purchased this book to get a taste of how much fun joining the social media party can be. I look forward to seeing you on Twitter and Facebook, and seeing your pictures on Instagram.

I dedicate this book also to my husband, Curt Buthman, who puts up with my late nights on social media (all for research — wink) and photobombs my pictures to make me smile; and my daughter, Susan Dickman, who critiques some of my posts with love.

Also to my dear friends on Twitter, Facebook, and Instagram who have embraced me as part of their community. I want to thank all of you for your help and support; you make the online world a fun place to visit for millions of people. Keep on doing what you're doing.

Author's Acknowledgments

This book couldn't have been written without the input from the thousands of wonderful people that I've met online from all over the world. You inspire me to work harder and do my best to help as many people as possible.

This book is filled with screen shots of the many friends I've made along my social media journey: If it wasn't for them, this book wouldn't be here. Also, thanks to my social media buddies — whose replies contain brilliant responses when I ask them questions or send them messages.

My editor, Maureen Tullis, is way cool. Her comments and compliments made writing this book a pleasure. She's a real asset to the process and this book wouldn't be as good as it is without her guidance. Many thanks to Scott Tullis who painstakingly copy edited this title, and Patti Louise Ruby who relentlessly reviewed every word and screen shot for accuracy.

Publisher's Acknowledgments

Executive Editor: Steve Hayes
Development/PM: Maureen Tullis
Copy Editor: Scott Tullis
Technical Editor: Patti Louise Ruby

Production Editor: Vasanth Koilraj
Cover Image: © Steve Smith/Getty Images

Leverage the power

Dummies is the global leader in the reference category and one of the most trusted and highly regarded brands in the world. No longer just focused on books, customers now have access to the dummies content they need in the format they want. Together we'll craft a solution that engages your customers, stands out from the competition, and helps you meet your goals.

Advertising & Sponsorships

Connect with an engaged audience on a powerful multimedia site, and position your message alongside expert how-to content. Dummies.com is a one-stop shop for free, online information and know-how curated by a team of experts.

- Targeted ads
- Video
- Email Marketing
- Microsites
- Sweepstakes sponsorship

20 MILLION PAGE VIEWS EVERY SINGLE MONTH

15 MILLION UNIQUE VISITORS PER MONTH

43% OF ALL VISITORS ACCESS THE SITE VIA THEIR MOBILE DEVICES

700,000 NEWSLETTER SUBSCRIPTIONS TO THE INBOXES OF

300,000 UNIQUE INDIVIDUALS EVERY WEEK

# of dummies

Custom Publishing

Reach a global audience in any language by creating a solution that will differentiate you from competitors, amplify your message, and encourage customers to make a buying decision.

- Apps
- Books
- eBooks
- Video
- Audio
- Webinars

Brand Licensing & Content

Leverage the strength of the world's most popular reference brand to reach new audiences and channels of distribution.

For more information, visit dummies.com/biz

PERSONAL ENRICHMENT

Staying Sharp	**Facebook**	**Guitar**	**Investing**	**Beekeeping**	**Digital Photography**
9781119187790	9781119179030	9781119293354	9781119293347	9781119310068	9781119235606
USA $26.00	USA $21.99	USA $24.99	USA $22.99	USA $22.99	USA $24.99
CAN $31.99	CAN $25.99	CAN $29.99	CAN $27.99	CAN $27.99	CAN $29.99
UK £19.99	UK £16.99	UK £17.99	UK £16.99	UK £16.99	UK £17.99

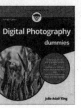

Meditation	**Pregnancy**	**Samsung Galaxy S7**	**iPhone**	**Crocheting**	**Nutrition**
9781119251163	9781119235491	9781119279952	9781119283133	9781119287117	9781119130246
USA $24.99	USA $26.99	USA $24.99	USA $24.99	USA $24.99	USA $22.99
CAN $29.99	CAN $31.99	CAN $29.99	CAN $29.99	CAN $29.99	CAN $27.99
UK £17.99	UK £19.99	UK £17.99	UK £17.99	UK £16.99	UK £16.99

PROFESSIONAL DEVELOPMENT

Windows 10	**AutoCAD**	**Excel 2016**	**QuickBooks 2017**	**macOS Sierra**	**LinkedIn**	**Windows 10**
9781119311041	9781119255796	9781119293439	9781119281467	9781119280651	9781119251132	9781119310563
USA $24.99	USA $39.99	USA $26.99	USA $26.99	USA $29.99	USA $24.99	USA $34.00
CAN $29.99	CAN $47.99	CAN $31.99	CAN $31.99	CAN $35.99	CAN $29.99	CAN $41.99
UK £17.99	UK £27.99	UK £19.99	UK £19.99	UK £21.99	UK £17.99	UK £24.99

SharePoint 2016	**Fundamental Analysis**	**Networking**	**Office 2016**	**Office 365**	**Salesforce.com**	**Coding**
9781119181705	9781119263593	9781119257769	9781119293477	9781119265313	9781119239314	9781119293323
USA $29.99	USA $26.99	USA $29.99	USA $26.99	USA $24.99	USA $29.99	USA $29.99
CAN $35.99	CAN $31.99	CAN $35.99	CAN $31.99	CAN $29.99	CAN $35.99	CAN $35.99
UK £21.99	UK £19.99	UK £21.99	UK £19.99	UK £17.99	UK £21.99	UK £21.99